I0793227

IMAGES
of America

AROUND TOMBSTONE

GHOST TOWNS AND GUNFIGHTS

ON THE COVER: Two prospectors (one not visible to the left) are setting out from the Tombstone Livery Stable. (Courtesy of Arizona Historical Society, Tucson, Arizona.)

IMAGES
of America

AROUND TOMBSTONE
GHOST TOWNS AND GUNFIGHTS

Jane Eppinga

Arizona Historical Foundation

ARCADIA
PUBLISHING

ISBN 978-0-7385-7127-0

Published by Arcadia Publishing
Charleston, South Carolina

Printed in the United States of America

Library of Congress Control Number: 2008940184

For all general information contact Arcadia Publishing at:
Telephone 843-853-2070
Fax 843-853-0044
E-mail sales@arcadiapublishing.com
For customer service and orders:
Toll-Free 1-888-313-2665

Visit us on the Internet at www.arcadiapublishing.com

Contents

ACKNOWLEDGMENTS

The work of a book is never entirely the output of one person and so it is with Images of America: *Around Tombstone: Ghost Towns and Gunfights*. Many individuals and organizations have helped the author. Nancy Lewis Sosa, whose roots run deep into Tombstone history, provided images and documentation on Tombstone's history. The Macias-Devere family provided photographs and documentation on Tombstone's rose tree. Charles and Betty Escapule gave freely of their family history of mining and ranching around Tombstone. Viji Winters provided material, both historical and mining, from her late husband, Wayne Winters, longtime editor of the *Tombstone Epitaph*.

Other contributors include Don Taylor of the O. K. Corral, Linda D'Ambrose, Shirley Gillette, and Barbara Lacy. People of organizations who have contributed to this work are Kate Reeve and the staff of Arizona Historical Society, Wendy Goen of the Arizona State Archives, and Art Austin and Tombstone State Park. No book sees the light of day without a publisher and an editor, such as Jared Jackson, Christine Talbot, and the Arcadia staff. Finally, the biggest contributors are those pioneers, good and bad, who left their stories and their mark on a place called Tombstone.

Introduction

Tombstone owes its beginning to Ed Schieffelin, who prospected the nearby hills. From nearby Fort Huachuca, Schieffelin told a soldier that the mountain's rich colors looked very promising for mineral wealth. The soldier sneered, "All you'll find in those hills is your tombstone." However, in February 1878, Schieffelin found a vein of rich silver ore and registered two claims—the Tombstone and the Graveyard. He took an ore sampling to his brother Al in Signal, Arizona, and they returned to Tombstone with assayer Richard K. Gird, who had found the ore to be very rich in silver. Along the way, Ed located two more silver claims, which he registered as the Lucky Cuss and the Tough Nut. Today the Good Enough, also one of Schieffelin's mines, founded in 1878, provides underground tours.

Although Tombstone acquired a reputation as a hell-raising settlement, the nearby towns of Charleston, Gleeson, and Milltown (also called Millville), as well as other places around Tombstone, had their fair share of local rowdiness. Those with the courage to administer the law did it swiftly with no appeal. These towns also had churches, some of which are still practicing; schools; banks; and local newspapers.

Tombstone is best remembered for the notorious gunfight at the O. K. Corral, where the feud between the Earp brothers, Doc Holliday, the Clantons, and the McLaurys erupted in the famous shoot-out that lasted for less than a minute on October 26, 1881. Just who shot first is still a matter of great historical debate and has been the subject of many barroom arguments and of *History's Mysteries*, a television show. What is known is that in a hail of gunfire and less than 30 seconds after the opening shot, three men lay dead and three were wounded. Virgil Earp had been shot in the leg and Morgan Earp through both shoulders. Only Wyatt Earp survived the fight unwounded.

As Tombstone's population grew, so did its political power. In 1881, the Arizona Legislature established Cochise County with Tombstone as the county seat. The beautiful Tombstone Courthouse, which is now on the National Register of Historic Places, was built in 1882 at a cost of $50,000. Many colorful characters, including Johnny Ringo, Johnny Behind the Deuce, Curly Bill Brocius, Three-Fingered Jack Dunlap, and Fatty Ryan, made Tombstone a special place.

Today the entire town of Tombstone is preserved and on the National Register of Historic Places. The Crystal Palace Saloon serves customers, and the O. K. Corral features reenactments of the famous shoot-out. Tourists stroll along Allen Street, once full of bars and bordellos. The original Cochise County Courthouse, now an Arizona State Historic Park, features exhibits and artifacts that tell of Tombstone's colorful past. Visitors walk along rows of graves in Boot Hill Cemetery, where many died with their boots actually on. The Bird Cage Theatre, the site where the song "She's Only a Bird in a Gilded Cage" was composed, showcases photographs and documents of people who visited Tombstone. And a person can still have lunch or dinner at the famous Nelly Cashman's.

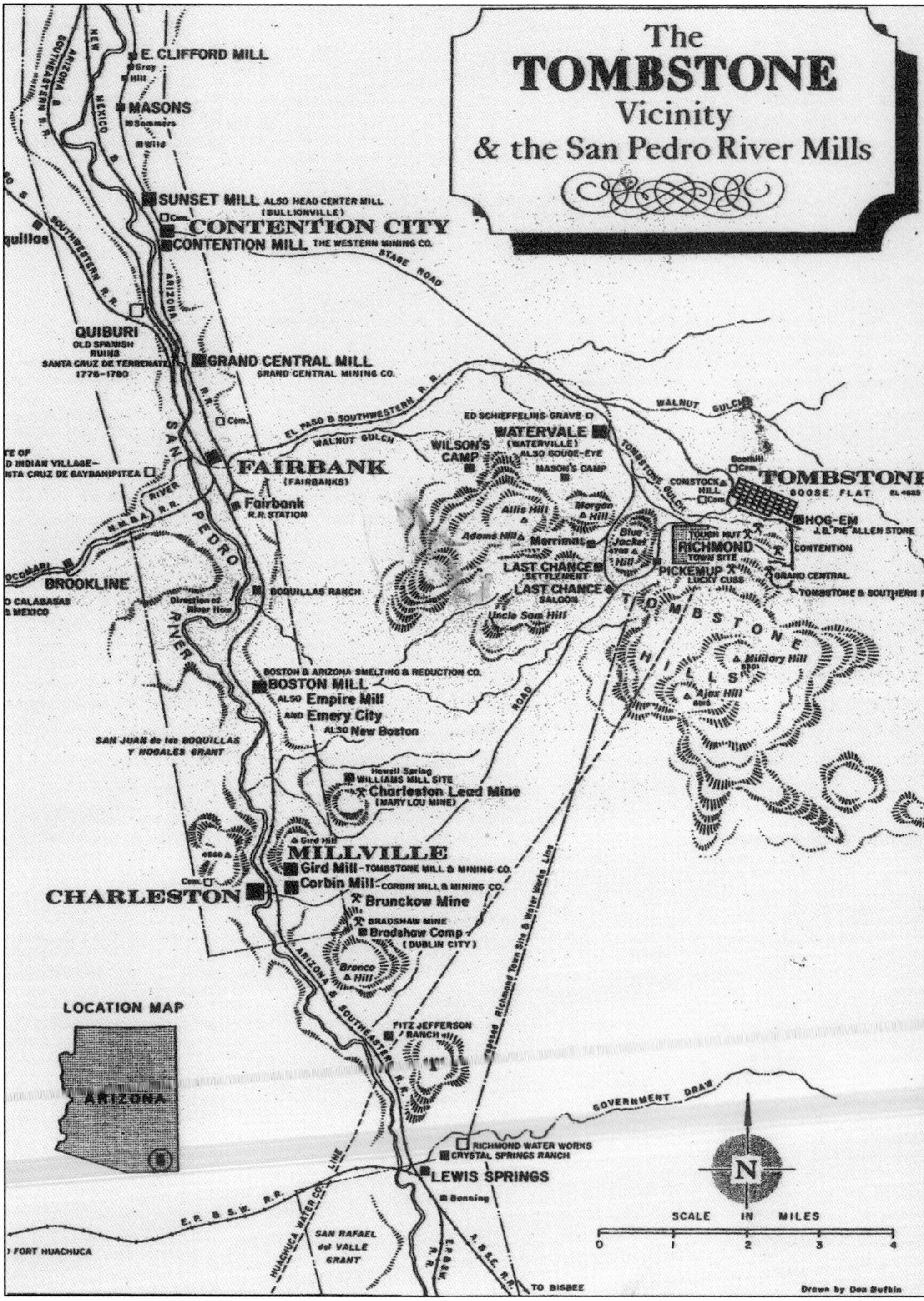

Pictured here is an 1880s map of Tombstone, Arizona. (Courtesy of the late Don Bufkin.)

One

Charleston

"If a corpse had a gun on him and the fatal shot came from the front, you didn't look for the killer." Such was one resident's memory of Charleston. Charleston was tougher and wilder than nearby Tombstone. Its post office was established on April 17, 1879, with Charles D. Handy, who gave the town its name, as the postmaster. The 1880 U.S. Census put Charleston's population at 350, but over the next two years, that figure rose to 800. Charleston had 13 to 15 saloons, four mercantile stores, butcher shops, restaurants, two Chinese laundries, a telegraph office, Mrs. Hugh's boardinghouse, the Eagle and Royal Hotels, a church, a school, corrals, and private homes. The Clantons, of the renowned gunfight, had the first boardinghouse in Charleston when Ike Clanton erected a canvas "hotel" structure, which was used until more substantial buildings were constructed.

Arizona Territory governor Anson P. K. Safford visited Tombstone in 1879 and offered to build a 10-stamp mill at the closest source of water, the San Pedro River. Millville provided the mill, and Charleston developed because of it. Taxes on gambling and prostitution funded education and local government administration. Charleston's justice of the peace, Jim Burnett, administered law and order in Charleston. He held trial any time and any place and served as both judge and jury. His swift justice held no appeals in his court. Burnett collected and pocketed the fines, leaving him with no shortage of funds. His career ended on July 7, 1897, when William Greene, a local rancher, shot and killed Burnett outside of the Can Can Restaurant in Tombstone. Burnett had destroyed a dam belonging to Greene. When the water swept down the wash, it drowned two little girls, and one of them was Greene's daughter. Greene never came to trial for killing Burnett.

A miners' strike in 1890, combined with a drop in silver prices, further reduced the ore output. Mill production declined, and in 1903 the addition of a railroad to Tombstone enabled the ore to be shipped cheap. People left to find work in other places. Today Charleston is administered by the Bureau of Land Management and located within the San Pedro Riparian Area. Most artifacts from Charleston have been removed, but the north side of town still has many petroglyphs. Across the river from Charleston are the remains of the old stamp mill.

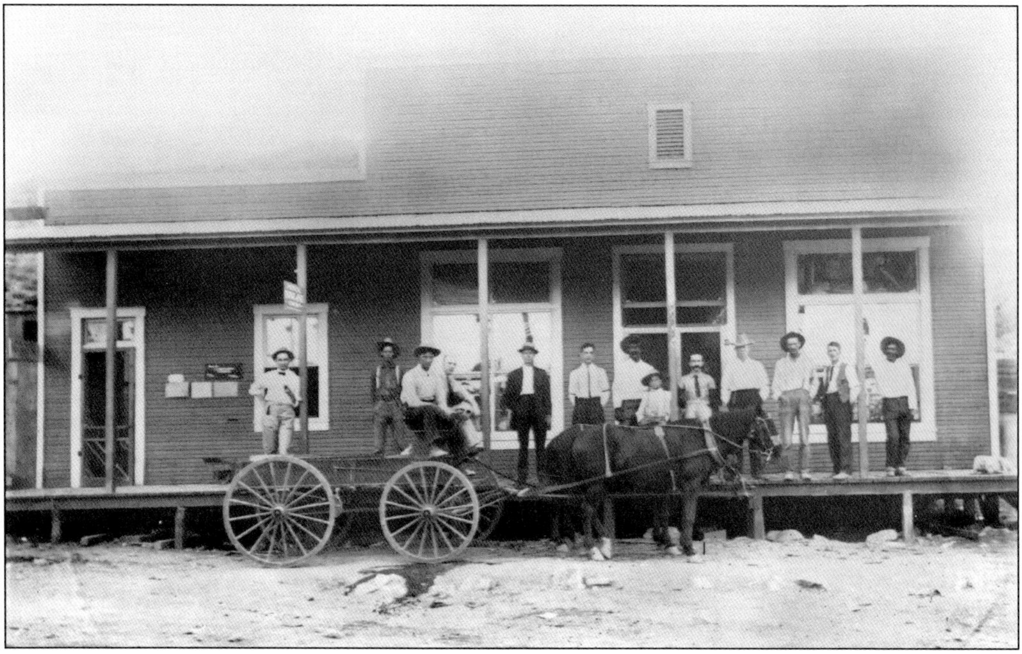

Photography was still a novelty in the 1880s, especially in a place remote even for its time, like Charleston. Everyone stopped what they were doing and put on their best smiles. This wagon is probably about to be loaded with groceries and other merchandise before returning home to a ranch. (Courtesy of Hayden Arizona Collection, Tempe, Arizona.)

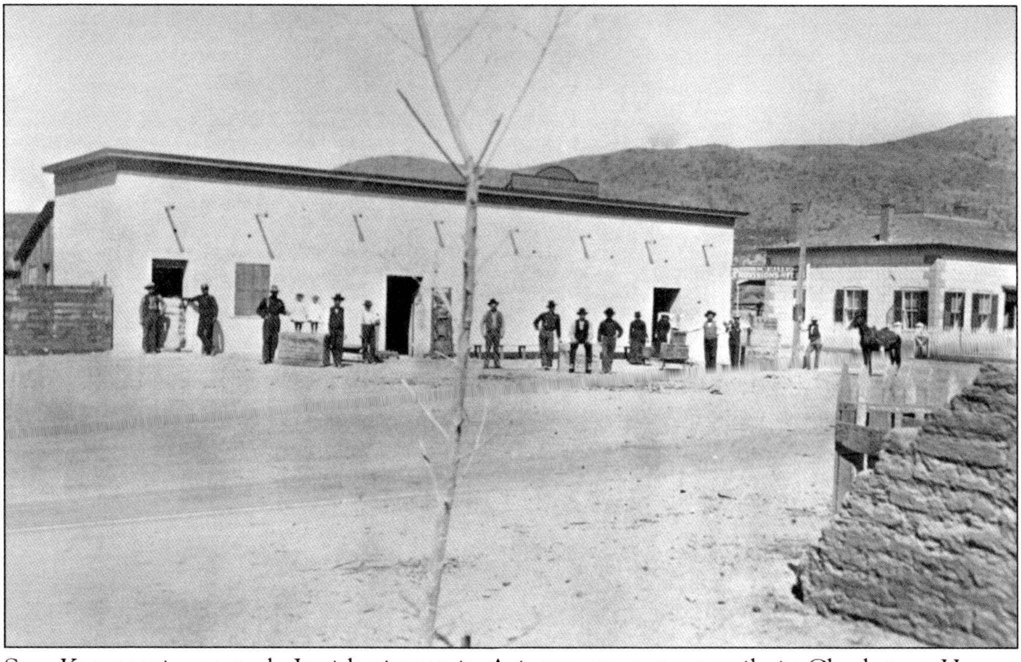

Sam Katzenstein, an early Jewish pioneer in Arizona, ran a mercantile in Charleston. He was a colorful character who played a concertina to entertain his children and nieces as well as his barroom patrons. Charleston, founded in 1879, served as a milling site for ore mined in the silver mines of nearby Tombstone. (Courtesy of Hayden Arizona Collection, Tempe, Arizona.)

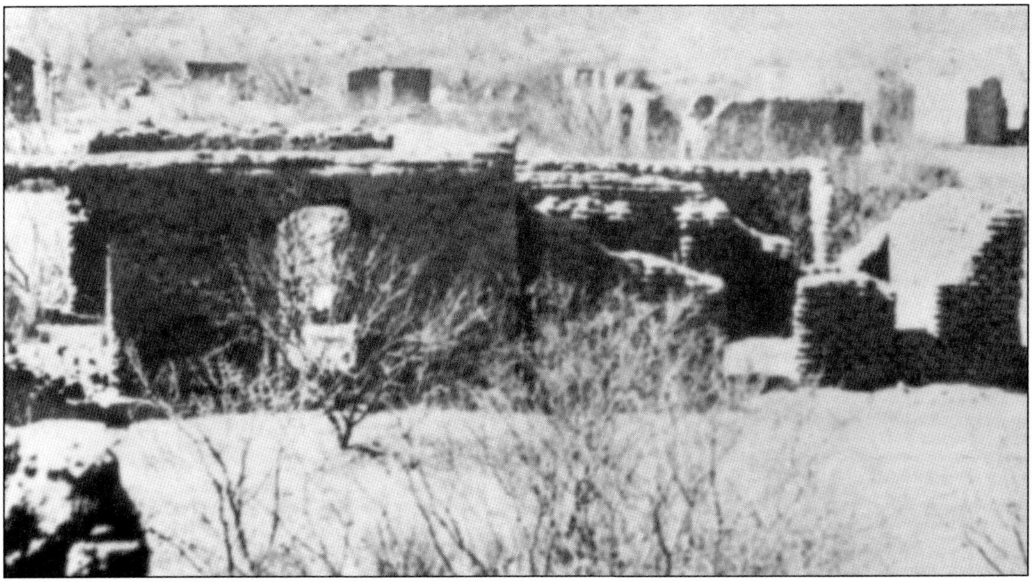

The Millville mill shut down at the end of 1885, striking the death knell for Charleston. An earthquake on May 3, 1887, believed to have been a 7.0 on the Richter Scale, left crumbling adobes and burning embers in southern Arizona Territory and northern Mexico. Thirty minutes of continued tremors reduced most of the adobe buildings to rubble, and Charleston was never rebuilt. The fires created from the falling rocks on extremely dry brush produced an ash that sifted down into the San Pedro River. A few people stayed for a few years after the earthquake, but the post office closed in 1888. (Photograph by Marshall Trimball; courtesy of Hayden Arizona Collection, Tempe, Arizona.)

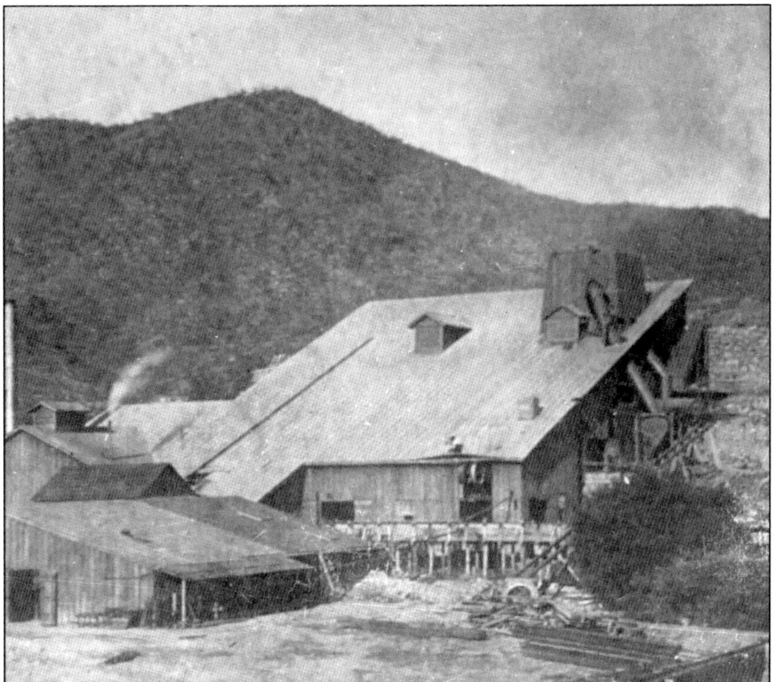

Charleston was the mill center for the reduction works of the Tombstone Milling and Mining Company. It was also the center for cattle thieves and soldiers from nearby Fort Huachuca, who were bent on having a rip-roaring good time. Although Tombstone did not have an adequate water source, Charleston was built on the banks of the San Pedro River, which had a year-round water supply. (Courtesy of Hayden Arizona Collection, Tempe, Arizona.)

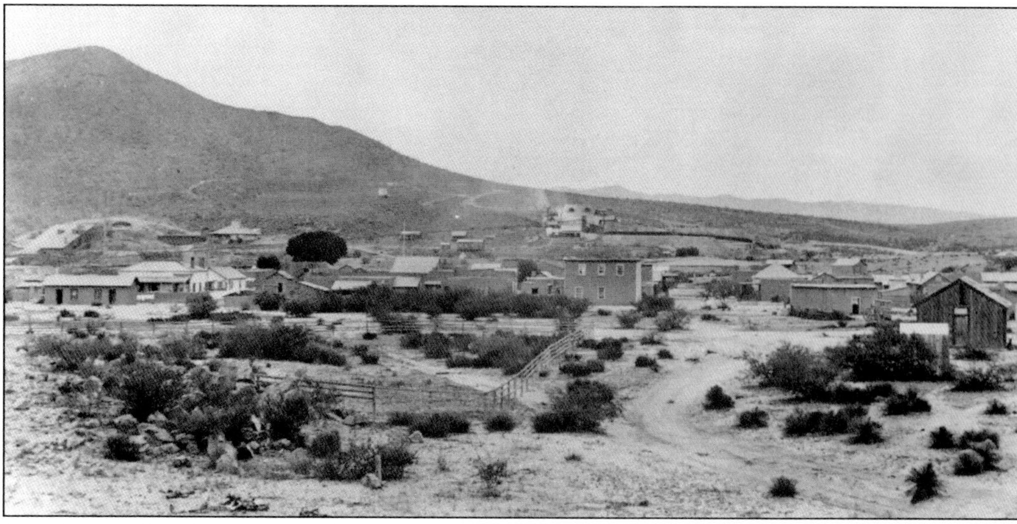

In its heyday, Charleston boasted a population of more than 350 people as well as a school, mercantile laundries, and plenty of saloons. The smoke in the distance comes from Millville, and the two-story house belonged to Richard Gird, who completed the original assay work on Ed Schieffelin's Tombstone discoveries. (Courtesy of Hayden Arizona Collection, Tempe, Arizona.)

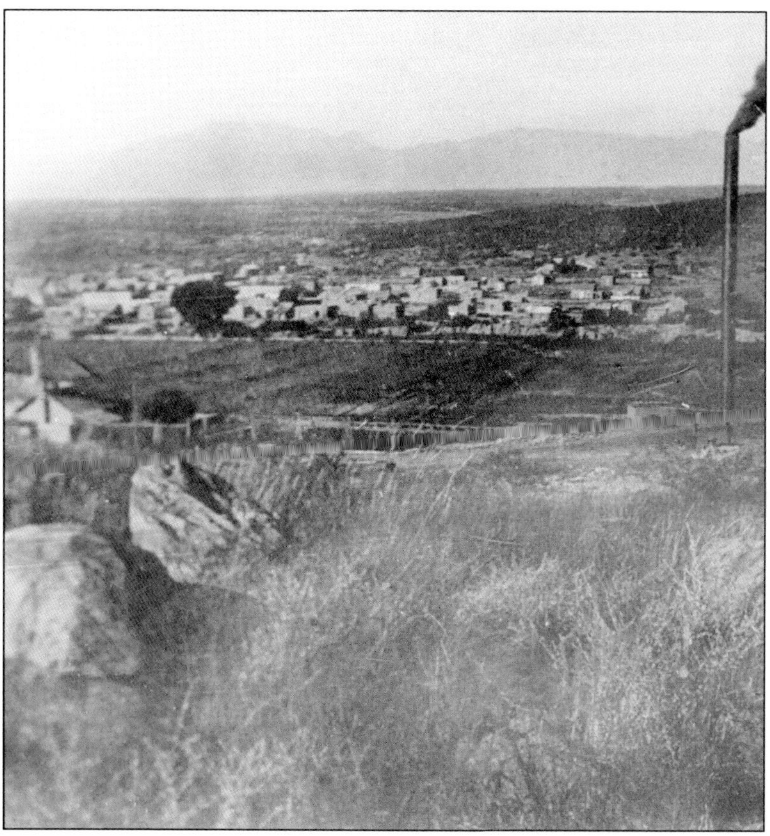

The Charleston smelter belched black smoke into the air as it refined the Tombstone ore. Nevertheless, belching smokestacks were what every town wanted to show off their prosperity. Little consideration was given to air pollution and miners' health. (Courtesy of Hayden Arizona Collection, Tempe, Arizona.)

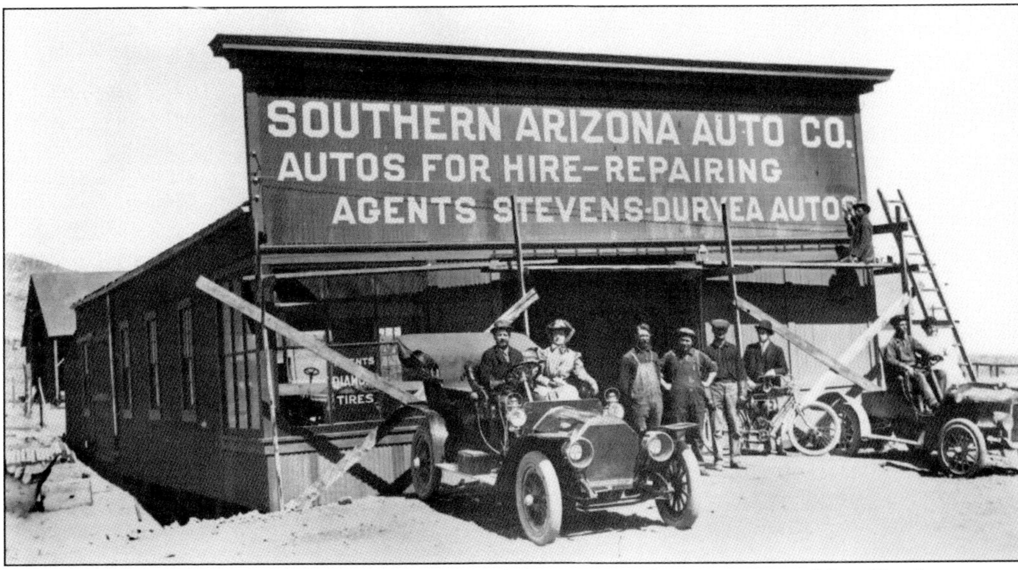

With the arrival of the automobile in the early 1900s, residents in towns like Charleston and nearby Courtland found themselves ready to get dressed in their finest outfits and take a spin. Pictured here is the Southern Arizona Auto Company. Stevens-Duryea was an early automobile manufacturer. The company established rental sites all over the United States, many with only one car. In 1901, J. Frank Duryea built the pilot model for the first Stevens-Duryea automobile as part of the J. Stevens Arms and Tool Company in Chicopee Falls, Massachusetts. This five-passenger car had Westinghouse air shock absorbers, a spring-loaded front bumper, and at the time was the only car with a one-piece windshield. It cost around $5,000, and today this grand old touring car would be worth at least a quarter of a million dollars. (Courtesy of Hayden Arizona Collection, Tempe, Arizona.)

Jacob W. Swarts bought Frank Stilwell's Charleston saloon in early 1881. Drinks were advertised for 12.5¢, which would have been one bit. Two bits in the United States is a quarter or 25¢. The "bit" expression dates from Colonial days, when a common unit of currency was the Spanish milled dollar. To make change, a dollar would have been cut into eight pie-shaped pieces called bits. Stilwell was involved in the events leading up to the gunfight at the O. K. Corral. Wyatt Earp considered Stilwell to be the main suspect in his brother Morgan's murder. (Courtesy of Arizona Historical Society, Tucson, Arizona.)

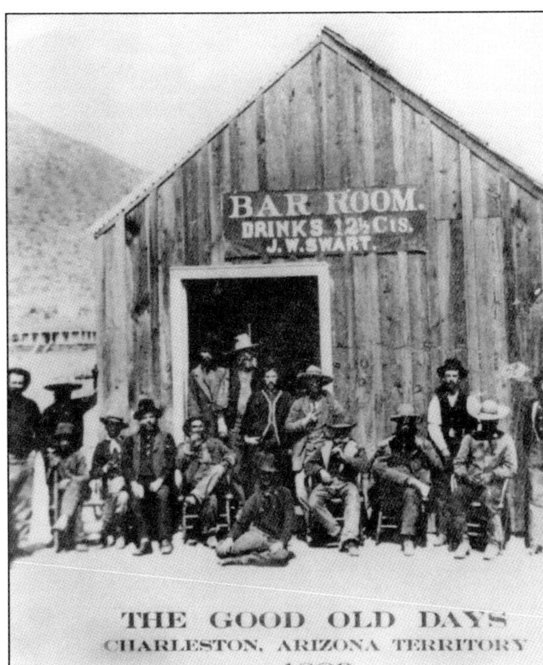

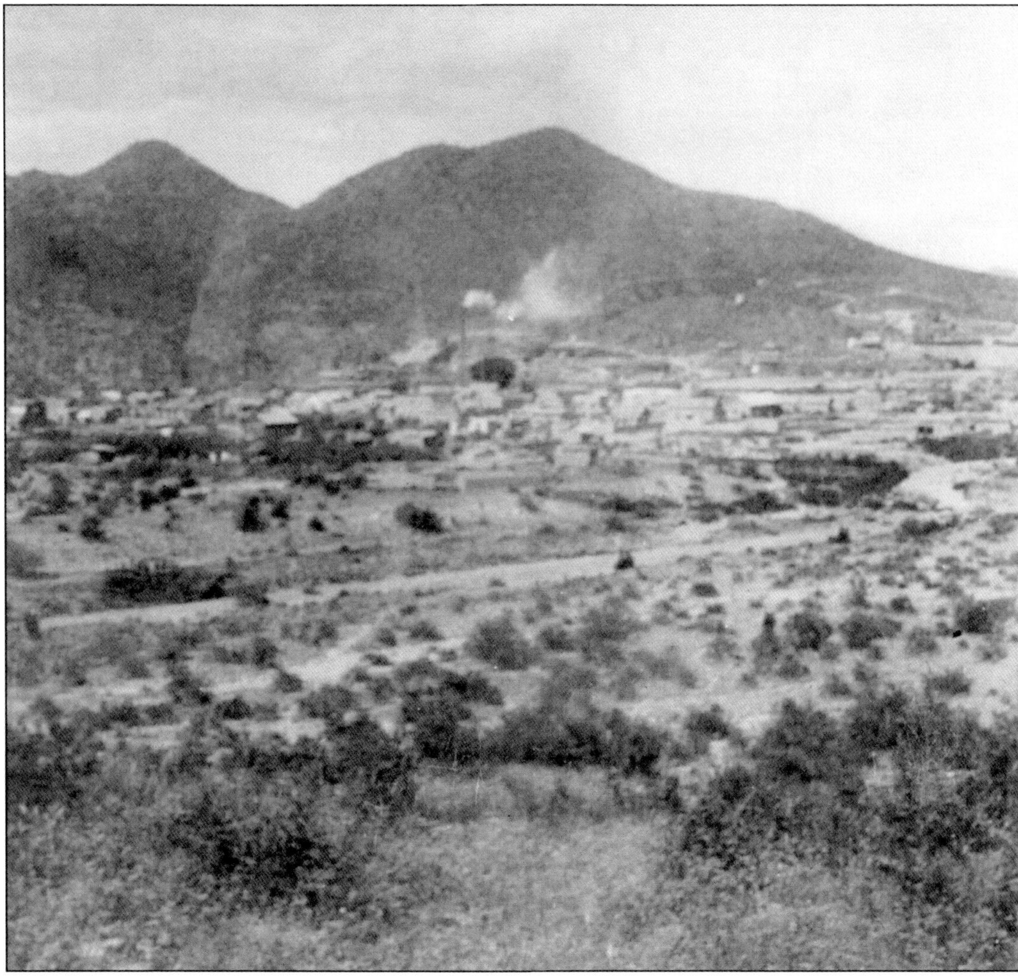

Pictured here is a view of Charleston around 1882. Interestingly, in 1943, troops from nearby Fort Huachuca used the old Charleston town site as a gunnery range for recruits to practice street fighting with live ammunition. It was dubbed "Little Tunisia" by the troops because Arizona and Tunisia in South Africa are approximately the same latitude and have a similar environment. (Courtesy of Hayden Arizona Collection, Tempe, Arizona.)

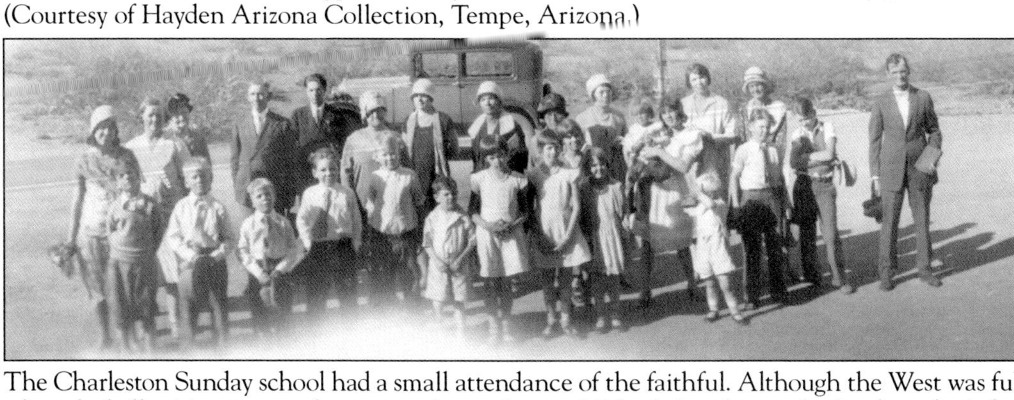

The Charleston Sunday school had a small attendance of the faithful. Although the West was full of rowdy, hell-raising towns, there were those who established churches and schools and tried to make the places like Charleston livable. (Courtesy of Arizona Sate Archives, Phoenix Arizona.)

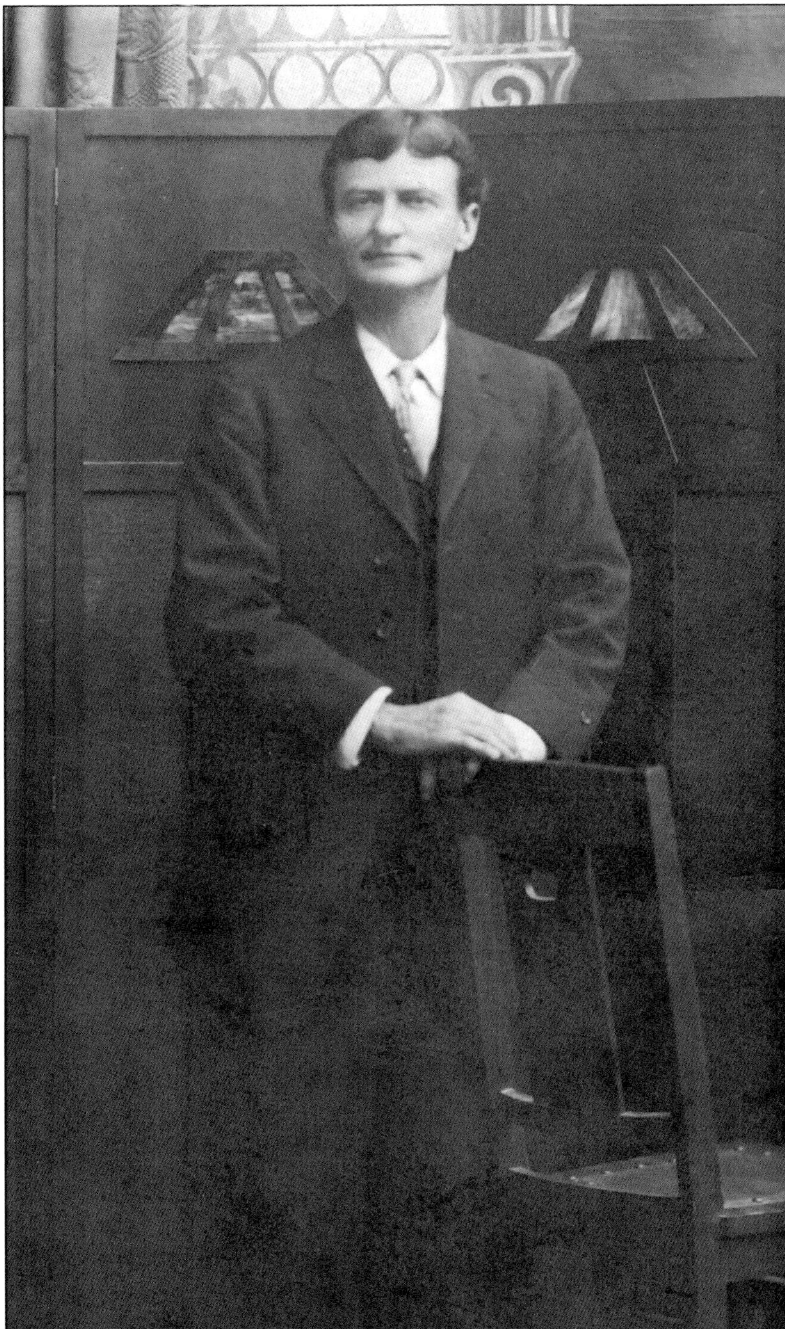

Billy Old, an Uvalde, Texas, native, was a member of the short-lived Arizona Rangers. In 1907, Lt. Billy Old's assignment was to clean out northern Arizona of thieves, murderers, and cattle rustlers above the Colorado River. He had five men to help him. He returned to Tombstone in October to testify before a grand jury concerning arrests he had made before his transfer. Old remarked, "It is certainly mighty fine to be back in the lowlands where it is not necessary to be bundled up in heavy woolens and overcoats." (Courtesy of Arizona Historical Society, Tucson, Arizona.)

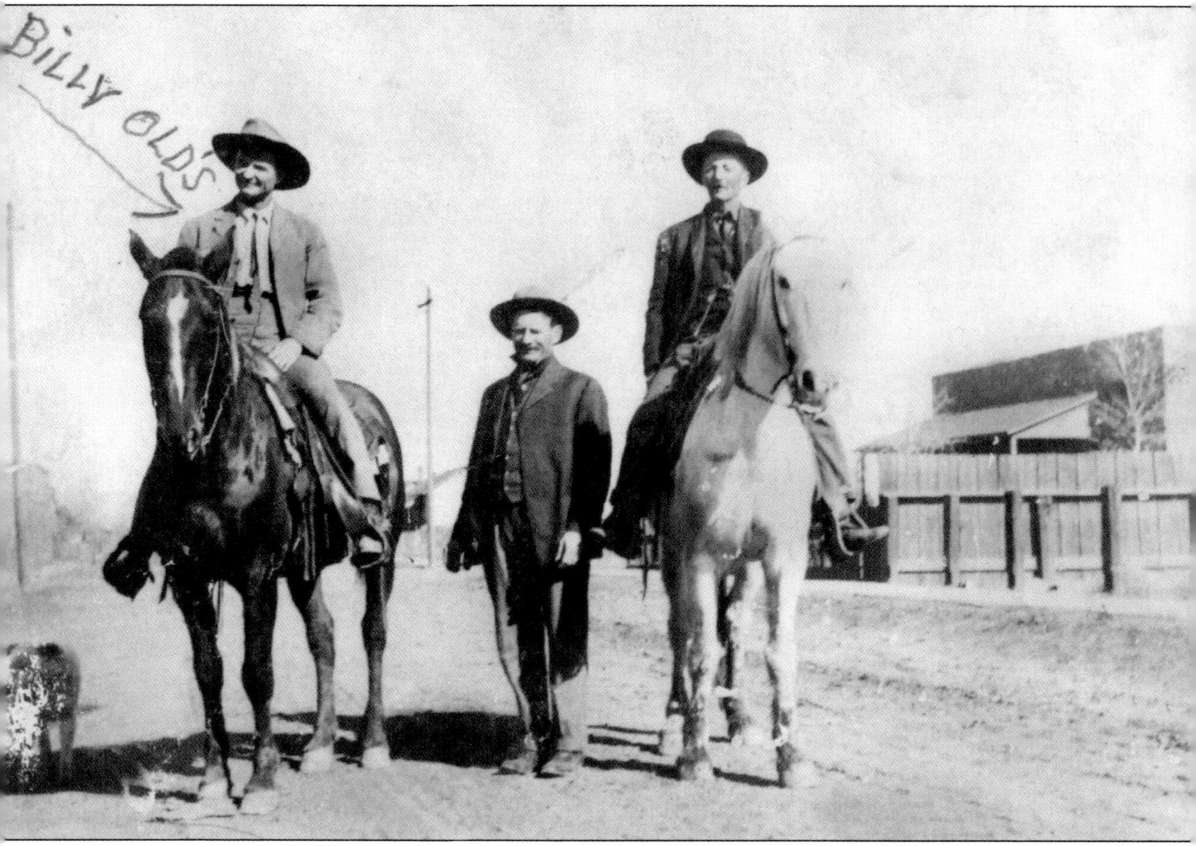

Pictured here are, from left to right, three members of the Arizona Rangers—Lt. William "Billy" Old, Pvt. Cy Byrne, and Pvt. Sam Black. Billy Old was small in stature and fast with the gun. However, Billy Old loved the ladies a little too much, and on April 28, 1914, he was shot and killed by his wife, Annie, in Pearce. He ran out into the street screaming for help, but it was too late. Annie appeared at his funeral in manacles. (Courtesy of Arizona Historical Society, Tucson, Arizona.)

Two

Courtland, Gleeson, St. David, Fairbank, and Pearce

Courtland, Gleeson, and Pearce, now ghost towns, were once thriving mining towns. Courtland's post office was established on March 13, 1909, and the area at one time had more than 2,000 residents. W. J. Young, owner of the Great Western Mining Company, named the town for his brother Courtland Young. A butcher store, mercantile, Wells Fargo office, Southern Arizona Auto Company (owned by Stevens and Duryea), and the Mexico and Colorado Railroad from Douglas all thrived in Courtland. For entertainment, there was a swimming pool and a cinema as well as baseball games and horse races. Unfortunately, when the mines played out, so did the town. The post office was discontinued on September 30, 1942. Almost nothing is left of Courtland except the ruins of the jail, stone walls, one collapsing store, a cemetery south of the town, and plenty of mines and mine shafts that tell the story of a more prosperous time.

In 1900, John Gleeson, an Irish miner from the town of Pearce, prospected in the old Turquoise area, found copper, and started the Copper Belle Mine. The area became known as Gleeson and had a population of about 500 people. The town was moved closer to water resources. In 1912, a fire burned down the town, but it was rebuilt because of the large body of copper ore produced there. John Gleeson sold his claims in 1914. Although copper production flourished during World War I, after the war prices dropped and the mines closed. The post office closed on March 31, 1939. The hospital, saloon, jail, and school ruins still exist along with the cemetery on the road to Tombstone.

The St. David community was founded in 1877 by Mormons who named the site after David W. Patten, an apostle in the Church of Jesus Christ of Latter-day Saints. Fairbank was named after Chicago investor Nathaniel Kellogg Fairbank, a railroad man who provided capital to open the Tombstone silver mines. On February 15, 1900, Fairbank was the scene of a gunfight between lawman Jeff Davis Milton and members of the Burt Alvord gang, resulting in the killing of Three-Fingered Jack Dunlop and the wounding of both Milton and Bravo Juan Yaos during the gang's attempt at a train robbery. Now it is a ghost town, but during the 1880s Fairbank was home to a post office, mills, railroad lines, a school, and a hotel. The last few residents were evicted in the 1970s when the buildings were declared unsafe. The remaining structures at Fairbank include a small stone schoolhouse, two wooden houses, and a wooden outhouse.

For several years, Johnnie Pearce and his wife lived in Tombstone, where he mined and she managed a boardinghouse. They ranched in Sulphur Springs Valley near present-day Pearce. One evening in 1894, while riding his range, Pearce stopped to rest at the top of a small hill, and his burro wandered off. While searching for the animal, Pearce found a rock that was heavier than it should be, and he knew he had struck gold. Pearce filed claim for the Commonwealth Mine, and people flocked to the area. A post office opened in Pearce in March 1896 and the Pearce railroad station opened in 1903. The mine was worked until 1904 when cave-ins caused a temporary shutdown.

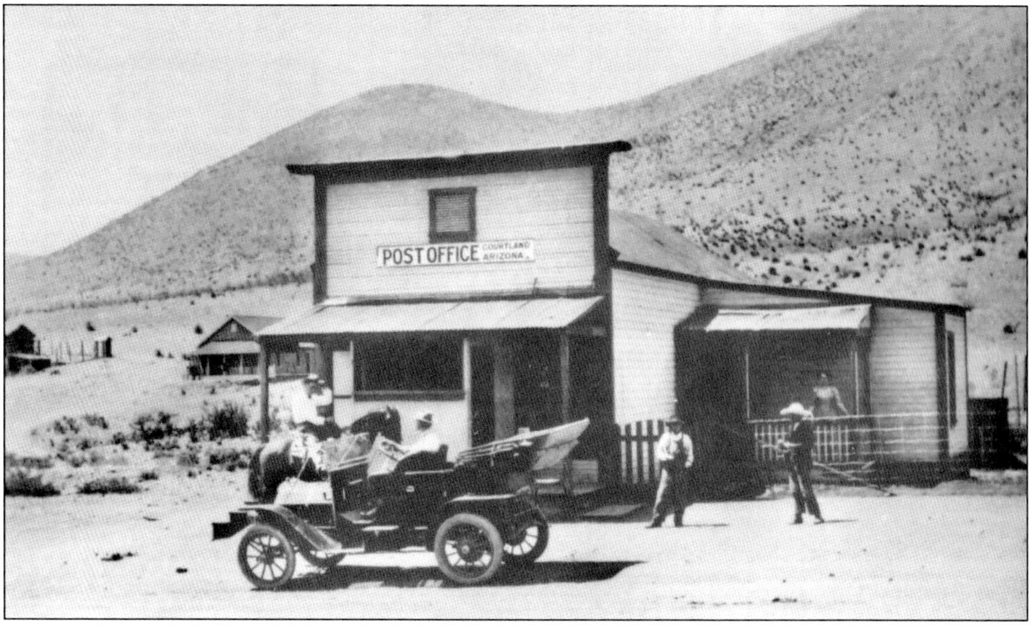

Courtland, Arizona, was named after Courtland Young, brother of W. J. Young who established the Great Western Mining Company, which operated several mines in the Tombstone area. The post office, which also housed the Wells Fargo office, was established on March 13, 1909, with Henry Locke as the postmaster. Folks now came in their automobile to pick up their mail. The post office was discontinued on September 30, 1942. (Courtesy of Arizona State Archives, Phoenix, Arizona.)

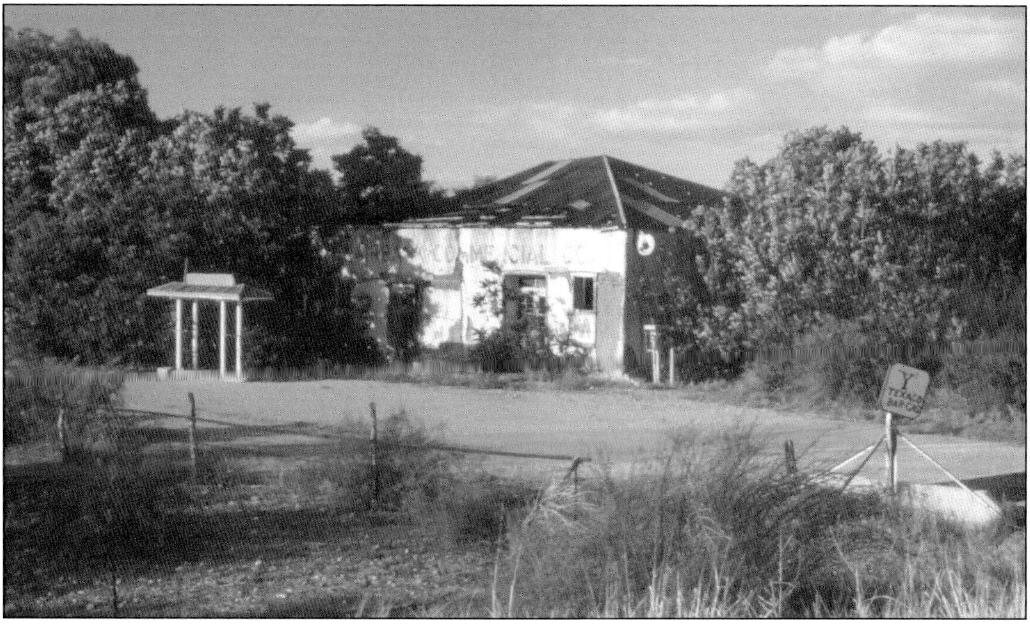

Only faded letters remain on the Commercial Company building, which was once the hub of Fairbank, Arizona. The town was named for Nathaniel K. Fairbank, who organized the Grand Central Mining Company in Tombstone. Fairbank was one of the stockholders in the railroad line that ran from Fairbank to Benson to Mexico. (Photograph by Marshall Trimble; courtesy of Hayden Arizona Collection, Tempe, Arizona.)

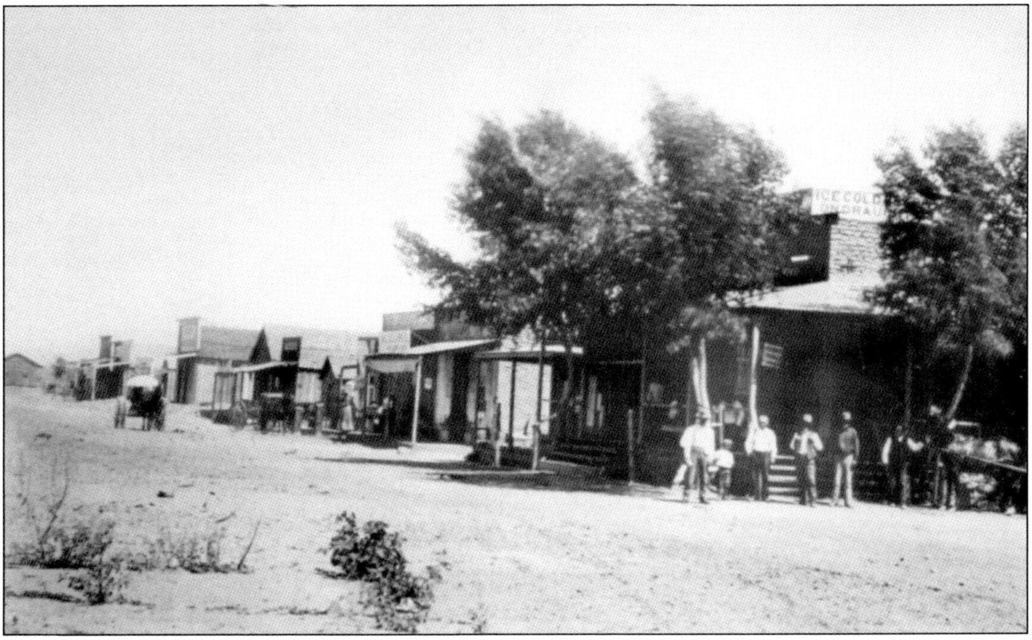

This is an early photograph of Nathaniel Fairbank (front left). The building in the shadows is an old hotel, which has stood since the early 1880s. Fairbank's early life was spent in New York where he became a journeyman bricklayer. He later went to Chicago where he learned the manufacture of soap and lye. After making $5 million in the Chicago Stockyards, he joined the Chicago Board of Trade. (Courtesy of Hayden Arizona Collection, Tempe, Arizona.)

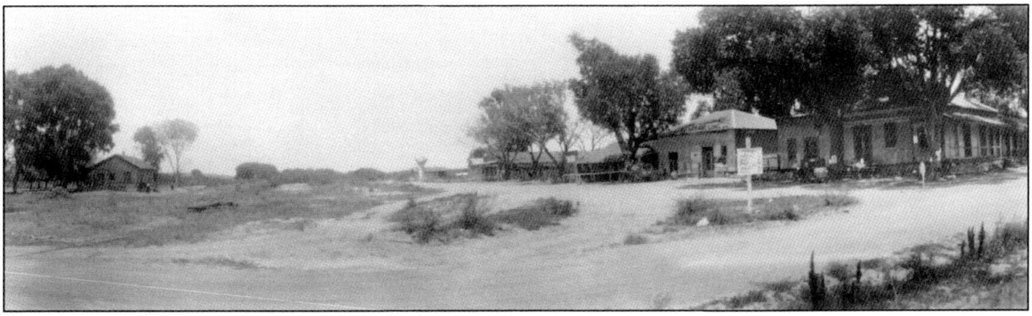

This is a view of the prosperous home of a Fairbank resident. In the early 1880s, Nathaniel Fairbank invested heavily in the Tombstone mines. He also promoted the Santa Fe, Prescott, and Phoenix Railroad. He later promoted the Congress Mine in central Arizona and the Maxwell land grant in New Mexico. Fairbank died in Chicago at the age of 73 on March 27, 1903. (Courtesy of Hayden Arizona Collection, Tempe, Arizona.)

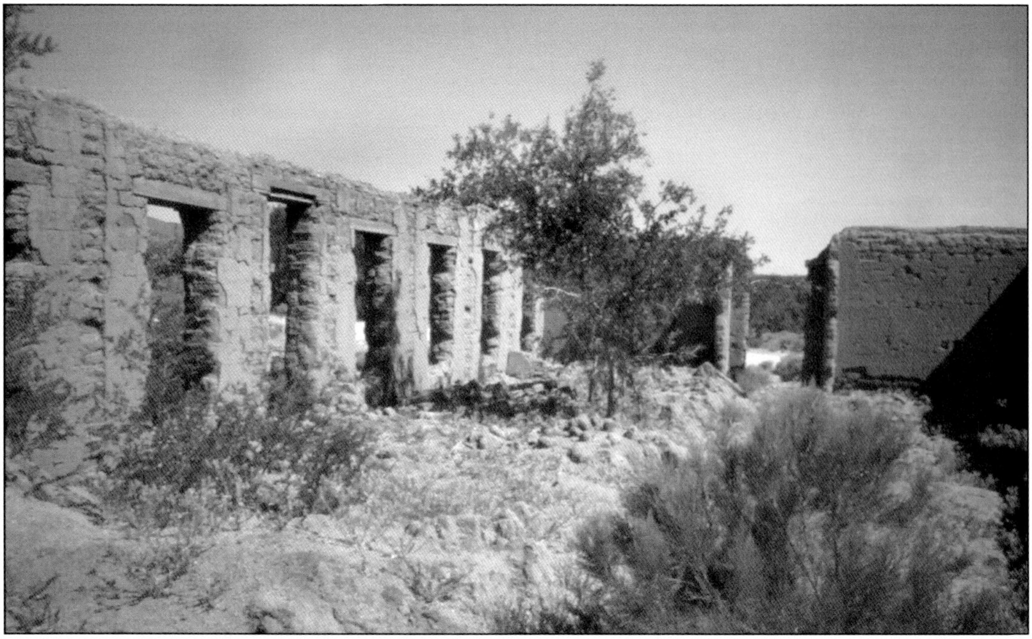

Only crumbling adobe walls remain of Gleeson, Arizona. In 1889, John Gleeson married Elizabeth Cummings from Syracuse, New York. They had eight children. John and Elizabeth, Irish immigrants, arrived in Tombstone via Iowa and Colorado in the 1880s. This frugal couple saved their money from John's earnings as a miner and Elizabeth's work running a boardinghouse. When the mines at Tombstone played out they moved, and John discovered rich mines in the Gleeson area. Long before the white man came to this area, Native Americans mined the Turquoise mines. In 1925, Gleeson's oldest son, Edward, who ran a garage at Bowie, Arizona, was killed in a car accident. (Photograph by Marshall Trimble; courtesy of Hayden Arizona Collection, Tempe, Arizona.)

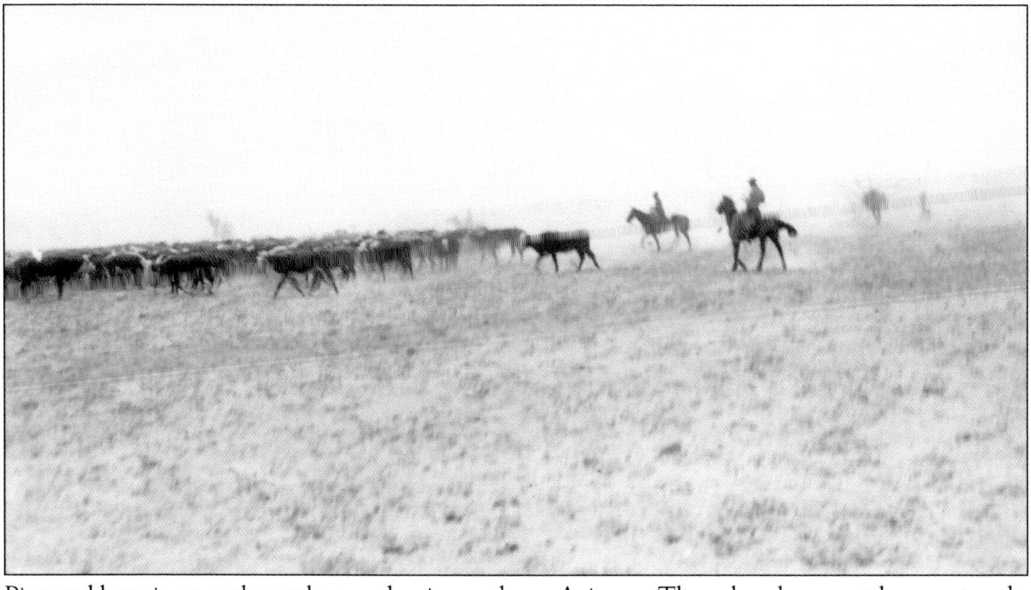

Pictured here is an early cattle roundup in southern Arizona. These longhorn cattle were tough, and they learned to forage for food and live on what the desert would produce until they were brought to market. (Courtesy of Hayden Arizona Collection, Tempe, Arizona.)

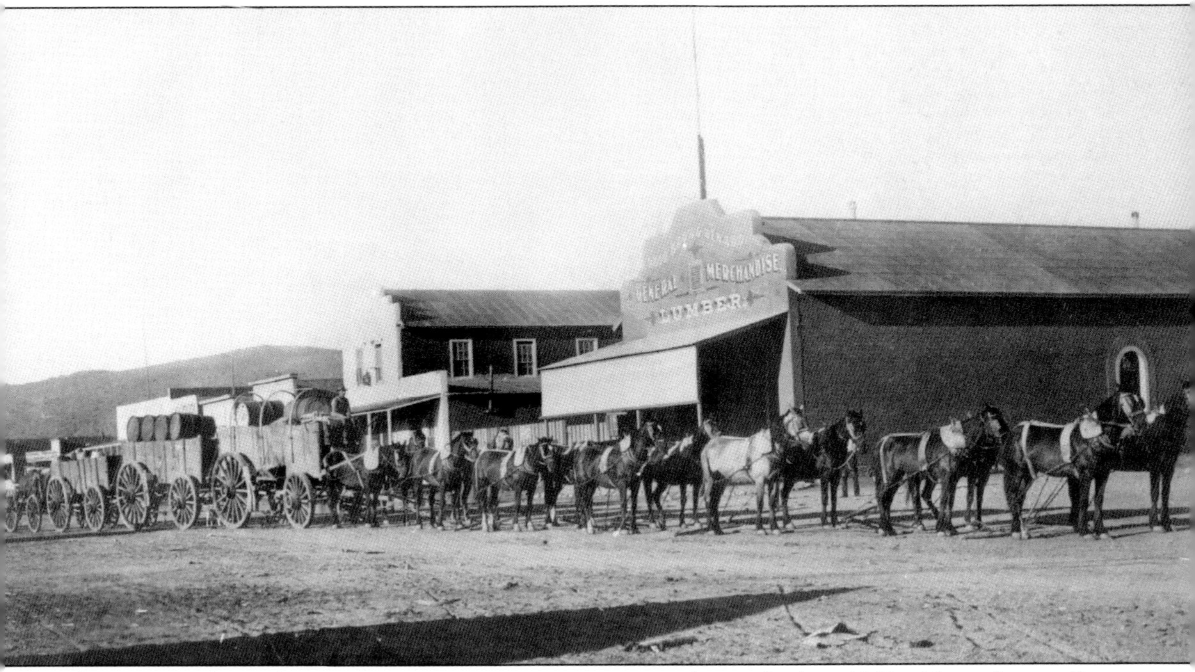

These magnificent long wagon trains were a common sight in the late 1880s. Note the small wheels on the front of the wagon, which would make for easier, safer turns. Here the train is picking up supplies in Pearce to take to the mine. On its return trip, it would take ore from the mines to places where it could be milled and shipped out by train. (Courtesy of Hayden Arizona Collection, Tempe, Arizona.)

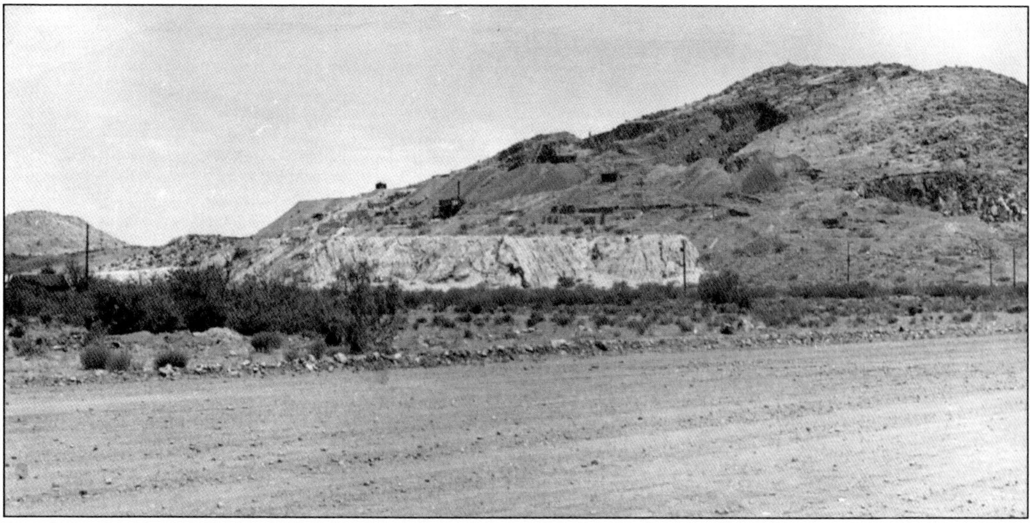

Roads had to be built through dangerous, rough country for the wagon trains. (Courtesy of Hayden Arizona Collection, Tempe, Arizona.)

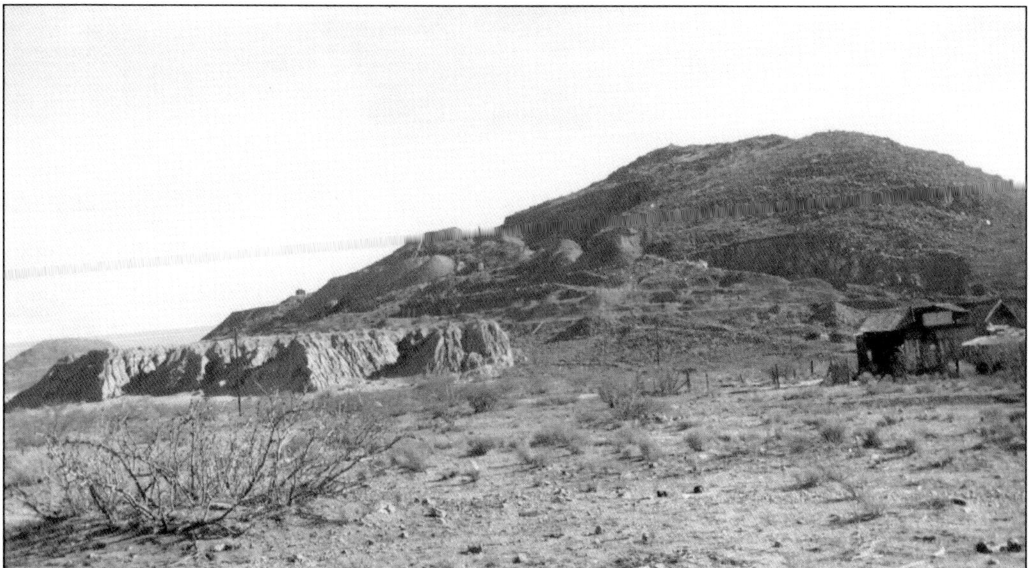

This road ran from the Graham Mountains to Pearce and then on to the Dragoon Mountains. (Courtesy of Hayden Arizona Collection, Tempe, Arizona.)

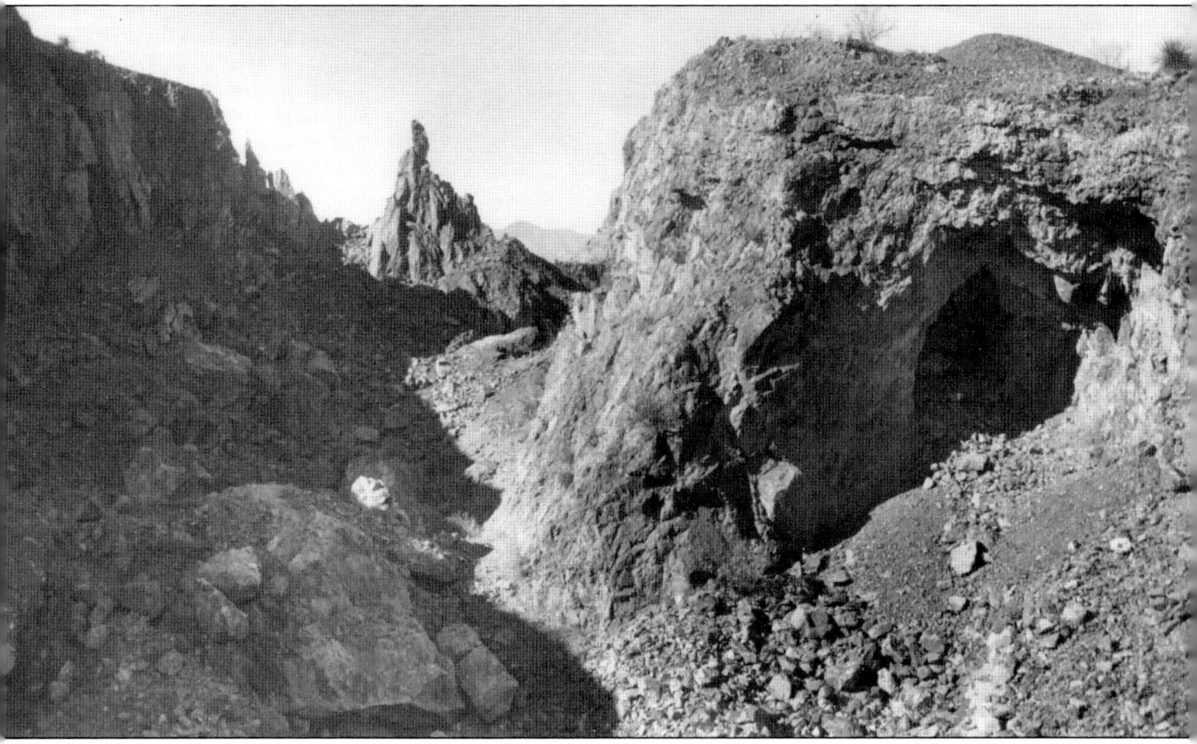

Frequently passages were narrow and treacherous. (Courtesy of Hayden Arizona Collection, Tempe, Arizona.)

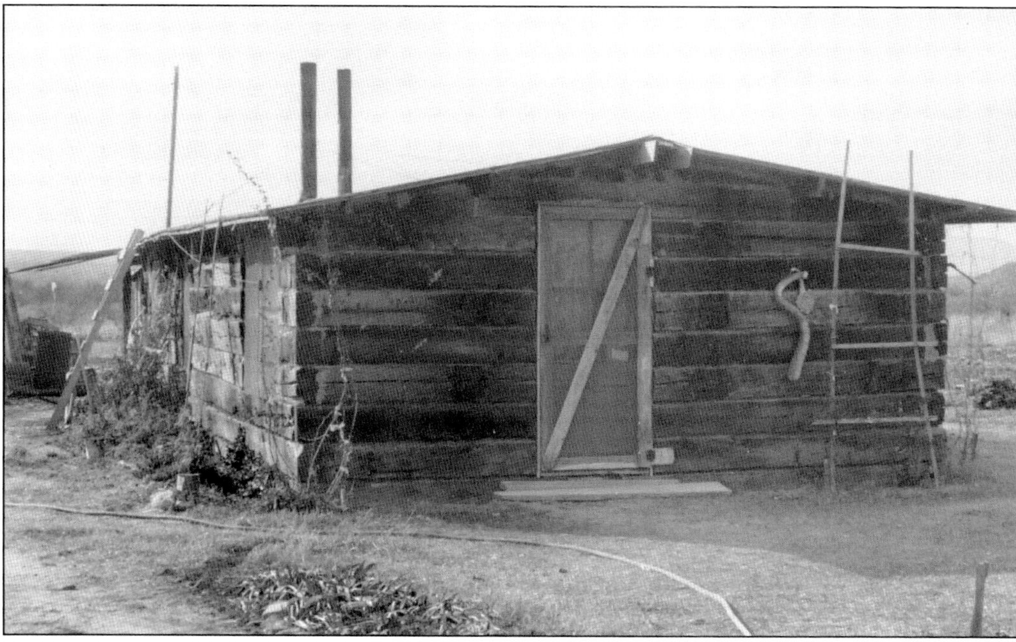

St. David was established as a Mormon colony around 1877. With a shortage of building supplies, at least one enterprising soul constructed his home out of old railroad ties. During the first year, the pioneers built a rock fort about 60 square feet in size. They also endured the hazards of malaria. (Courtesy of Shirley Gillespie, St. David, Arizona.)

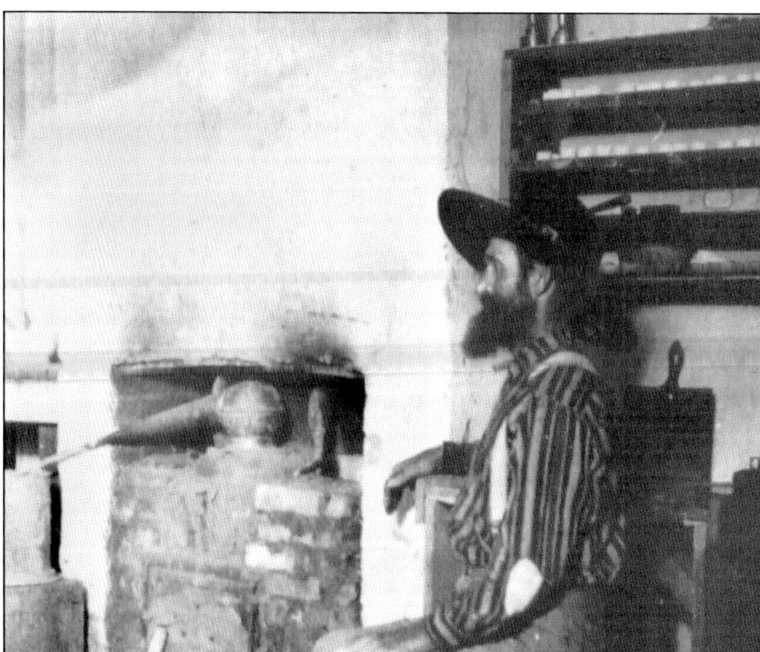

Pictured is John Reid, just one of the many mining pioneers. He appears to be quite comfortably off for his occupation and the time. (Courtesy of Shirley Gillespie, St. David, Arizona.)

Three

The Rogue of the Mascot Mine

In 1857, a stage station was built by the San Antonio and San Diego Stage Lines (Butterfield-Overland) in Ewell Springs. By the time Fort Bowie was established four years later, the station had been destroyed by Apache Indians in the area. In 1864, the first American mining claims appear to have been filed by 17 soldiers/prospectors.

During the 1870s, the town grew. There was a barbershop, brewery, general store, brickyard, hotel, blacksmith, three saloons, a stamp mill for gold ore, and a population of approximately 300 people. A post office was established on April 8, 1879, and the name of the town was changed to Dos Cabezas. Dos Cabezas ("two heads" in the Spanish translation) was named after two bald peaks in the Dos Cabezas mountain range, located on the east side of Sulphur Springs Valley. Another stage station was built by the National Mail and Transportation Company in 1884.

Thomas McCauley was the owner of the Dos Cabezas Mascot Mine; the property is now known as Dos Cabezas Spirit and Nature Retreat. McCauley, known to some as an angel and to others as a rogue, called the property the Hospitality House. Here McCauley wined and dined prospective clients who bought worthless shares in his worthless copper mine. Entry to the Dos Cabezas Mascot Mine lent credence to Mark Twain's description that "a mine is a hole in the ground with a liar at the other end."

Dos Cabezas prospered well into the 20th century as a transportation center and mining town, as people mined for about 80 years here. Some of the richest mines on the gold-bearing ledge near the town were the Silver Cave, Greenhorn, and Murphy.

However, when the mines closed, the businesses and settlers started leaving. By 1960, Dos Cabezas was well on its way to becoming a ghost town, and the post office officially closed on January 31, 1960, although the building is still standing.

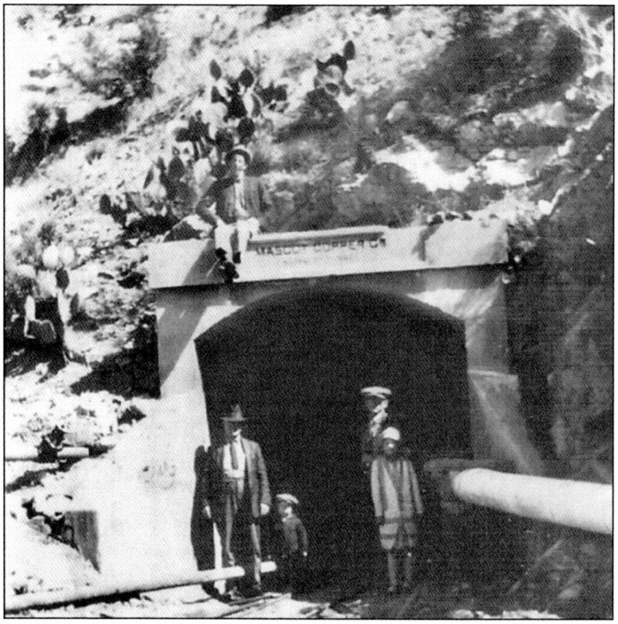

The entry to the Dos Cabezas Mascot Mine lent credence to Mark Twain's description that "a mine is a hole in the ground with a liar at the other end." It was a worthless mine. The *Copper Handbook of 1908* mentioned that a mysterious man by the name M. Page, accompanied by a mining engineer, had appeared on the Dos Cabezas scene. M. Page was actually Thomas McCauley. (Courtesy of Phyllis de la Garza.)

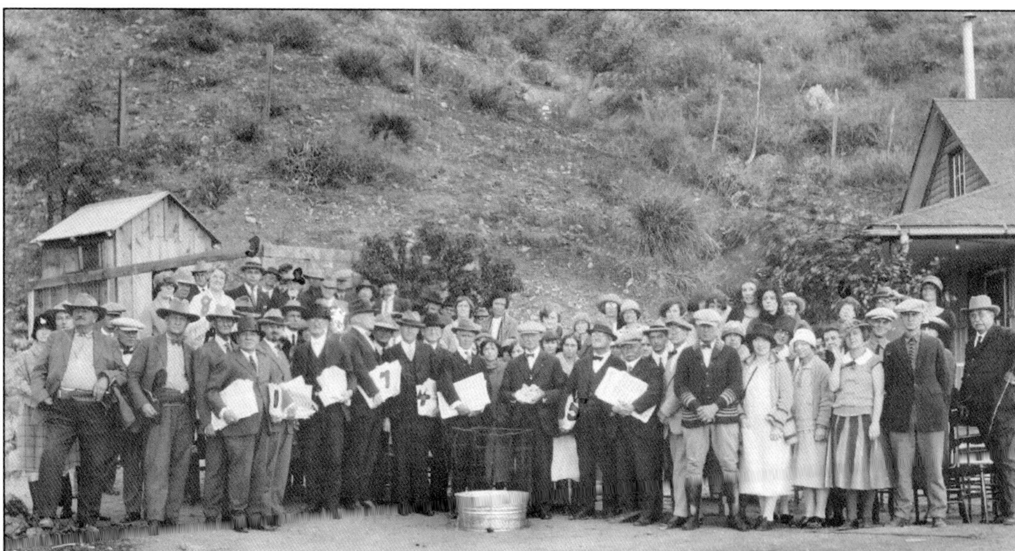

Everyone was thoroughly encouraged by the burning of the bond that indicated that the mine was clear of debt. Thomas N. McCauley brought a bevy of beautiful secretaries from Chicago. The local cowboys were enchanted with the ladies and decided there had to be a dance. The ladies decided they had to have baths before attending the dance. However, scarcity of water was a problem. The *Engineering Mining Journal Press* wrote, "Now one of the problems at this property is a scarcity of water. Only about 20 gallons per minute are available, but the New York stenographers knew nothing about water scarcity. The girls all took a bath and went to the dance. Had a swell time too, they say. But the mine had to shut down until the tanks were replenished. It is understood that there is an opening for an efficiency engineer who can figure out a plan to provide baths for the stenographers and supply enough water to keep the mine going at the same time. The problem is most serious on Saturday night." (Courtesy of Arizona Historical Society, Tucson, Arizona.)

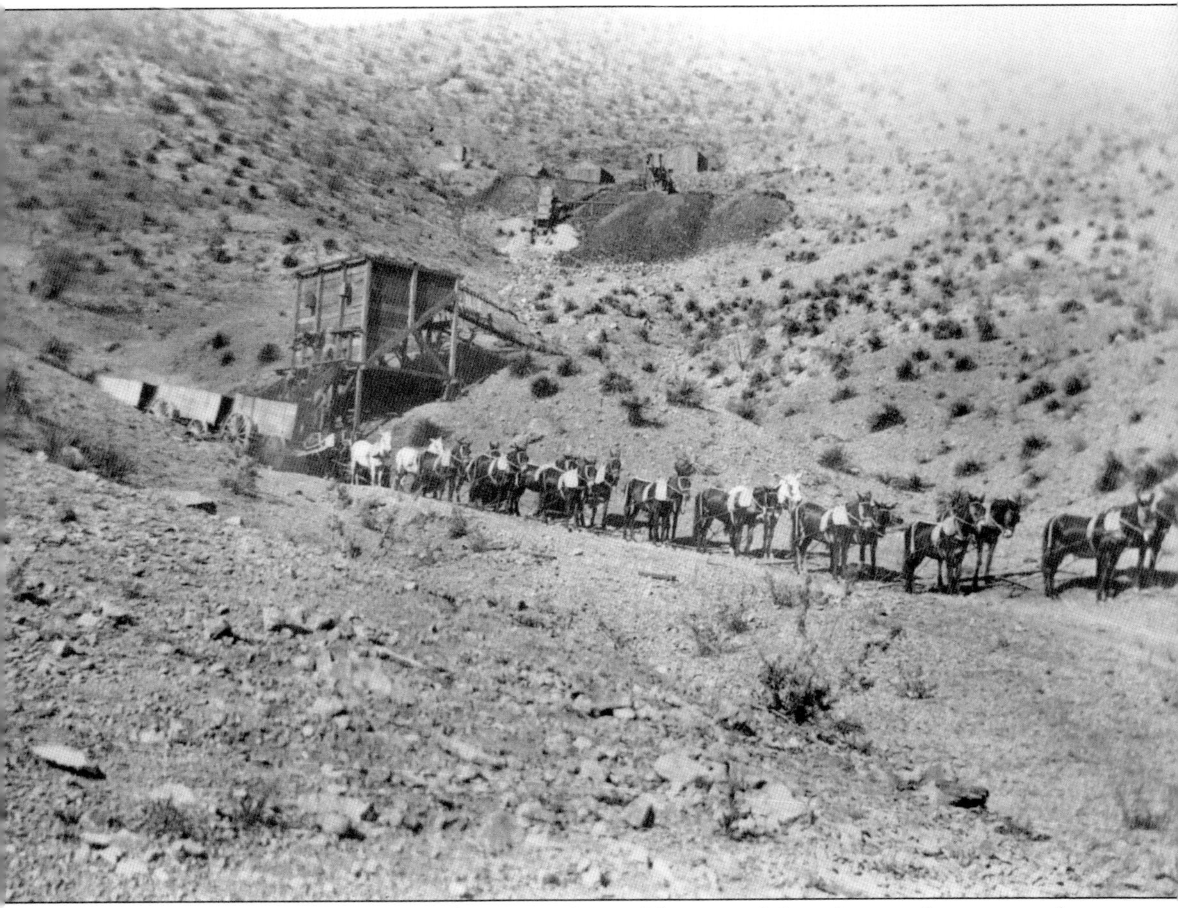

A small wagon train hauls ore from the Mascot Mine. The mine did produce ore but not nearly enough to cover the millions that McCauley fleeced from his stockholders. He gave grand banquets in places like San Francisco to encourage investment, but the investors never saw a dividend or even a share of stock. (Courtesy of Arizona Historical Society, Tucson, Arizona.)

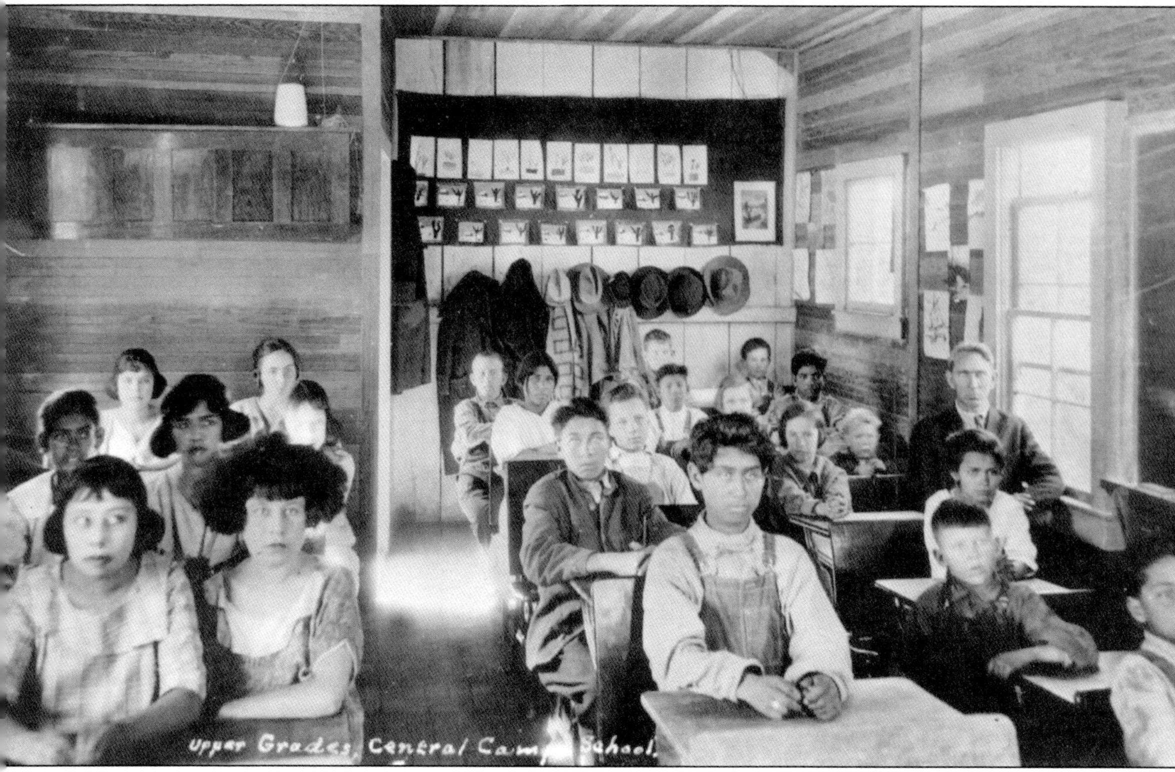

There was enough money in the town to hire a teacher and open the Dos Cabezas School. Still the town watched carefully when McCauley brought in important investors and herded them into the local newspaper office to expound on the value of the Mascot Mine. (Courtesy of Arizona Historical Society, Tucson, Arizona.)

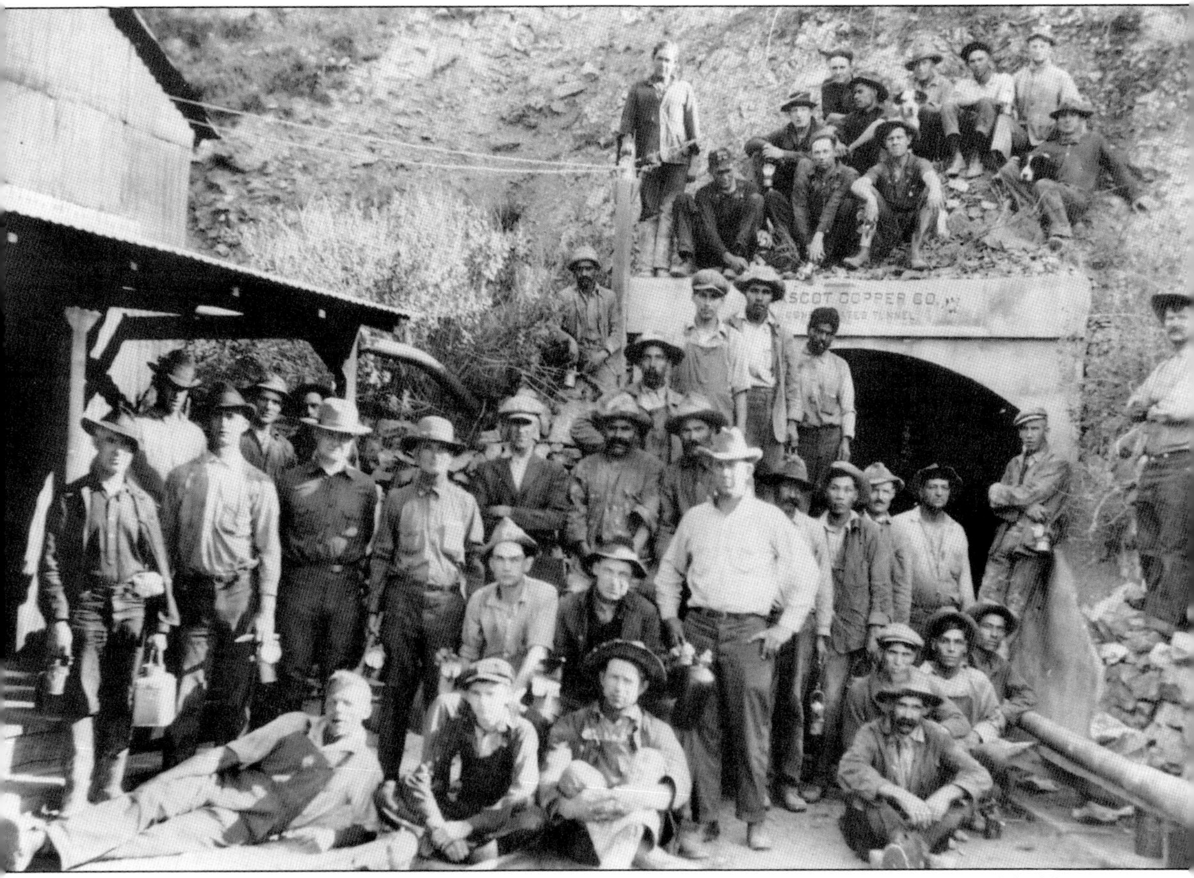

Miners take a break to have their picture taken in front of the Mascot Copper Company. Stockholders were becoming disillusioned, but McCauley calmed them down by saying, "Great mines always take time to develop." The Mascot Copper Company's push for stock sales ended just before World War I. The Central Copper Company was formed to acquire the Elma mine and to assume the Mascot Copper's holdings when the lease that company had with American Smelting and Refining Company (ASARCO) was surrendered. It operated copper mines on the southwestern slopes of the Dos Cabezas Mountains. A rail line from the mine to the main rail line at Wilcox was completed in 1915 and ore was shipped to El Paso for smelting. The Mascot continued to operate under a lease, and the two mines operated until 1930. Total production, chiefly copper, amounted to about $800,000. The property was then sold to ASARCO, which after nine months was returned to its owners. (Courtesy of Arizona Historical Society, Tucson, Arizona.)

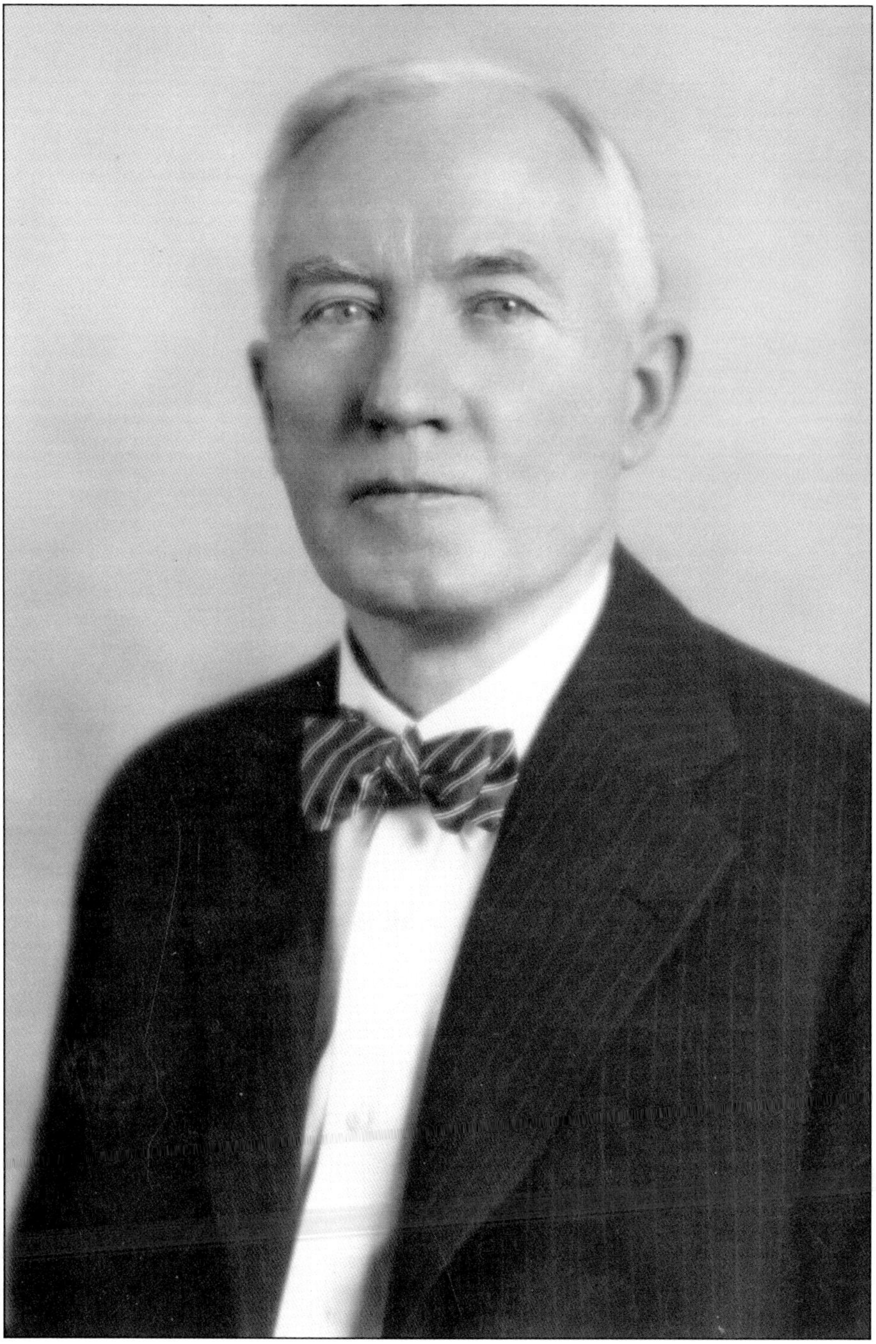

Thomas N. McCauley moved to Tucson where he started a securities company, which managed to fleece even more stockholders. One lady described him as a "fine Christian gentleman," but most referred to him as the "Rogue of the Mascot Mine." He was last seen on a yacht outside the 3-mile limit near San Francisco and is supposed to have died shortly thereafter in that city. No one was ever tried or indicted for any of his schemes. Most of the secretaries stayed in Arizona and married the cowboys they had met at that first dance. (Courtesy of Arizona Historical Society, Tucson, Arizona.)

Four

Gunfight at the O. K. Corral

The soldiers from Fort Huachuca, who were scouting the desert, asked Ed Schieffelin, "What are you looking for?" The crusty prospector with his long flowing mane and piercing black eyes, tersely muttered one word, "Gold!" The soldiers laughed and said, "All you'll find here is your tombstone."

Schieffelin discovered not gold but a rich mother lode of silver. When his brother Al called him a lucky cuss, Ed named his first claim the Lucky Cuss. Prospectors swarmed into the tent city of Tombstone. Other silver strikes included the Tough Nut, the Grand Central, and the Contention, each richer than the one before. Tombstone sprang up almost overnight with gunslingers, miners, bawdy house girls, gamblers, and a variety of persons of dubious reputation. Around the clock the bat-wing doors of the saloons swung open and shut while glasses clinked and the chips kept changing hands. Cattle rustling and stagecoach robbing became popular sports. Through legends and the gunfight at the O. K. Corral, Tombstone secured its place in Western history.

Even today, Tombstone capitalizes on its lurid reputation. Nevertheless, early Tombstone had many upstanding, respectable citizens. Rev. Endicott Peabody established a church, which still stands. Nellie Cashman, the angel of Tombstone, never turned anyone away hungry from her restaurant, and miners were ready to pull a gun on the stranger who dared criticize her cooking. Today visitors can dine at Nellie Cashman's secure that the gunfight is only a reenactment—maybe.

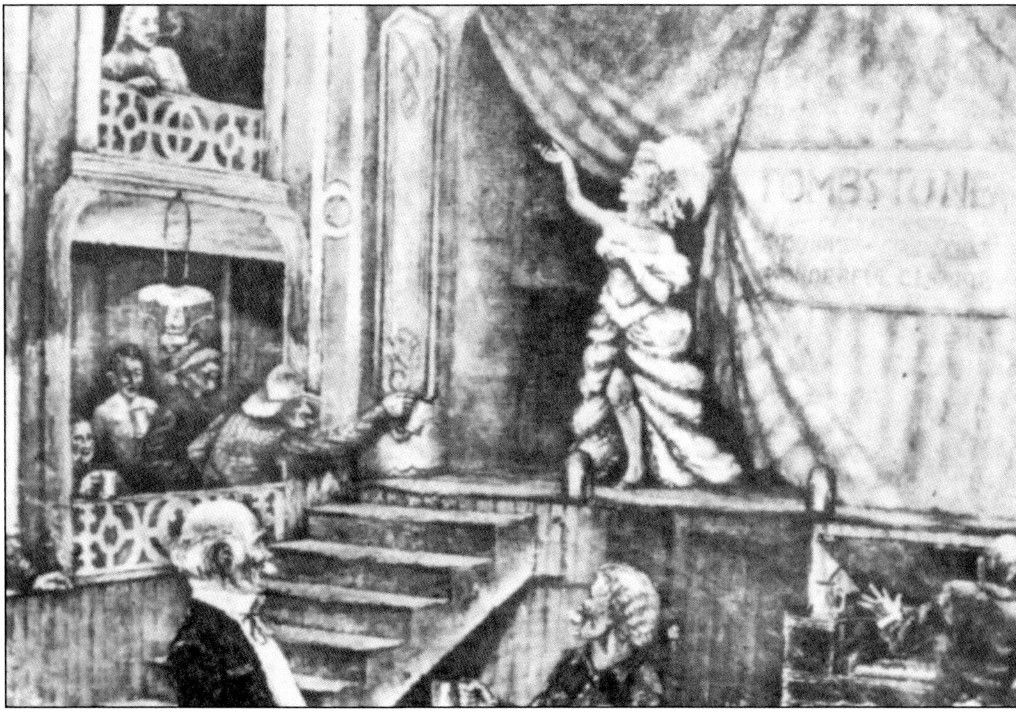

Tombstone's legends added much to the popularity of the town. Many were created in the saloons and the Bird Cage Theatre. Once, an eastern dude wandered into a Tombstone saloon and said, "Why this town isn't tough! I thought this was supposed to be a tough town." A quiet hush fell over the gathering as a Tombstoner reached into his pocket, pulled out a rattlesnake, and without a word threw it on the floor in front of the dude. With a grandiose hurdle, the stranger departed Tombstone. (Courtesy of Arizona Historical Society, Tucson, Arizona.)

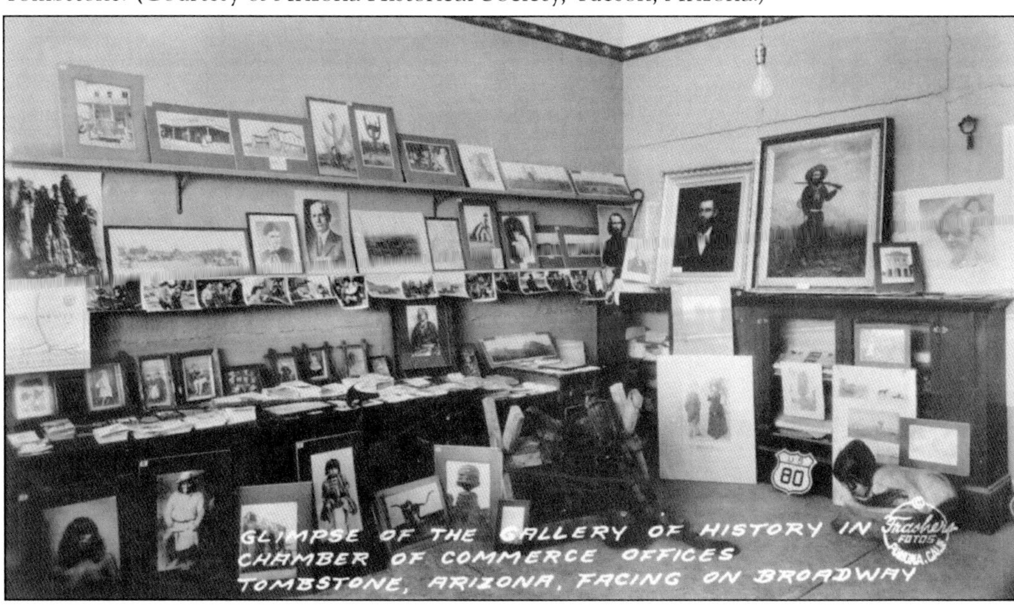

Pictured here are images of the colorful characters that made Tombstone a memorable place. (Courtesy of Arizona Historical Society, Tucson, Arizona.)

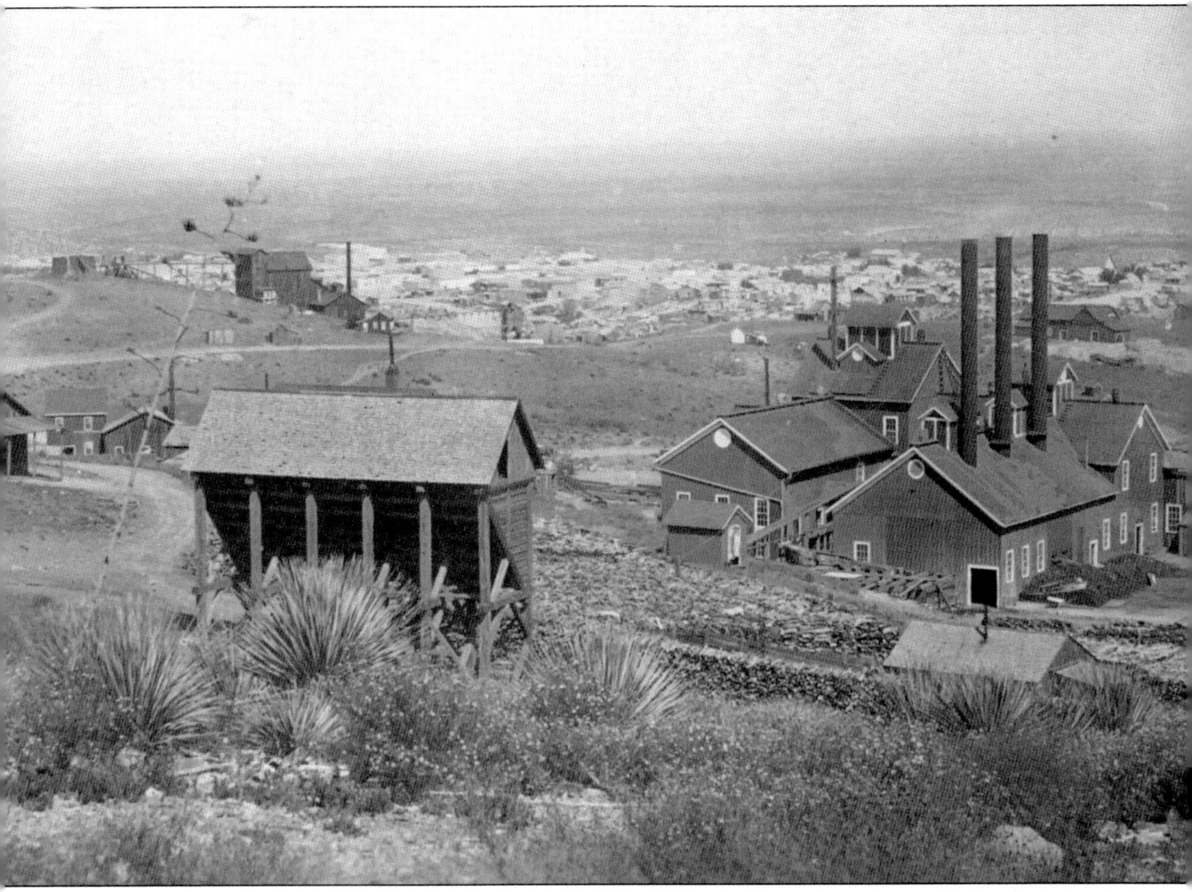

In 1879, the *Arizona Daily Star* reported that Contention City would soon rival Tombstone in importance. It got its name from the constant squabbling among investors. D. T. Smith and John McDermott sold lots and on March 4, 1880, the *Star* reported that Contention City was "a landscape for the pencil and fancy of an Italian painter." Three stamp mills served the mines, and the first passenger train reached town on January 10, 1882. This is a view of the Contention Consolidated Mine, which acquired some of the most valuable Tombstone mining property for a mere $10,000. The mine failed, however, when underground water flooded the works. (Author's collection.)

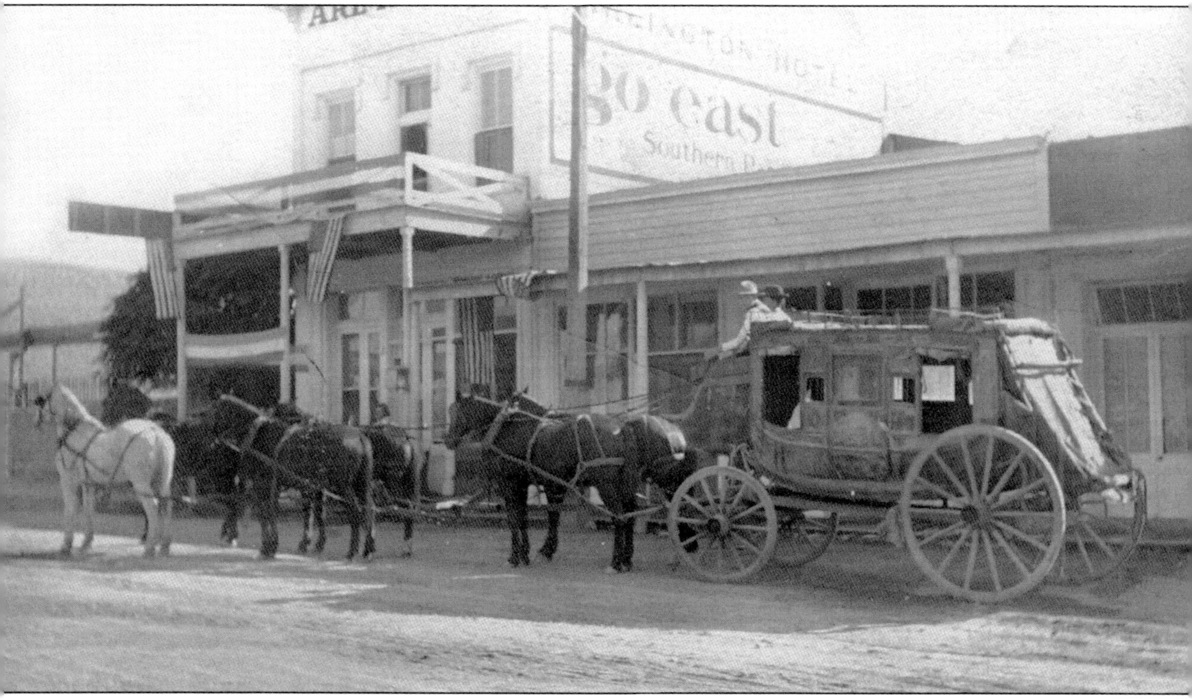

While many were advised to go west to find their fame and fortune, Tombstone advertised that it would take people east on its stagecoach. The trip would be miserable as the coach lurched over rocky, treacherous roads, and passengers were strapped in with early seat belts. They would pause for refreshment at the stage stops and hope that they would get through the trip without being attacked by highwaymen or Native Americans. (Courtesy of Arizona State Archives, Phoenix, Arizona.)

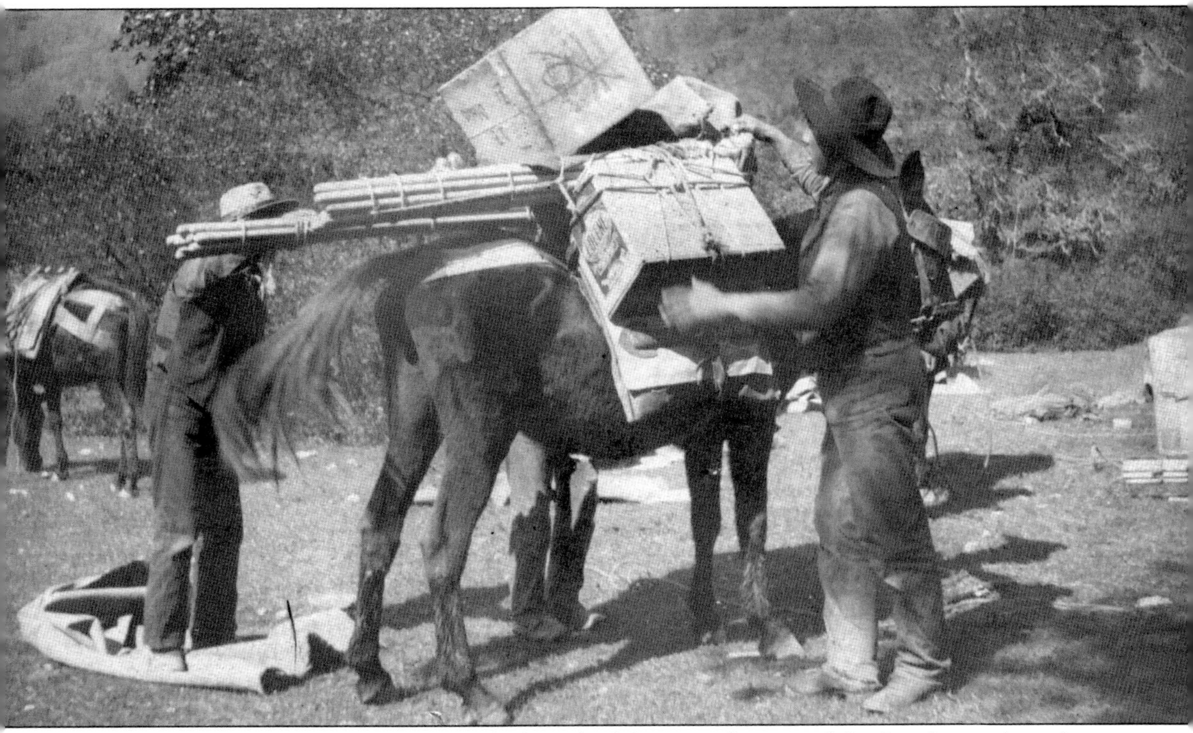

No animal is more closely associated with the colorful mining history of the Southwest than the burro. Prospectors were very careful about how they packed their animal. The little burro might willingly carry a heavy load but would kick up a storm and become ornery, lazy, stubborn, and many words not fit to print if the packing was unbalanced. Tents, mining gear, and food were usually packed on the animals using a diamond hitch. (Courtesy of Arizona State Archives, Tempe, Arizona.)

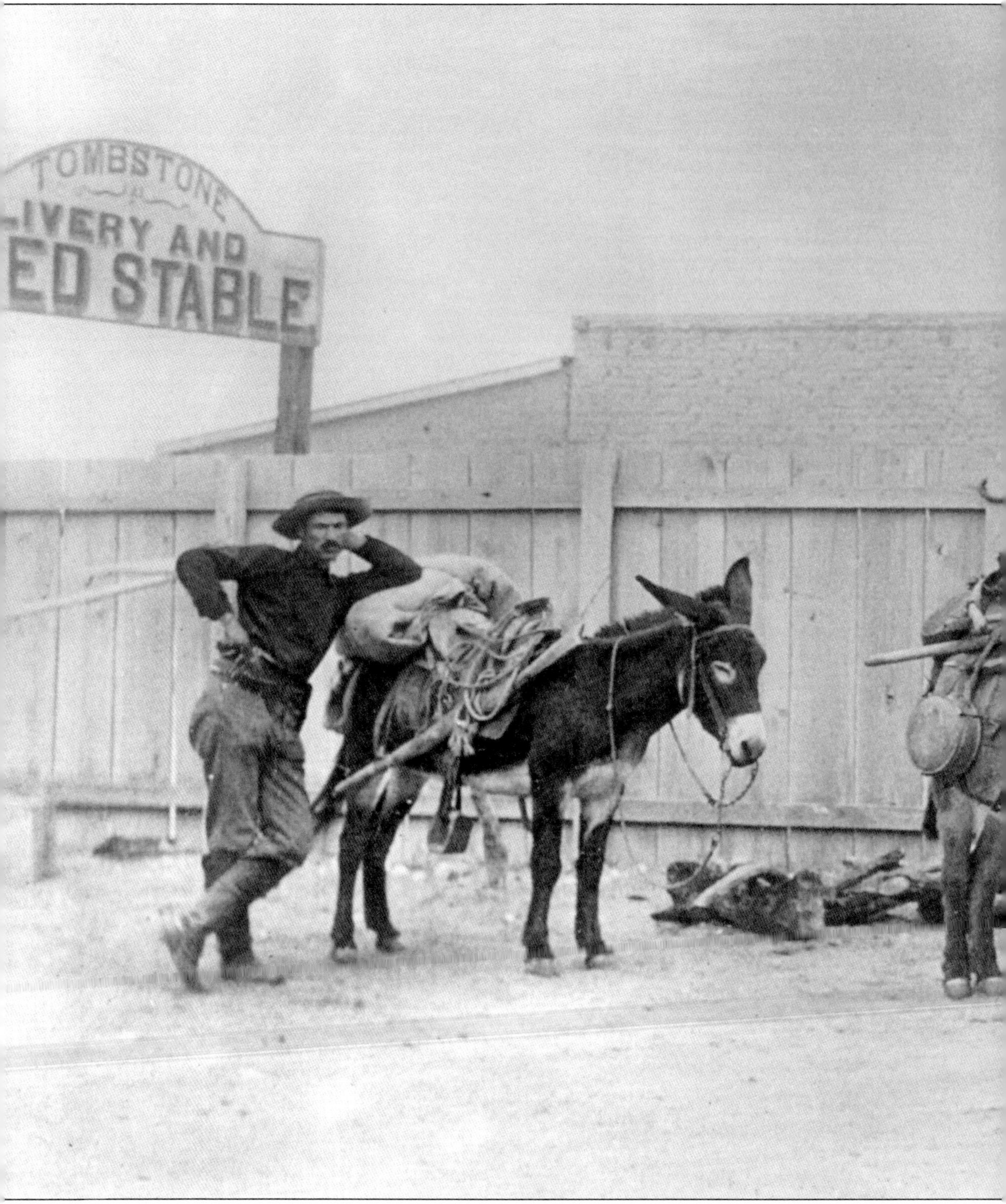

Two prospectors are setting out from the Tombstone Livery Stable, most certainly hopeful that on this day they will find their fortune. Note that each man carries guns, a blanket, and water with him. One burro carries only the prospecting gear, food, and pots and pans for cooking. The

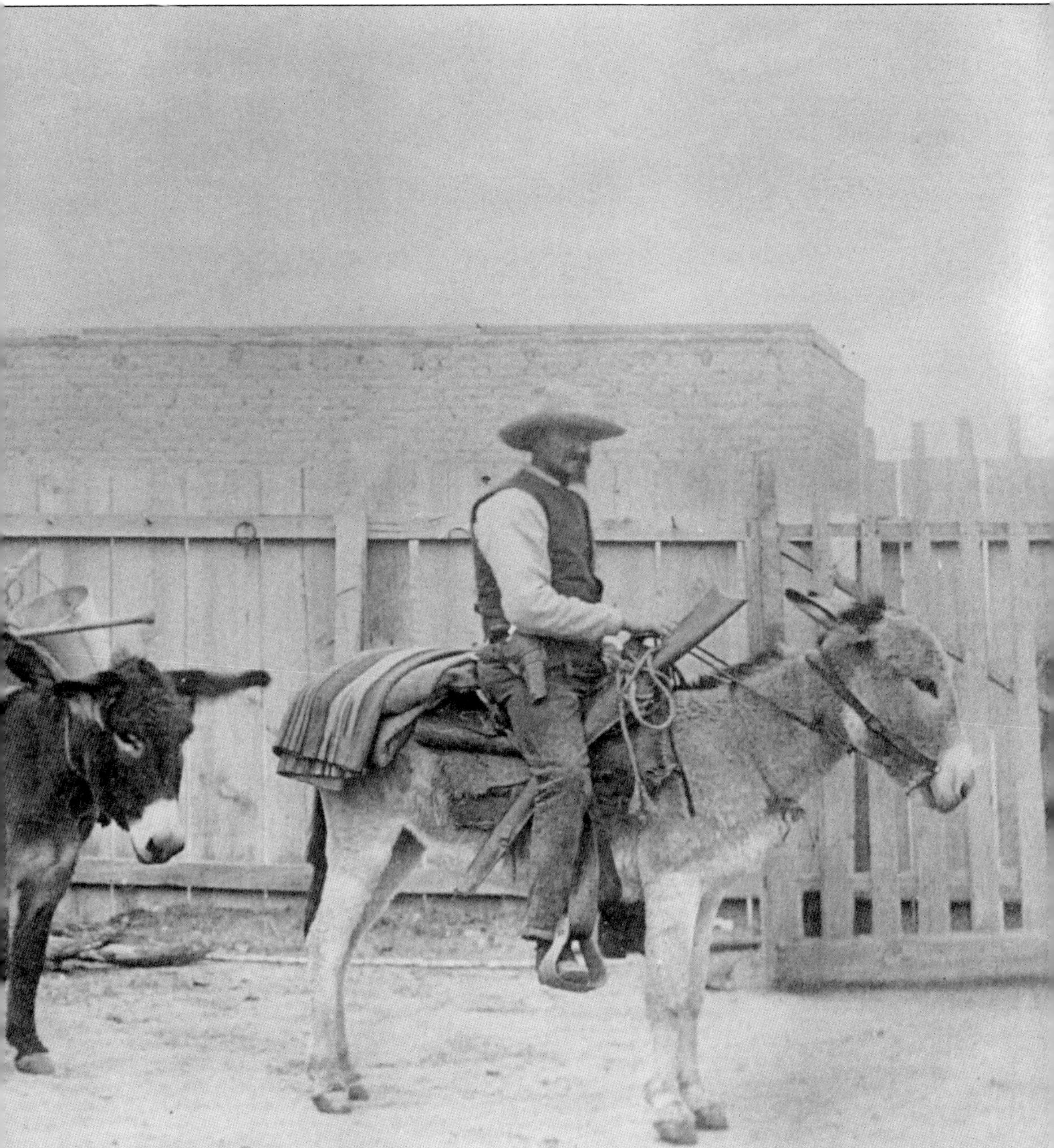

burros have a sad, gentle expression, almost as if they know it will be another day of fruitless searching. (Courtesy of Arizona Historical Society, Tucson, Arizona.)

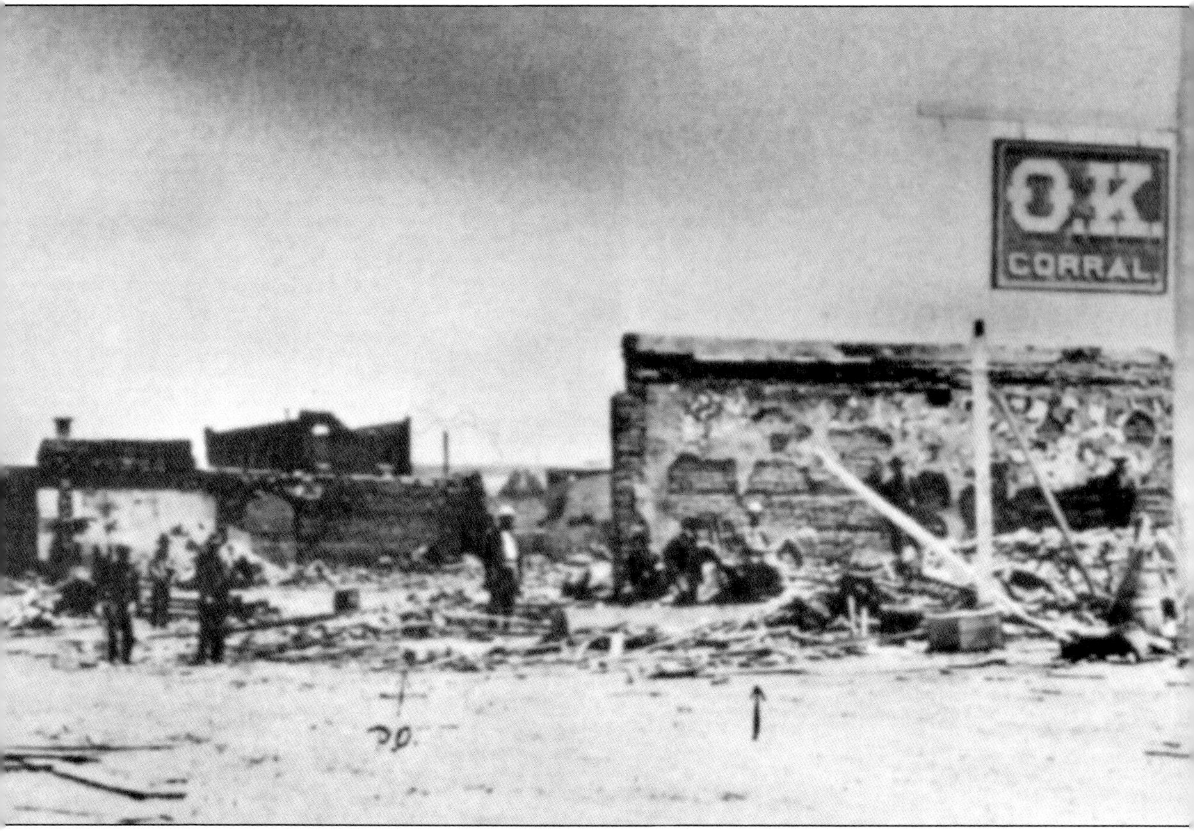

Fires were common in frontier towns such as Tombstone. Most of these towns depended on volunteer firefighters but had a poor water supply. On June 22, 1881, a fire destroyed much of Tombstone's business district. With no water to put out the fire, buildings in the fire's path were dynamited to slow the engulfing flames. Tombstone citizens blamed Marshal Ben Sippy for not controlling the looting that followed the fire, and Virgil Earp, the senior deputy, was soon appointed marshal, a move that further antagonized the Clantons. On May 25, 1882, another fire devastated Tombstone, again destroying Tombstone's business district, including the O. K. Corral. Here the men are waiting for the insurance adjuster to arrive. (Courtesy of Viji Winters.)

Five

TOMBSTONE, ARIZONA

Cochise County, created on February 1, 1881, from the southeast corner of Pima County, started out with so much trouble that the governor threatened to declare martial law. The booming silver mining town of Tombstone won the county seat over its contenders, Bisbee and Willcox. The county's creation with its lucrative appointments of federally appointed county officers contributed to the famous gunfight on October 26, 1881. From its inception, Tombstone and Cochise County had been plagued with the "Cowboy Gang," an alliance of cattle thieves who had been run out of Texas and New Mexico and who stole, murdered, and committed mayhem at will on both sides of the U.S.-Mexico border. The Clantons, the McLaurys, Johnny Ringo, Curly Bill Brocius, Buckskin Frank Leslie, Billy Claiborne, and other infamous outlaws helped themselves to cattle belonging to legitimate ranchers.

Tombstone residents looked forward to special entertainment. On July 4, 1879, an itinerant circus proprietor routed Mayor Carr out of bed at the ungodly hour of 8:00 a.m. to get permission to exhibit his fabulous attractions. The mayor said it would cost him $250 to set up a tent. The proprietor exploded and then set up his tent just outside the town limits. Tombstone turned out in high expectation only to be disappointed by a menagerie of emaciated, melancholy animals.

Tombstone has always been one of the few places in Arizona where one cannot "wear your guns to town, son." Although there are those who are working to get that law revoked.

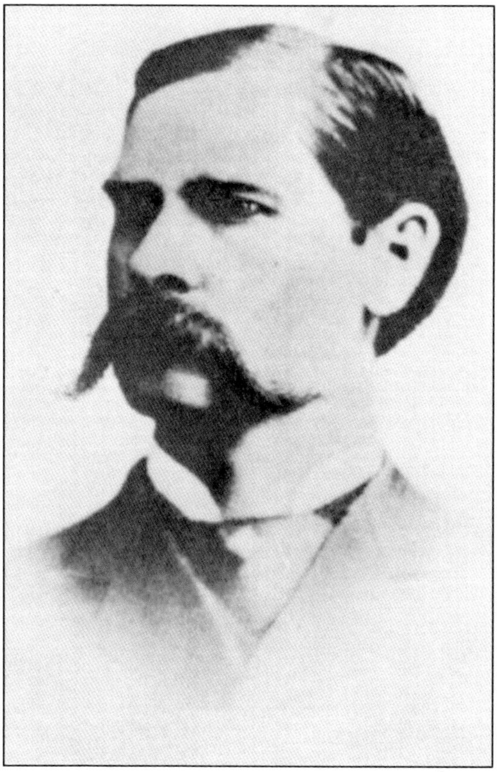

The Earps were sons of a Midwest farmer, Nicholas Porter Earp. Wyatt Berry Stapp Earp was born in Monmouth, Illinois, on March 19, 1848. Two years later, the Earp clan moved to Pella, Iowa, where Wyatt's brothers Morgan and Warren were born. After the Civil War, Wyatt and Virgil, another brother, left the farm and worked as freighters and lawmen in Dodge City. In December 1879, Virgil and Wyatt Earp arrived in Tombstone to open a stage line. After discovering that this business would be very competitive as two small stage lines were already in place, they turned to gambling and saloon keeping. Brother Morgan joined the Earps in their saloon venture. Their other partners included Bat Masterson, who became famous as a sports writer, and ne'er-do-well Luke Short. One good thing to be said for Short was that he supported many good causes, such as fund-raising a beautiful baby contest. (Courtesy of Arizona State Archives, Phoenix, Arizona.)

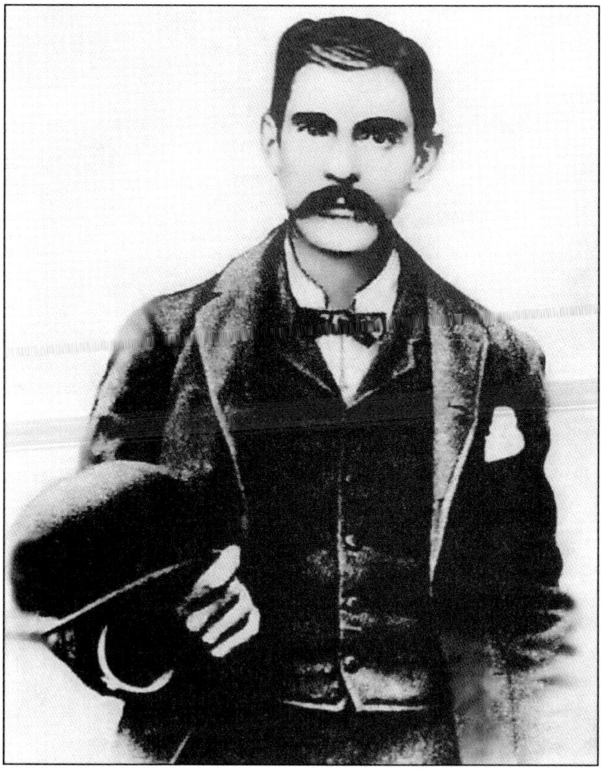

John Henry "Doc" Holliday, born in Georgia and trained as a dentist, became an alcoholic and bitter about life when his tuberculosis made it impossible for him to practice his profession. Doc Holliday, a fair-haired Southern gentleman, was well educated, with impeccable manners, and was a sophisticated dresser. Margaret Mitchell's second cousin was John Henry "Doc" Holliday. Mitchell was the author of the all-time best seller *Gone With the Wind.* There are pictures of the Holliday family in Mitchell's Atlanta home. (Author's collection.)

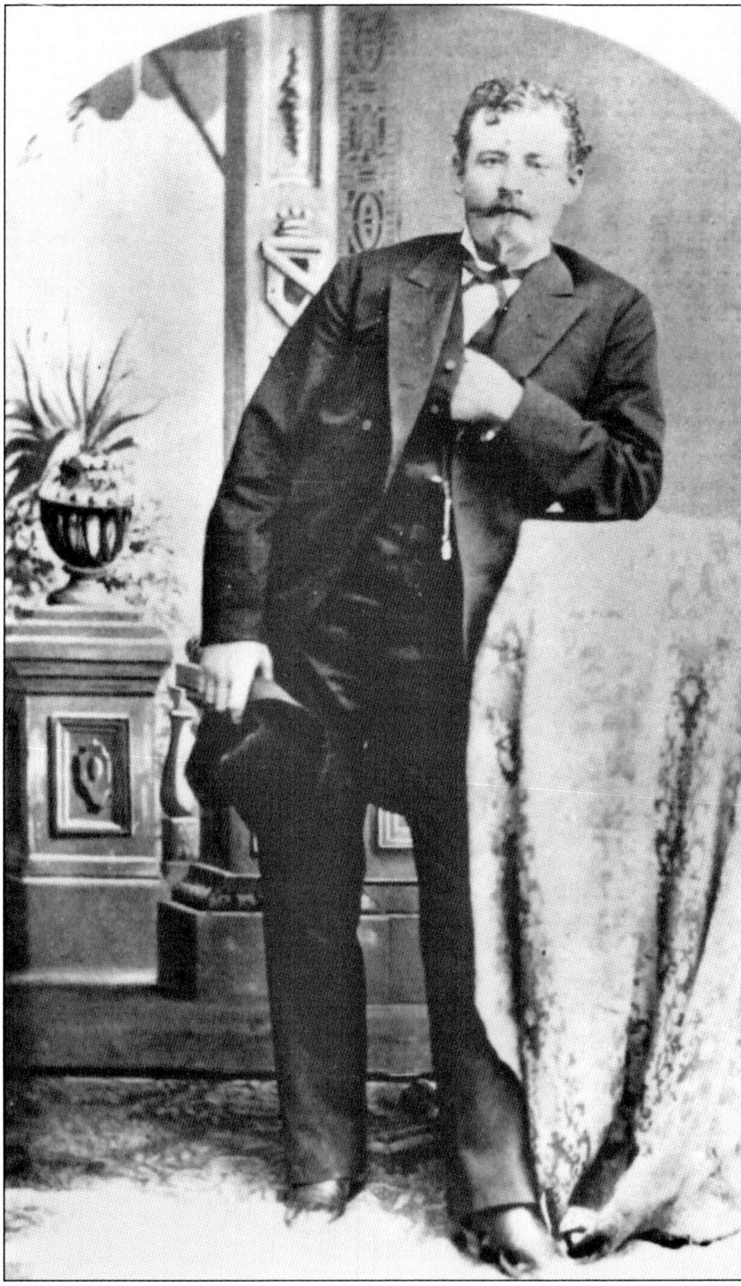

Joseph Isaac "Ike" Clanton (1847–June 1, 1887) was born in Callaway County, Missouri, as one of seven children to Newman "Old Man" Haynes Clanton (1816–1881) and his wife, Maria Sexton (Kelso) Clanton. Clanton's mother died in 1866. Ike stayed with the family when they moved to Tombstone, Arizona Territory, about 1877. Old Man Clanton worked as a day laborer, a gold miner, a farmer, and not infrequently as a cattle rustler and rancher in the Arizona Territory. The Clantons were accused of rustling cattle across the U.S.-Mexico border. By 1878, Ike was selling lunches at the Tombstone Mill site in Millville, and he was well known for talking too much. Ike, through either good sense or accident, escaped being in the famous gunfight at the last minute. (Courtesy of Viji Winters.)

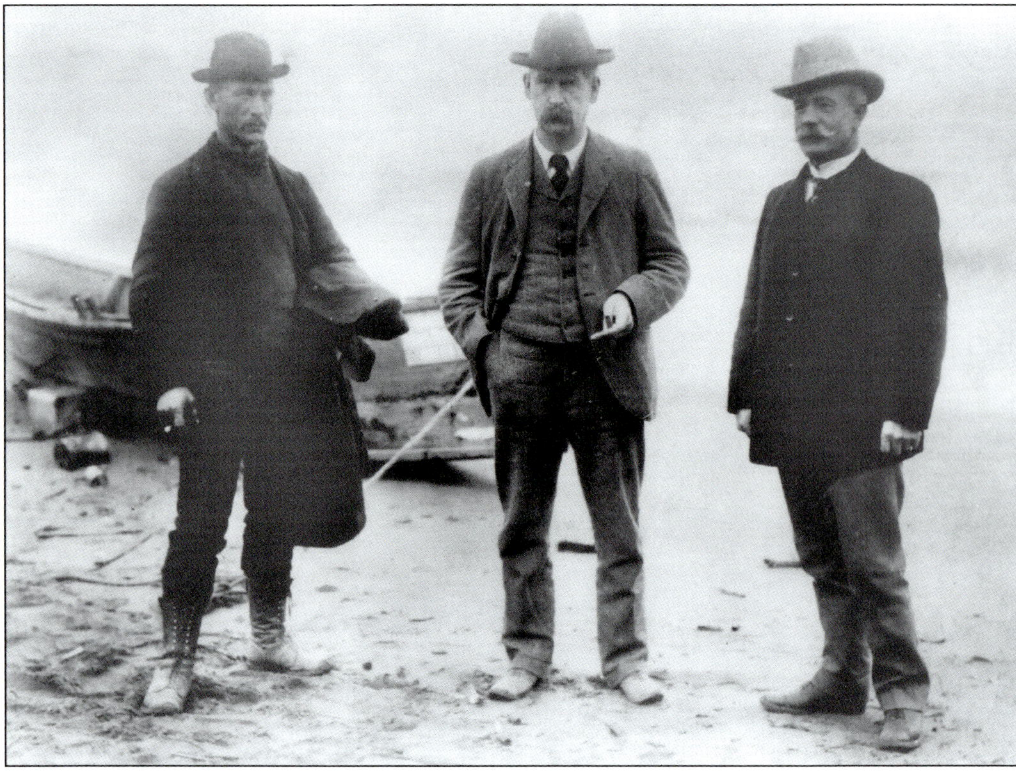

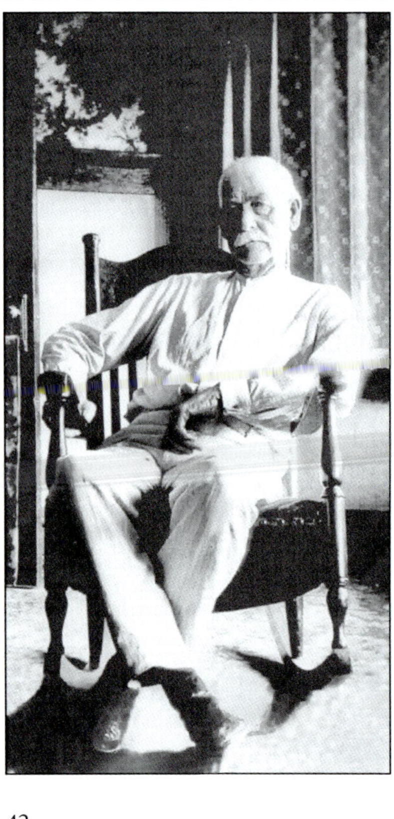

Pictured here near Nome, Alaska, around 1898 are, from left to right, Wyatt Earp, Ed Englestadt, and John Clum. Earp was a principal in the famous Tombstone shoot-out. Englestadt, a Norwegian immigrant, who reputed to have married a Russian woman of wealth, was a typical rugged frontiersman who also had a beautiful singing voice. Among his many jobs, Clum ran a newspaper in Tombstone and was in charge of postal service in Alaska. (Courtesy of Arizona Historical Society, Tucson, Arizona.)

Wyatt Earp outlived most of his enemies and friends. A few days before he died, Earp wrote to William S. Hart, "Only to move back ten years! That would be worth a world fortune. But it can't be done now. I will have to be satisfied for the ten years that are ahead—and that's a mighty lot. And, I can't plan anymore to climb the hills and hit the drill. Just now it would seem great to be drowsing out in the sun instead of being right here on my back." Wyatt Earp died on the morning of January 13, 1929 in Los Angeles, California. His funeral was held at the Congregational Church on Wilshire Boulevard. Following the service, he was cremated, and his ashes were interred in the Marcus family plot at Little Hills of Eternity, a Jewish cemetery in Colma, California. (Courtesy of Arizona Historical Society, Tucson, Arizona.)

Little is known about Mrs. Jackson, one of many Tombstone residents to have their picture taken at the C. S. Fly Studio. Camillus Fly served both as a premier photographer and Cochise County sheriff. He married Mollie Goodrich, who was an excellent photographer in her own right. The high point of his career as sheriff was tracking down the High Five Gang, including Three-Fingered Jack Dunlap, Black Jack Christian, and George Musgrove. However, the outlaws gave Fly the slip and escaped in Mexico. The last years of his life were very difficult with illness, financial problems, and a separation from his wife, Mollie. (Courtesy of Arizona State Archives, Phoenix, Arizona.)

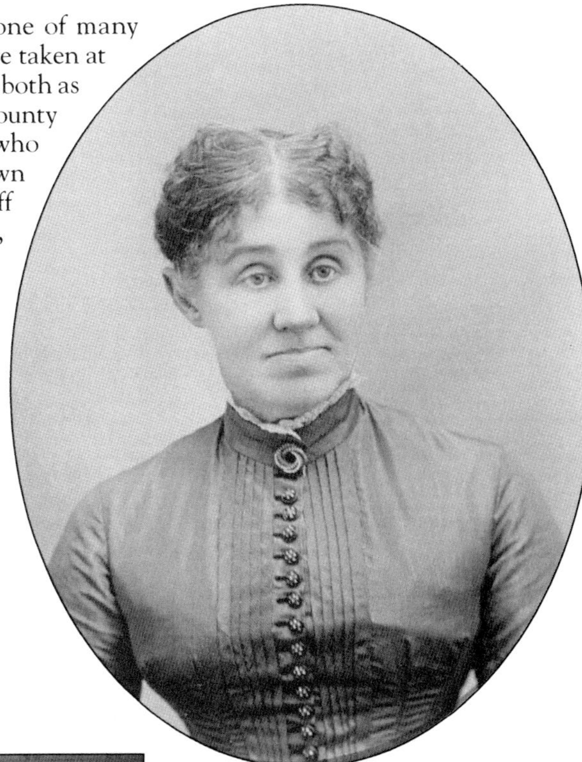

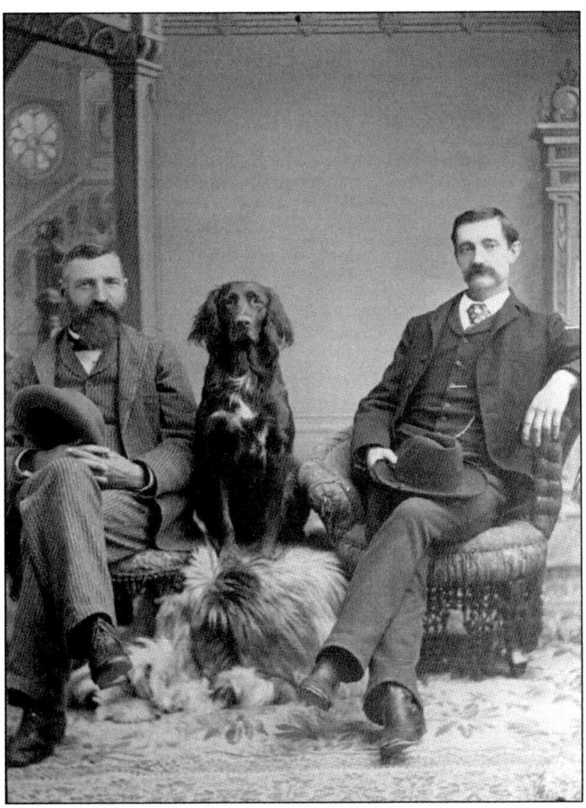

Andrew J. Ritter (left), his handsome dog, and an unidentified gentleman are photographed here in the C. S. Fly Studio around 1900. Ritter's name appears frequently as a witness to Tombstone marriage certificates, and he listed his occupation as cabinetmaker. (Courtesy of Arizona State Archives, Phoenix, Arizona.)

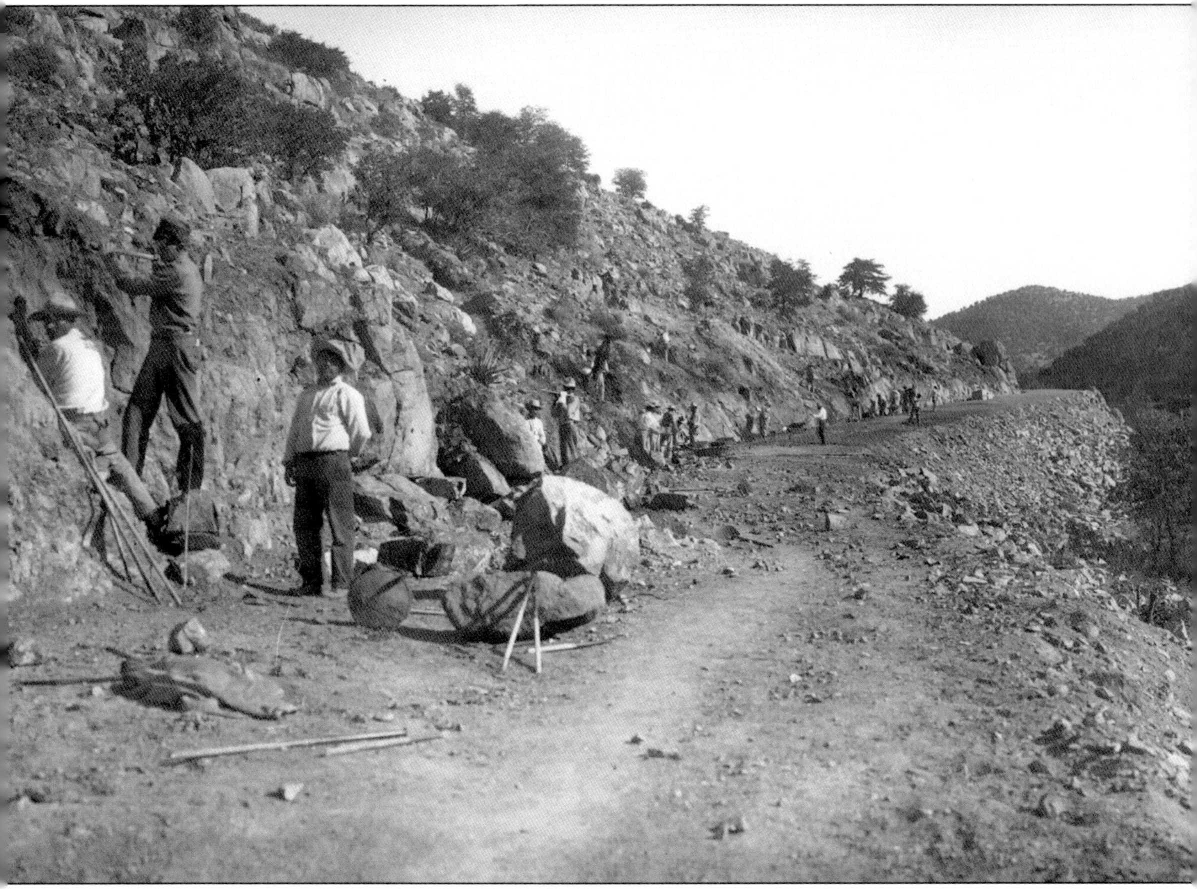

With the advent of the automobile, it became more important to build good roads to the various towns in the area. (Courtesy of Arizona State Archives, Phoenix, Arizona.)

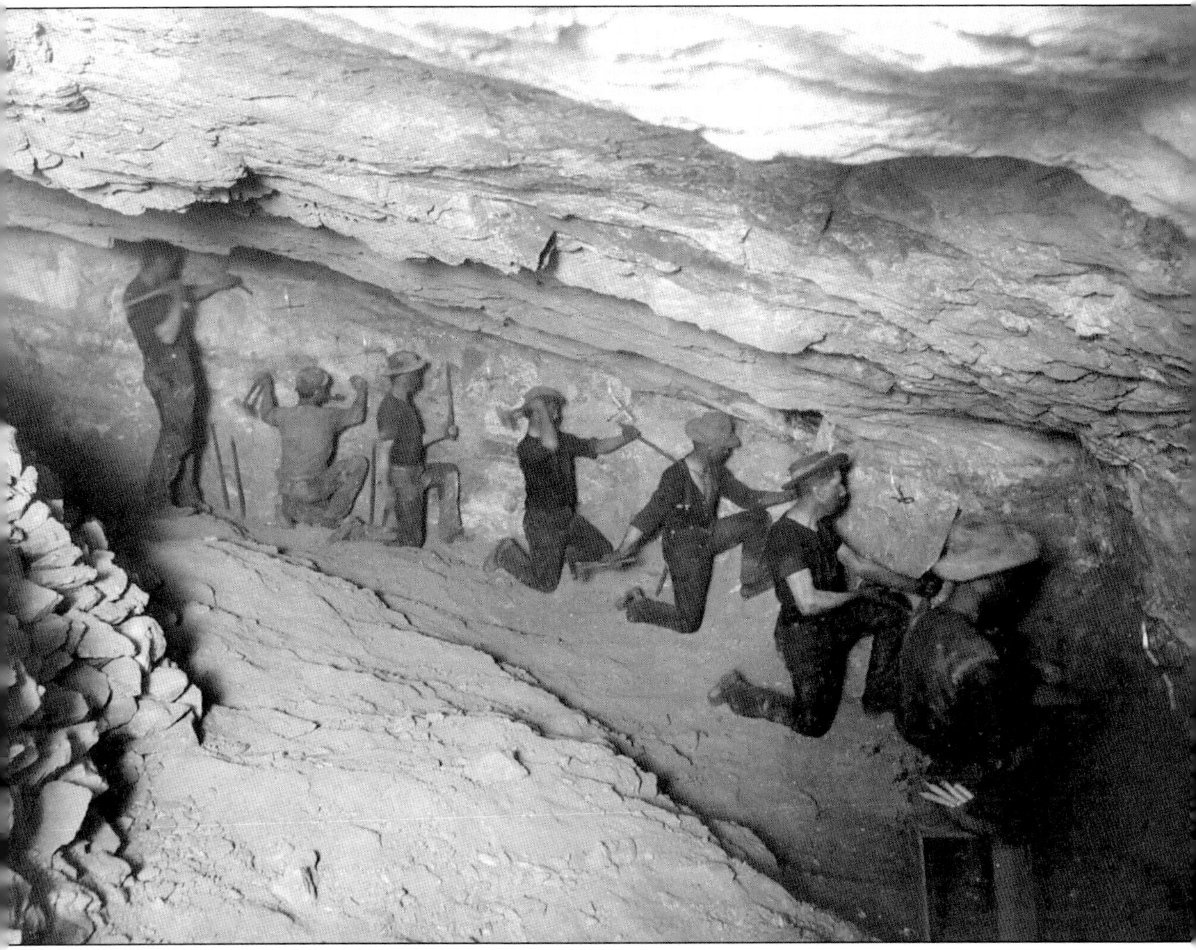

The underground blasting and mining of silver ore was a dangerous business. (Author's collection.)

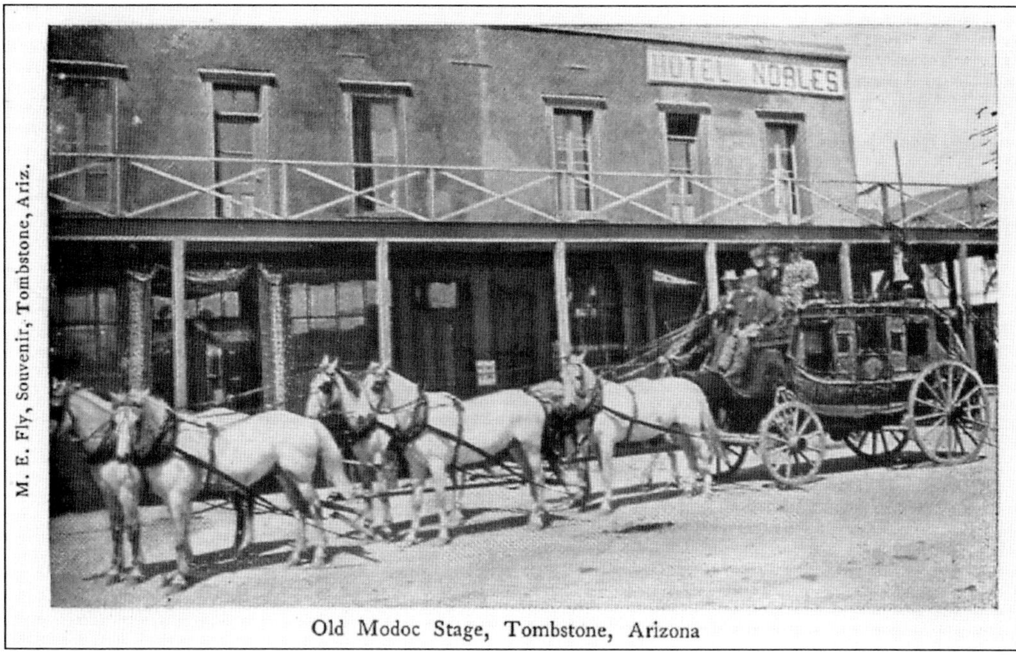

Here the Modoc stagecoach picks up guests at the Hotel Nobles. Built in Concord, New Hampshire, by the famous wagon-building company Abbot-Downing, the Modoc was designed as a 12-passenger mail stage to be pulled by a team of six horses. The stage was named after the Native America tribe in California, but it was sold to a stagecoach company in Tombstone. Mollie Fly took this photograph. (Courtesy of Arizona State Archives, Phoenix, Arizona.)

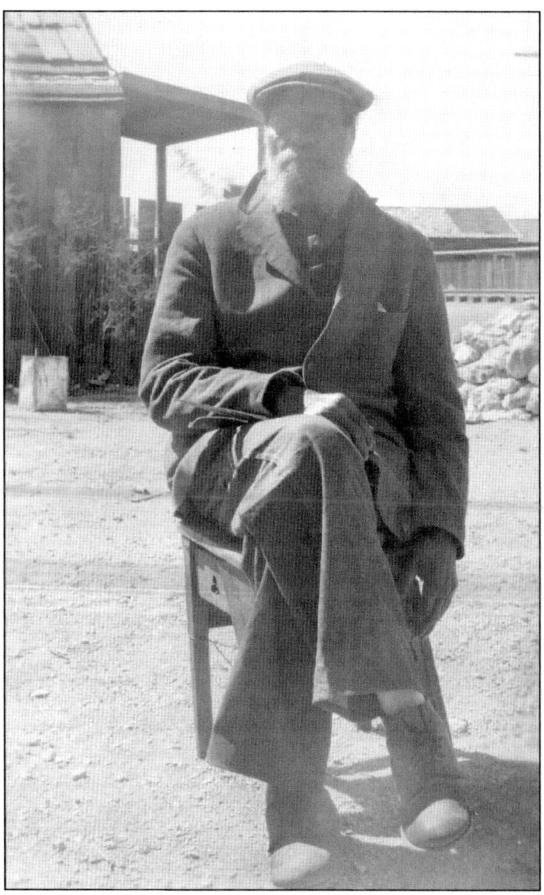

James Young, born a slave in Nashville, Tennessee, married Rosa Romero, a Mexican, and is mentioned as being a grave digger and cemetery caretaker in Tombstone. There are accounts of him working in the Allen Street cemetery. He died in January 1935. (Courtesy of Arizona State Archives, Phoenix, Arizona.)

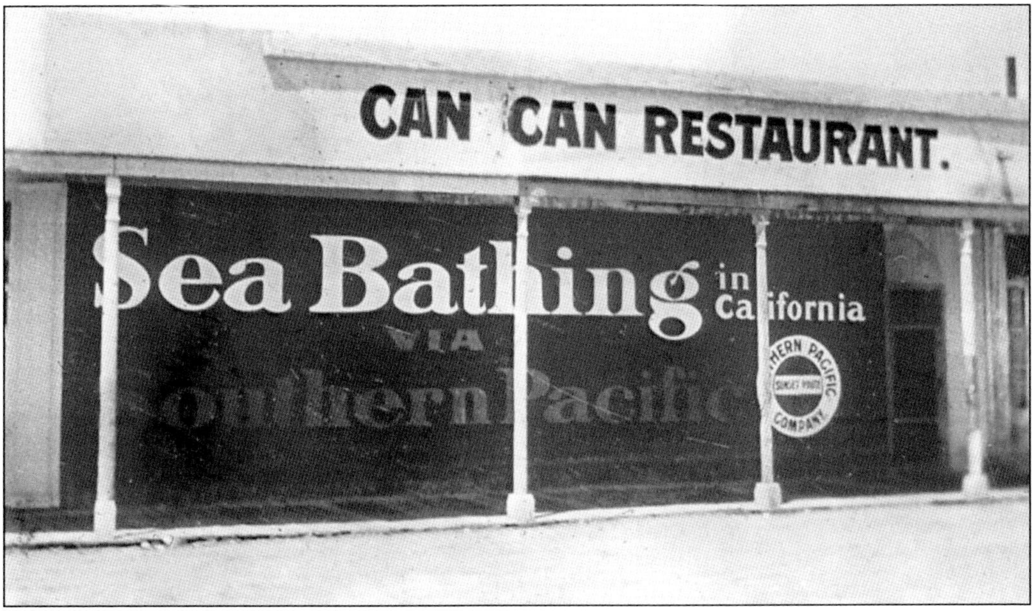

Quong Kee took over Ah Sing's Can Can Restaurant after arriving in Tombstone. The Can Can served excellent food, including steaks, ham, and Chinese food. Some of the Can Can customers included Billy Clanton, Wyatt Earp, and Curly Bill Brocius. Just why he chose to advertise sea bathing in California is a curiosity. (Courtesy of Arizona State Archives, Phoenix, Arizona.)

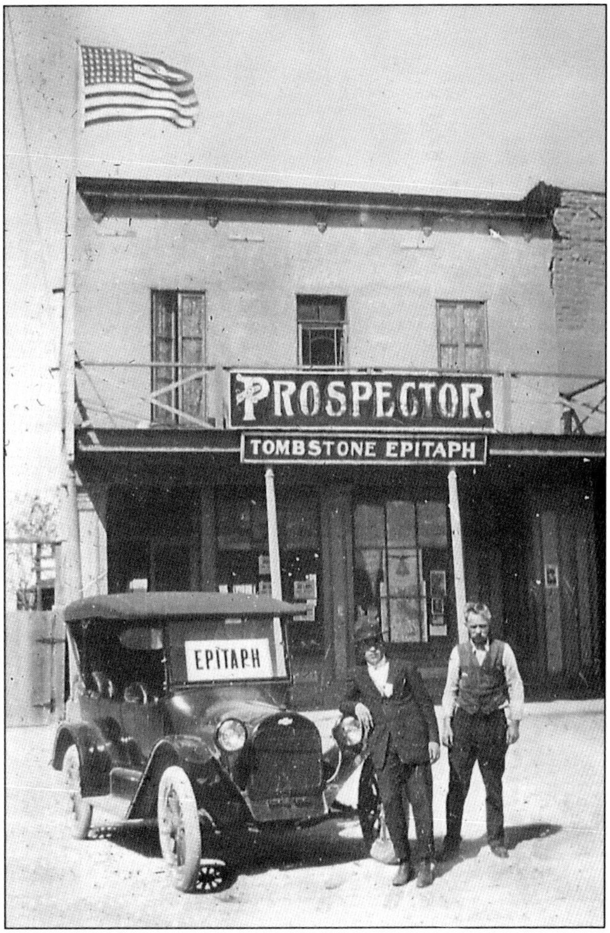

The *Tombstone Prospector* and the *Tombstone Epitaph* were competing newspapers in Tombstone. By the time this picture was taken, though, their competition was friendly, and newspapers were delivered to various areas by automobile. (Courtesy of Arizona Historical Society, Tucson, Arizona.)

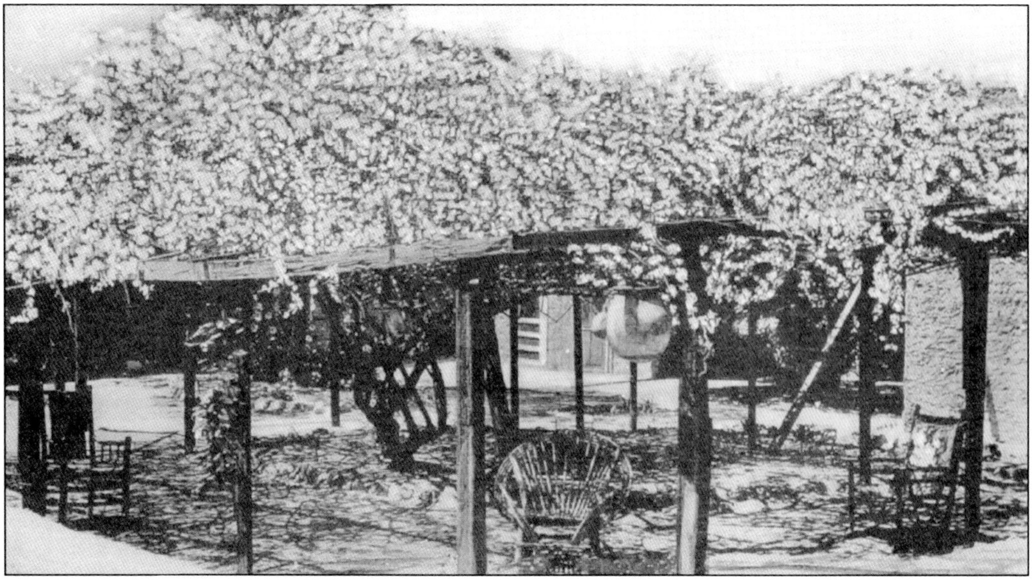

The Rose Tree Museum is home to the world's largest Lady Banksia rose tree, which covers approximately 8,500 square feet. It is the second-oldest rose tree in the world; the oldest is in Queen Elizabeth's Kew Gardens in London. The Lady Banksia white rose was brought to England from China by William Kerr, who discovered it in a Canton garden and brought it to London on behalf of the Royal Society. The flower is named for Lady Banks, the wife of the director of Kew Gardens. In 1930, Robert Ripley visited Tombstone and wrote about the rose tree in his column, "Believe It or Not." At present, it is listed in the *Guinness Book of World Records*. Every April, the rose tree produces millions of fragrant white blossoms and Tombstone celebrates with the Rose Tree Festival. (Courtesy Macia-Devere family.)

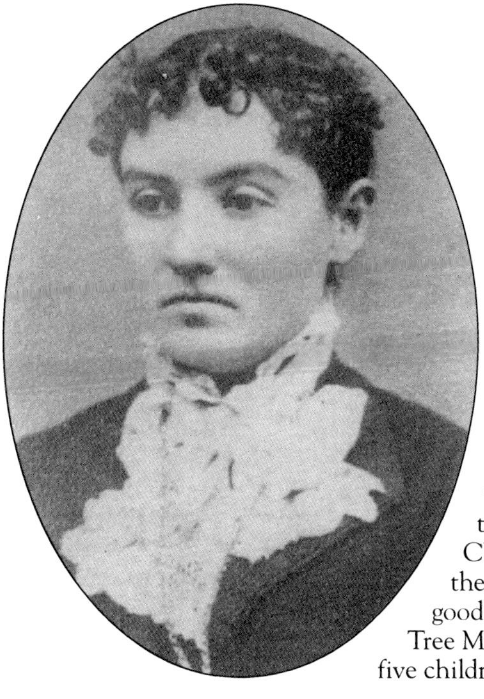

The Rose Tree Inn, now the Rose Tree Museum, eventually came into the hands of the Macia-Devere family. Alice and Chris Robertson were married on October 19, 1880, in Leadville, Colorado. Three days later, they set out in a covered wagon for Tombstone, where they hoped to make their fortune in the silver mines. They arrived on Christmas Eve, and Alice set up housekeeping in their wagon until a house could be built. Many of the goods she brought to Tombstone are now in the Rose Tree Museum. Alice died in 1895 at the age of 31, leaving five children. (Courtesy of Macia-Devere family.)

Chris Robertson worked in the mines and built a two-room house of rough-hewed wood on the east side of Tombstone. After his wife's death, Chris moved the family to Pearce, where he established a mercantile and livery stable. At this time, he sent his oldest daughter, Ethel, who would come to be known as the "Lady of the Rose" because she lived on the property and took care of the rose tree, to the University of Arizona. In 1899, Chris witnessed a train robbery near Cochise Station and was shot to death by one of the robbers. (Courtesy of Macia-Devere family.)

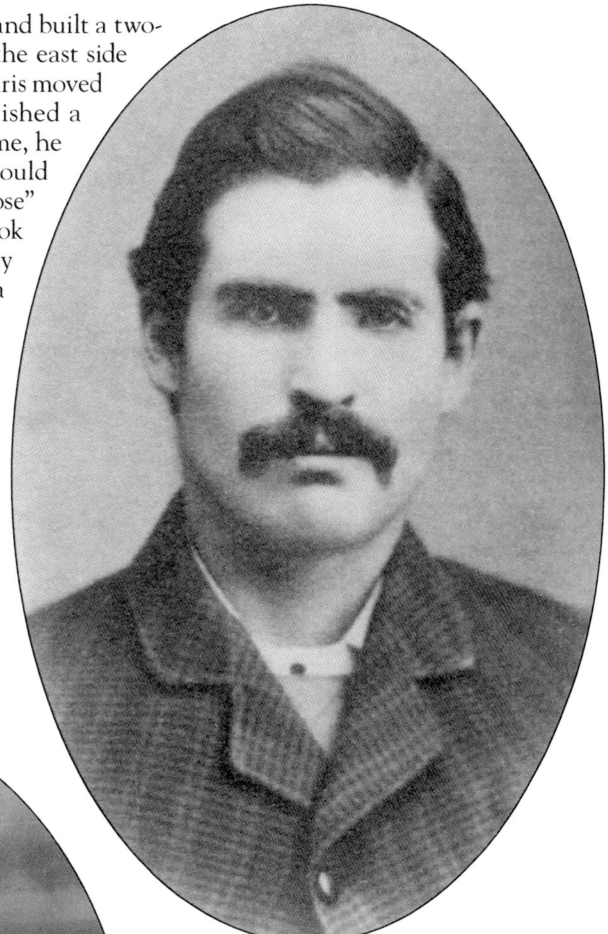

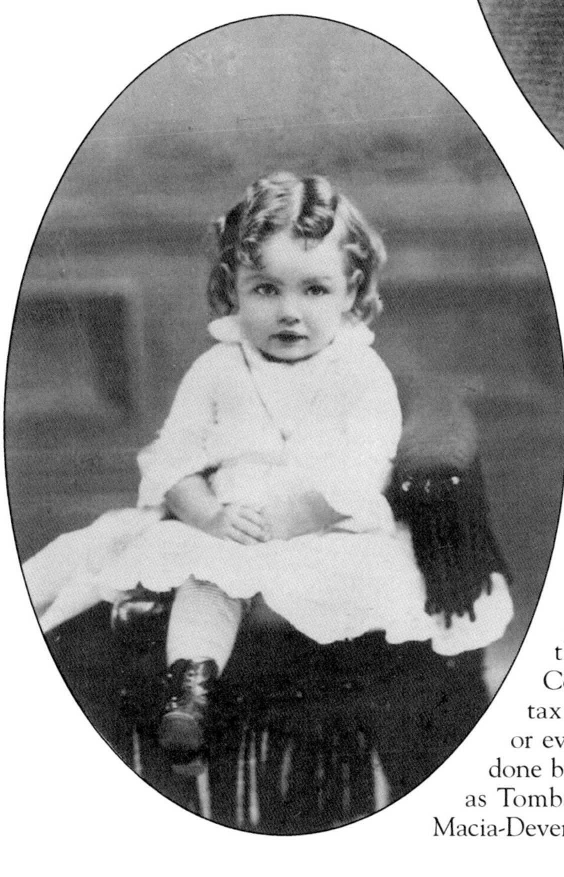

Ethel Robertson, pictured here at age two, would live all of her 83 years in Tombstone. After her mother's death, she dropped out of the University of Arizona and worked at the Cochise County Court House recording the tax rolls. This was before the days of computers or even typewriters, and everything had to be done by hand. She eventually came to be known as Tombstone's "Lady of the Rose." (Courtesy of Macia-Devere family.)

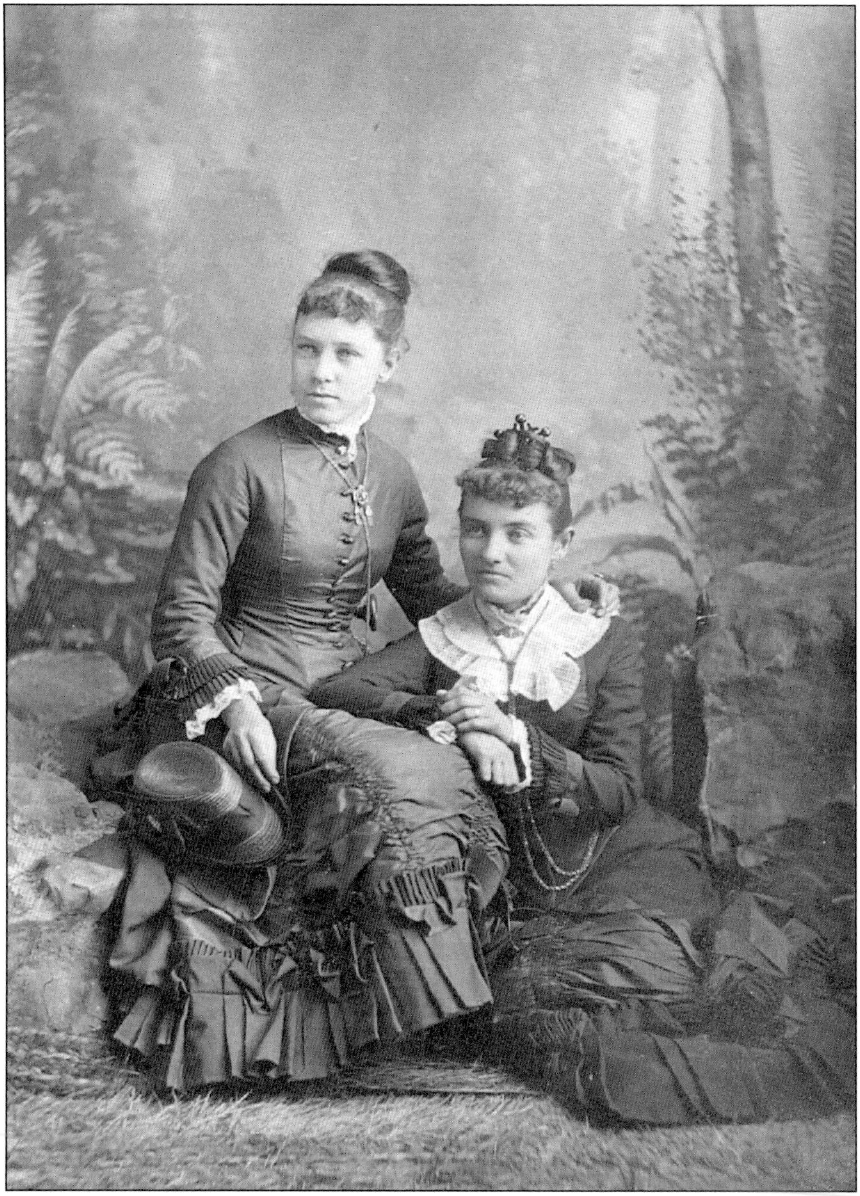

The Rose Tree Inn, one of the first adobe structures constructed in Tombstone, was built as offices and a boardinghouse for the Vizina Mining Company. In 1885, a newly married couple from Scotland—Henry, a mining engineer, and Mary Gee—lived in the boardinghouse. Mary, homesick for her native Scotland, made friends with Amelia Adamson, the Rose Tree Inn caretaker. When Henry and Mary built a permanent home, Mary's family sent her a box of plant cuttings from Scotland, including a white Lady Banks rose. Mary gave a cutting of the rose to Amelia, who planted it at the Rose Tree Inn. In 1930, Ethel Robertson Macia took over the inn. By now, the rose bush had grown to a "rose tree," covering more than 8,000 square feet. It holds the title of world's largest rose tree in the *Guinness Book of World Records* and has appeared in *Ripley's Believe It or Not.* Every spring the rose tree spreads millions of fragrant white blooms around. The Rose Tree Inn is still in the Macia-Devere family, but the building now serves as a small museum. Located at Fourth and Toughnut Streets, the museum is open daily. (Courtesy of Macia-Devere family.)

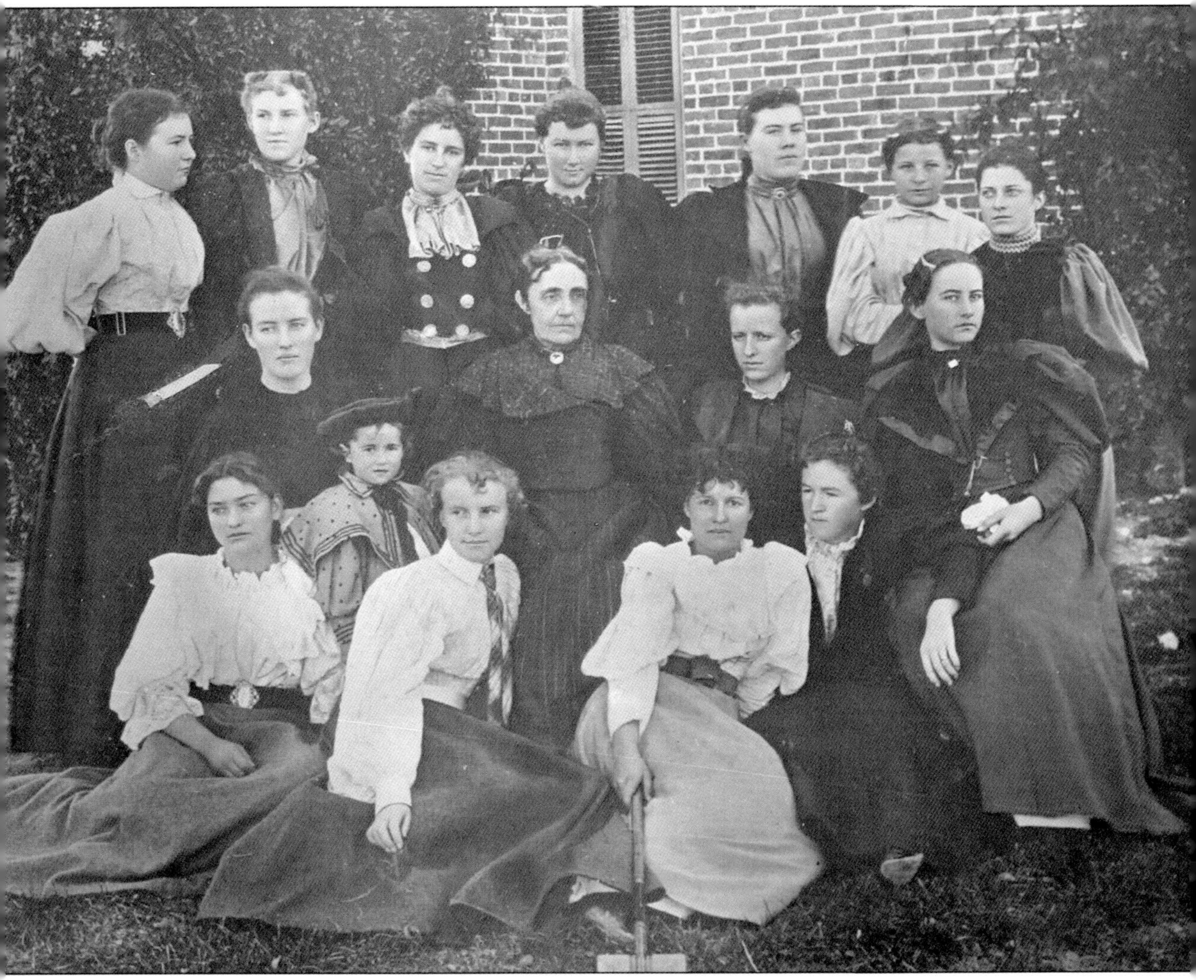

Ethel Robertson, second row at far left, was a member of the 1897 University of Arizona class along with several young women from Cochise County. However, when her mother passed away, she had to drop out to find work and take care of her four younger siblings. Around 1902, Ethel met James Herbert Macia, who was in charge of a crew sinking a boom shaft into the Grand Central Mine in the Tombstone hills. The crew moved on after the job was complete, but Bert stayed and married Ethel on February 4, 1904. (Courtesy of Macia-Devere family.)

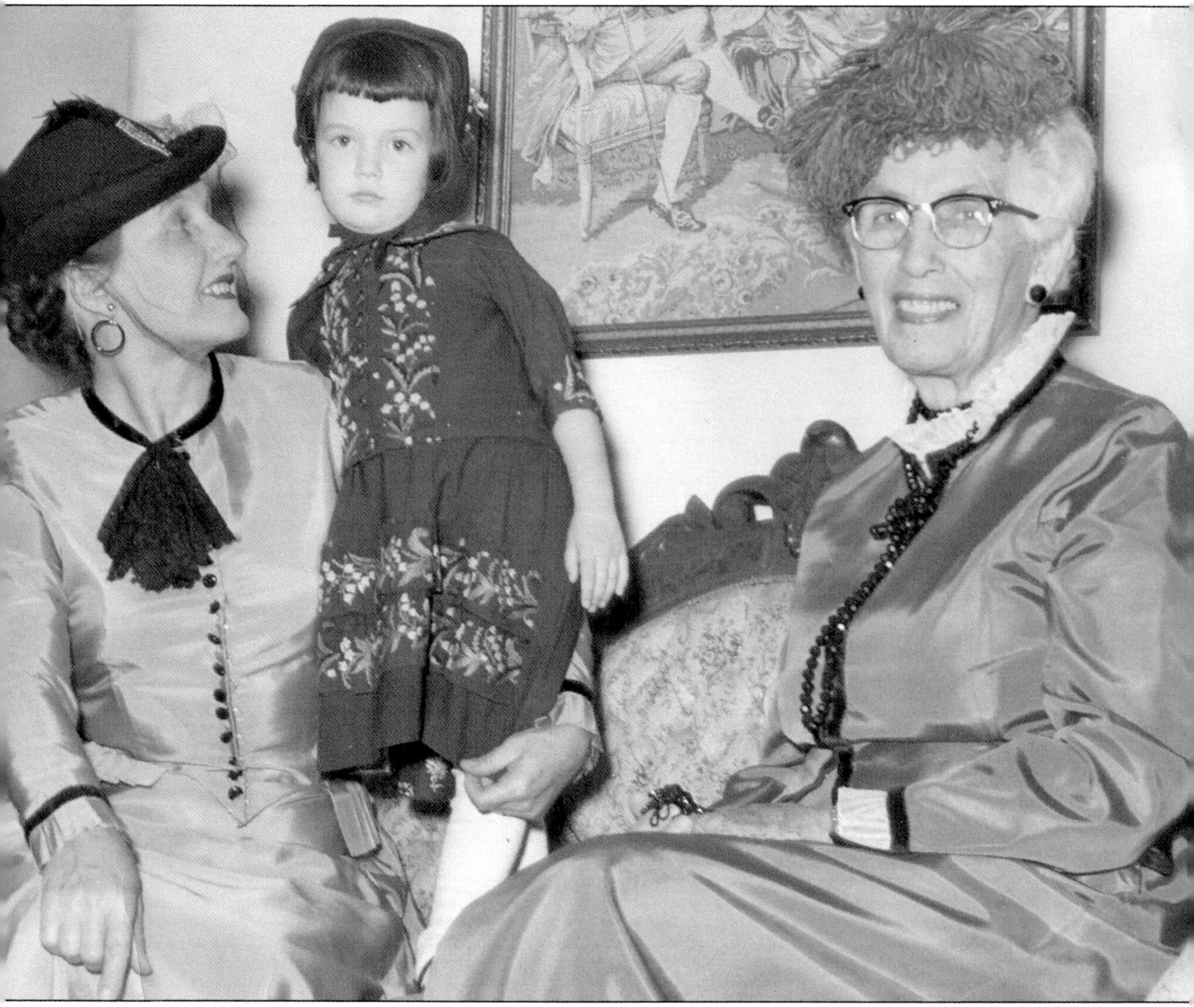

Bert and Ethel (right) Macia had three children: Jeanne (left), James Jr., and Iris. Ethel operated the Rose Tree Inn as the Arcade Hotel, and Bert trained the rose bush over trellises and built supports from wooden posts and metal pipe. The rose tree attracted worldwide attention, and in 1937 the Arcade Hotel became the Rose Tree Inn. In 1951, Bert died and his mining collection became part of the Macia Memorial in the Cochise County Court House. Ethel became much in demand as the Tombstone historian and appeared on the NBC program *Wide Wide World* in 1955. Her memory was flawless. Ethel Robertson Macia, the Lady of the Rose, died in August 1964. (Courtesy of Macia-Devere family.)

Challie was the undisputed king of Tombstone's Chinatown. Early Chinese migrant workers arrived in Arizona through an employment contractor for whom they were to work for a stated term. The business of hiring and managing the employees' affairs in Tombstone was controlled by China Mary and Challie. The Chinese Consolidated Benevolent Association of San Francisco, known as the Chinese Six because it represented the six different regions of Guangdong province, dealt with U.S. immigration matters at the city level. The Chinese Six Companies, which is still in existence, was the most powerful organization acting on behalf of the Chinese outside of China. (Courtesy of Macia-Devere family.)

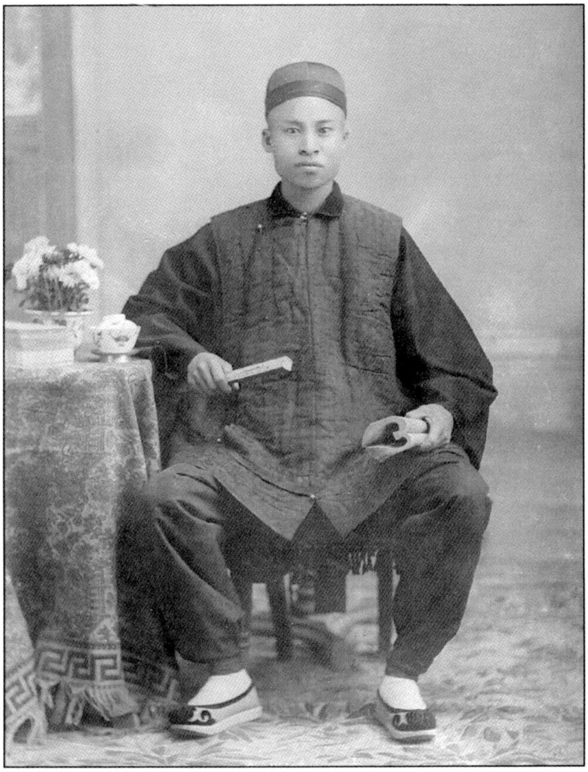

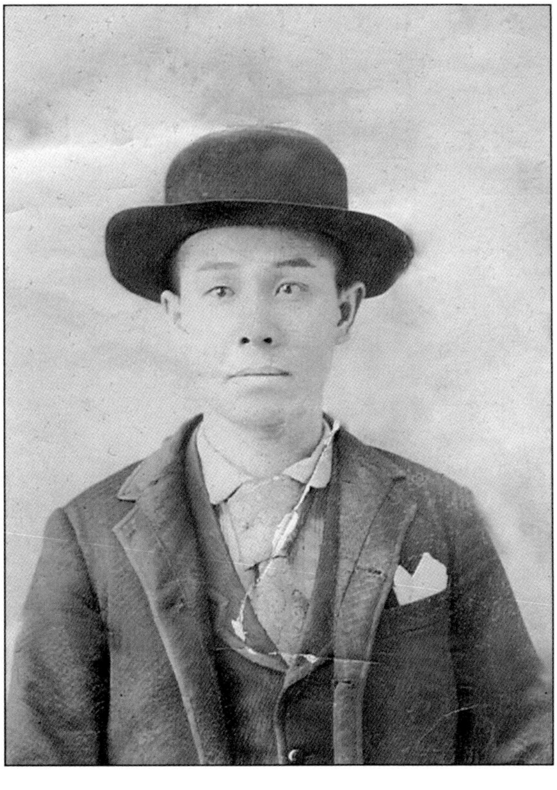

Challie Young, seen here around 1884, was disappointed with this picture because he thought it was too small. The Chinese workers would work hard for a few years so they could pay off their debt to the Six Company, and then they worked so they could return to China and raise a family. If they died on foreign soil, they were buried in the Chinese section of Boot Hill Cemetery. Eventually caretakers dug up the bodies, soaked the bones in brandy wine, and sealed them in an urn. (Courtesy of Macia-Devere family.)

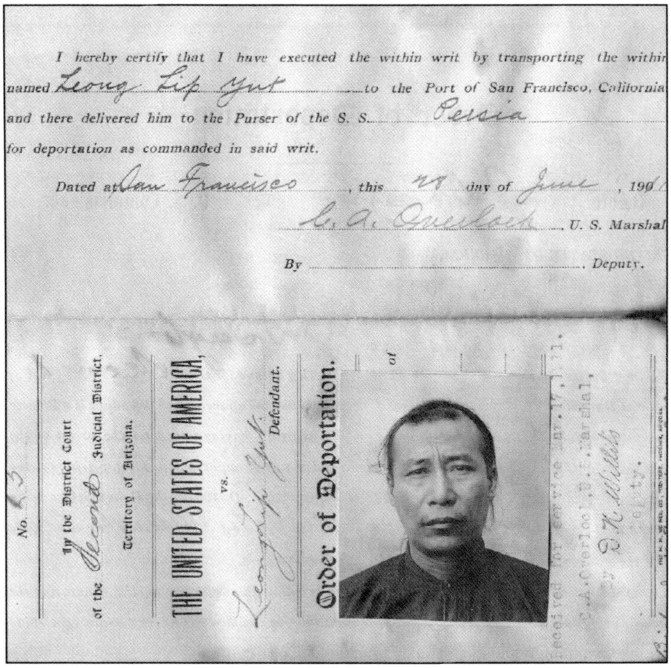

I hereby certify that I have executed the within writ by transporting the within named Leong Lip Yut to the Port of San Francisco, California and there delivered him to the Purser of the S. S. Persia for deportation as commanded in said writ.

Dated at San Francisco, this 28 day of June, 1911

C. A. Overlock U. S. Marshal

By .... Deputy.

No. 13

In the District Court of the Second Judicial District, Territory of Arizona.

THE UNITED STATES OF AMERICA, vs. Leong Lip Yut Defendant.

Order of Deportation.

Leong Lip Yut was probably glad to be deported. Frequently the early Chinese decided they had enough money or were homesick and would get in a fight to precipitate an order of deportation. Life could be dismal and lonely for the Chinese, and they often smoked opium at night. Running an opium den resulted in fines of $10 for Ah Sing (1881) and $23 for Gee Wah (1886). In 1905, a doctor reported that Yee Hing, a Chinese Tombstone resident, died from opium poisoning at Cochise County Hospital. Mah Jong and poker also served as entertainment in Tombstone's Chinatown, known then as Hoptown. (Courtesy of Macia-Devere family.)

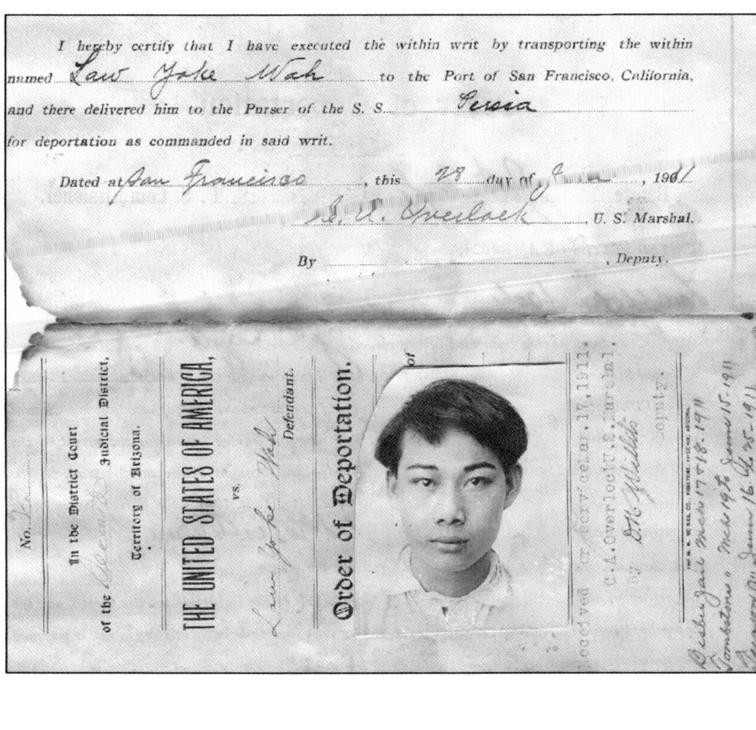

I hereby certify that I have executed the within writ by transporting the within named Law Yoke Wah to the Port of San Francisco, California, and there delivered him to the Purser of the S. S. Persia for deportation as commanded in said writ.

Dated at San Francisco, this 28 day of ______, 1911

C. A. Overlock U. S. Marshal.

By .... Deputy.

In the District Court of the Second Judicial District, Territory of Arizona.

THE UNITED STATES OF AMERICA, vs. Law Yoke Wah Defendant.

Order of Deportation.

Law Yoke Wah appears to be a very young Chinese immigrant. He, too, was probably quite happy with a deportation order, so he could return home for free. He would be delivered to the SS *Persia* for deportation from the port of San Francisco. (Courtesy of Macia-Devere family.)

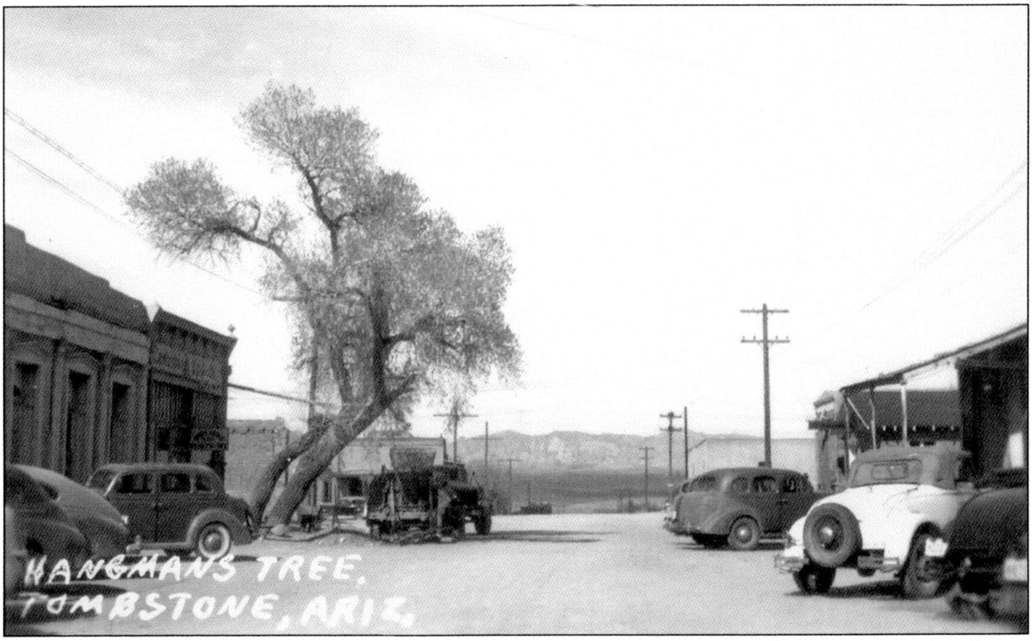

Although there is no hard documentation to support the premise that there were any lynchings in Tombstone and all legal hangings were conducted in the courthouse yard, this is purported to be Tombstone's hanging tree on Allen Street. (Courtesy of Don Taylor.)

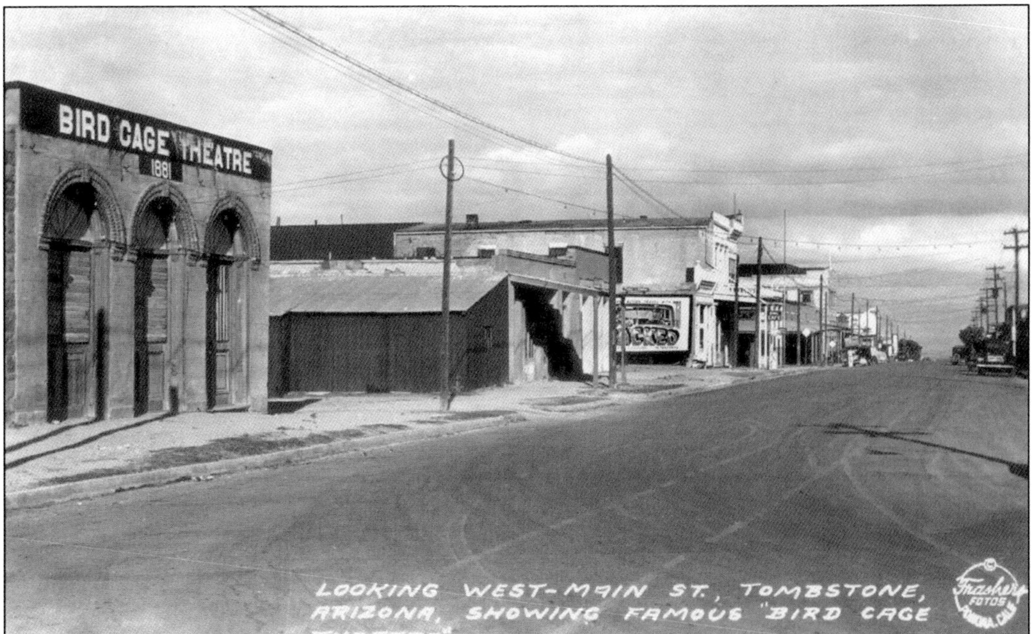

It was at the famous Bird Cage Theatre where the song "She's Only a Bird in a Gilded Cage" was composed. Actually the birds in the gilded cages were prostitutes who plied their trade in the cubicles above the theater. The Bird Cage Theatre was Tombstone's most infamous bawdy house. It was a one-stop sex shop. (Courtesy of Don Taylor.)

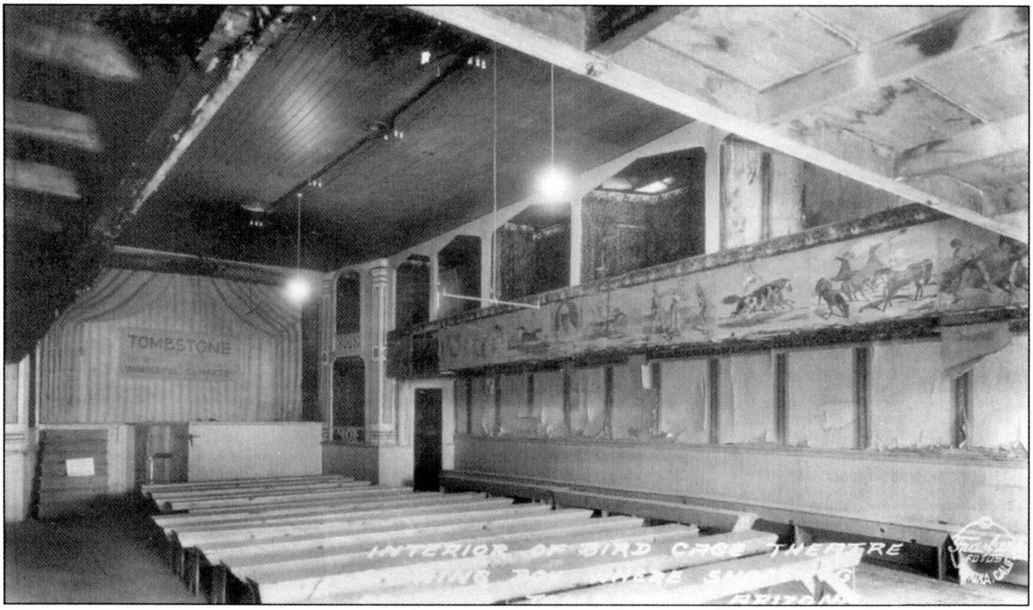

The interior of the Bird Cage Theatre, with its many wall paintings, is still intact. Visitors can see several of the cages where the soiled doves plied their trade. (Courtesy of Don Taylor.)

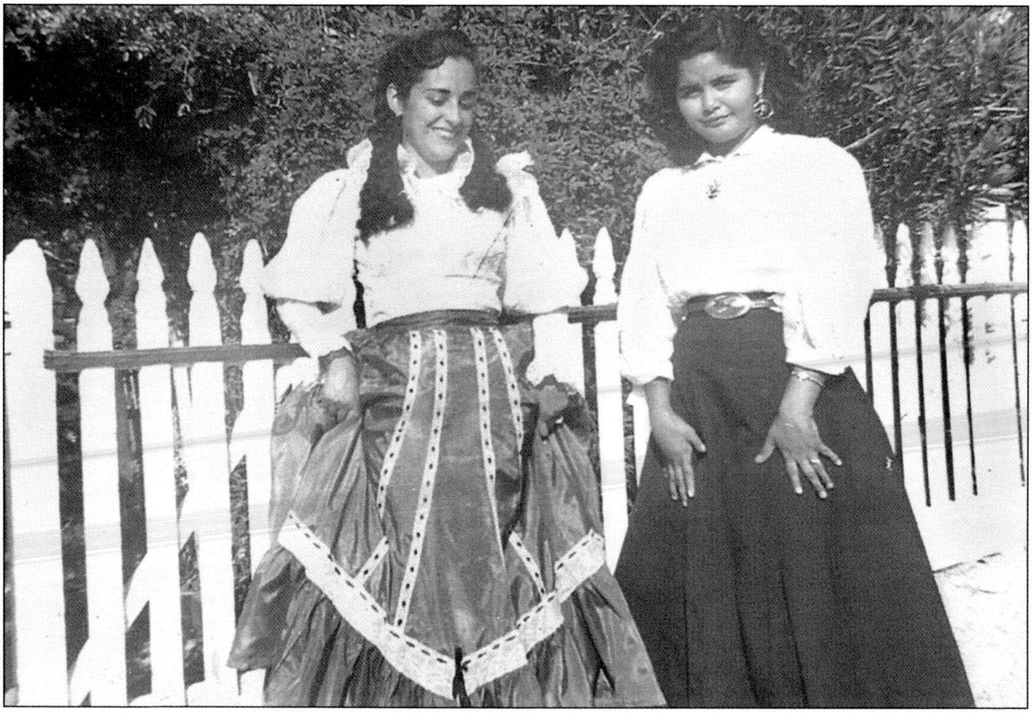

Alicia Lopez (right) recalled how she hated it when her mother made her dress in costumes for Helldorado Days. Here she is with her friend Consuela, and do they not look beautiful? An old-timer, Billy Breakenridge (on page 58) said that instead of finding the riches of El Dorado (the golden one) that most men found only Helldorado. Today Helldorado is Tombstone's oldest festival. Started in 1929, it celebrates the rip-roaring days of the 1880s. (Courtesy of Nancy Lewis Sosa.)

Alicia Lopez (left) poses with a friend for this photograph in Tombstone. Alicia's father, Ramon Lopez, came to Tombstone around 1910 with two brothers, and all of them worked in the Tombstone mines. Ramon, who had what was commonly referred to as "black lung disease," died in 1944 from the effects of working in the mines. He was also blind. Maria del Carmen Soto came to Tombstone when she was about four years old in 1910. Ramon and Carmen had both left Mexico to escape the civil war that was going on there. Their daughter Alicia was born in Tombstone in 1940, the last of 10 children. (Courtesy of Nancy Lewis Sosa.)

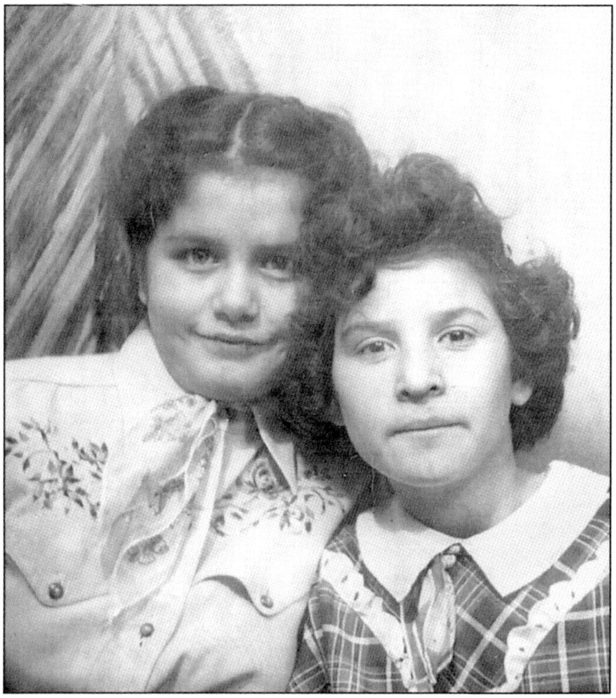

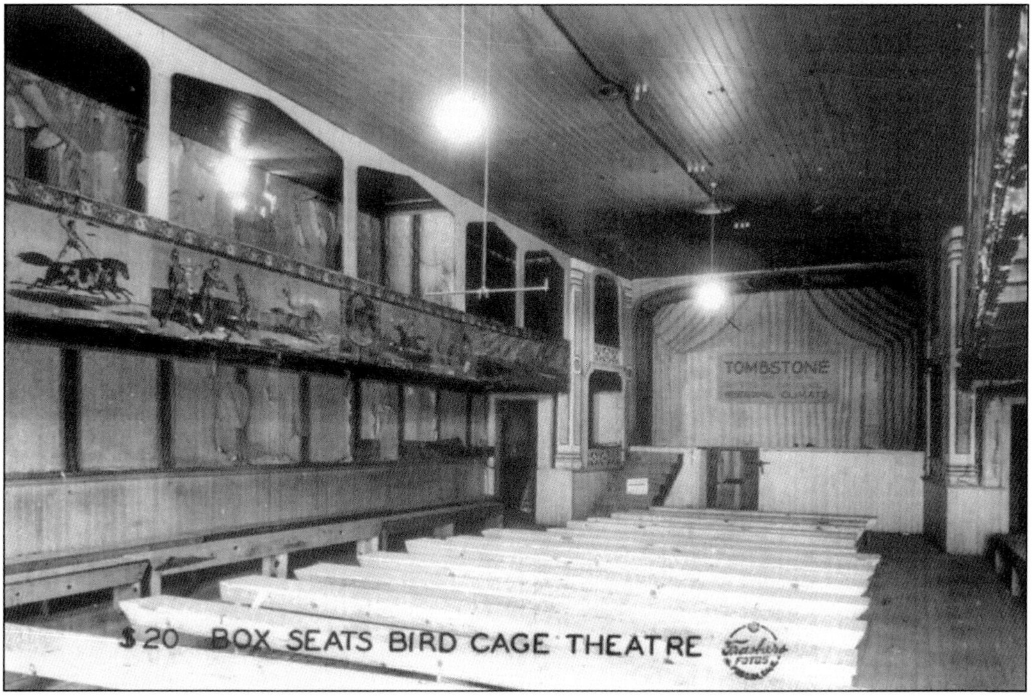

The Bird Cage Theatre, open 24 hours a day, seven days a week, boasted 20 upper-level box seats, and $20 bought a show, a bottle of whiskey, and a lady for the night. The longest poker game in history was played in the basement. It ran nonstop for eight years, five months, and three days. The buy in was a $1,000 minimum, and many of the old West's most famous personalities participated in this game. (Courtesy of Library of Congress, Washington, D.C.)

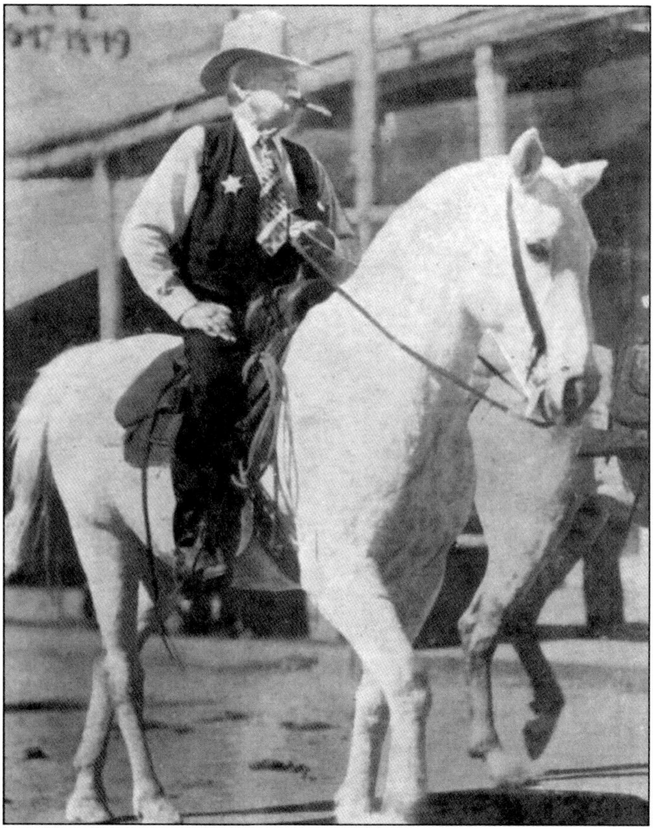

William Milton Breakenridge was born on December 25, 1846, in Wisconsin. He served as a Cochise County lawman. He also served as a Cochise County deputy sheriff, deputy U.S. Marshal, surveyor, and engineer and brought outlaws in to pay their taxes. When interviewed about Tombstone, he said that people came searching for El Dorado, but all they ever found was Helldorado. Here he is riding in the first Helldorado parade. Breakenridge died in Tucson on January 31, 1931, and is buried in Tucson's Evergreen Cemetery. (Courtesy Arizona Historical Society, Tucson, Arizona.)

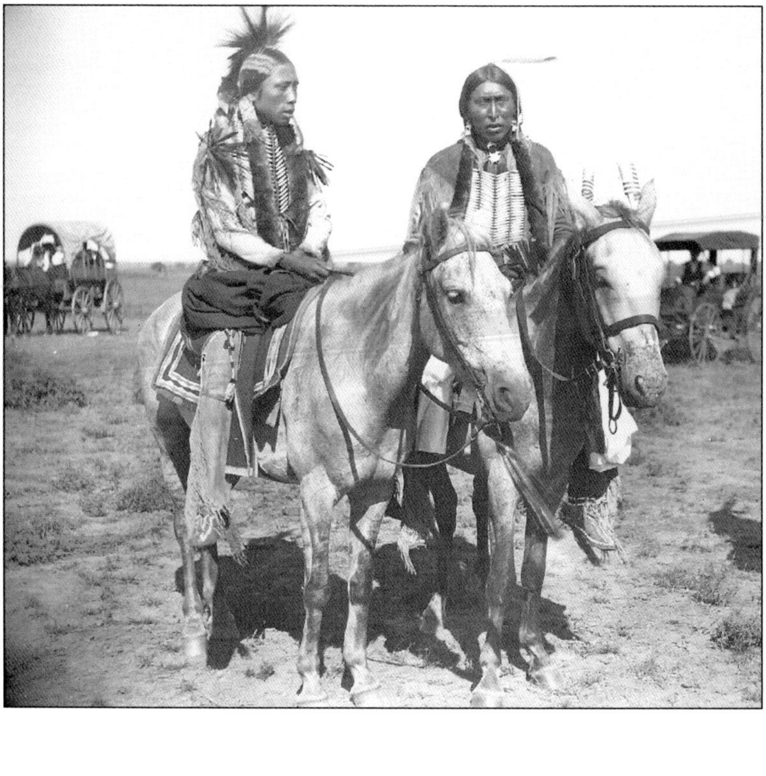

Helldorado, started in 1929, is held every third weekend in October. It consists of gunfight reenactment shows, street entertainment, fashion shows, and a family-oriented carnival. The original brochure claimed that a dead man would be served for breakfast every morning. Native Americans were brought in to participate but were often Anglos made up to look like Native Americans as in the movies. (Courtesy of Library of Congress, Washington, D.C.)

Photo booths were set up during the early Helldorado Days, and little Consuela seems a tad dubious about having her picture taken. (Courtesy of Nancy Lewis Sosa.)

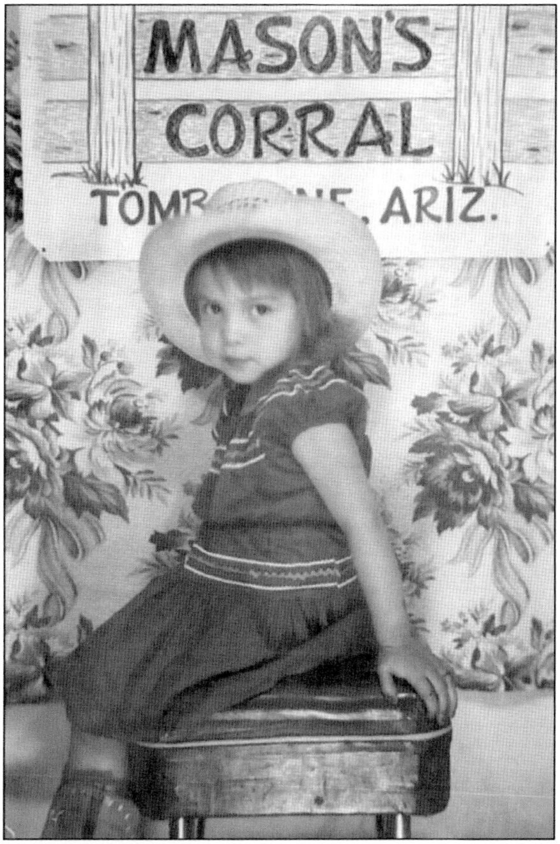

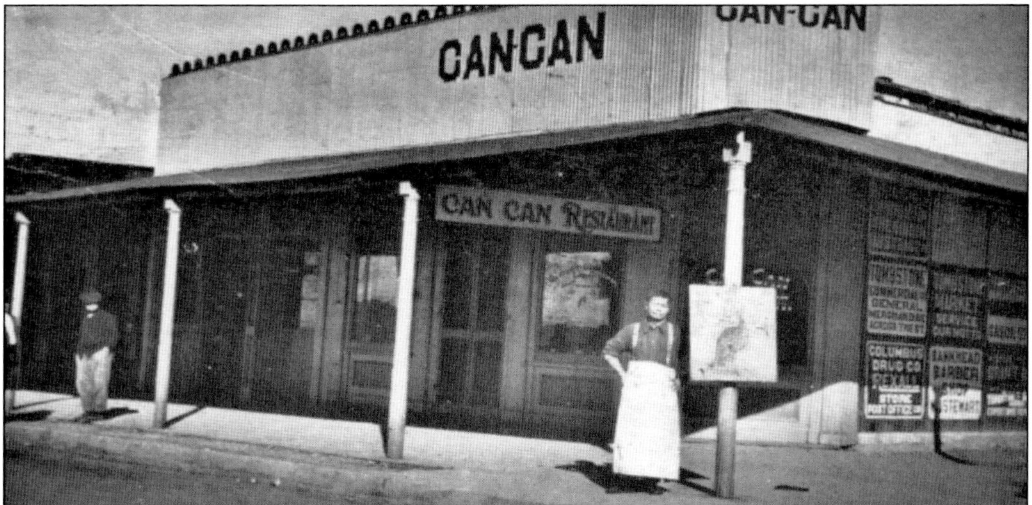

The Can Can Restaurant served excellent meals, including steaks and Chinese food. Quong Gu Kee took over Ah Sing's Can Can Restaurant after arriving in Tombstone. The restaurant is supposed to have been well furnished with paintings, fine white tablecloths, and oak chairs. Quong's customers included Billy Clanton, Wyatt Earp, and Curly Bill Brocius. Quong said Billy Clanton always ate at the Can Can and paid his bill. Curly Bill Brocius ate a lot and was never bad to Quong. (Courtesy of Don Taylor.)

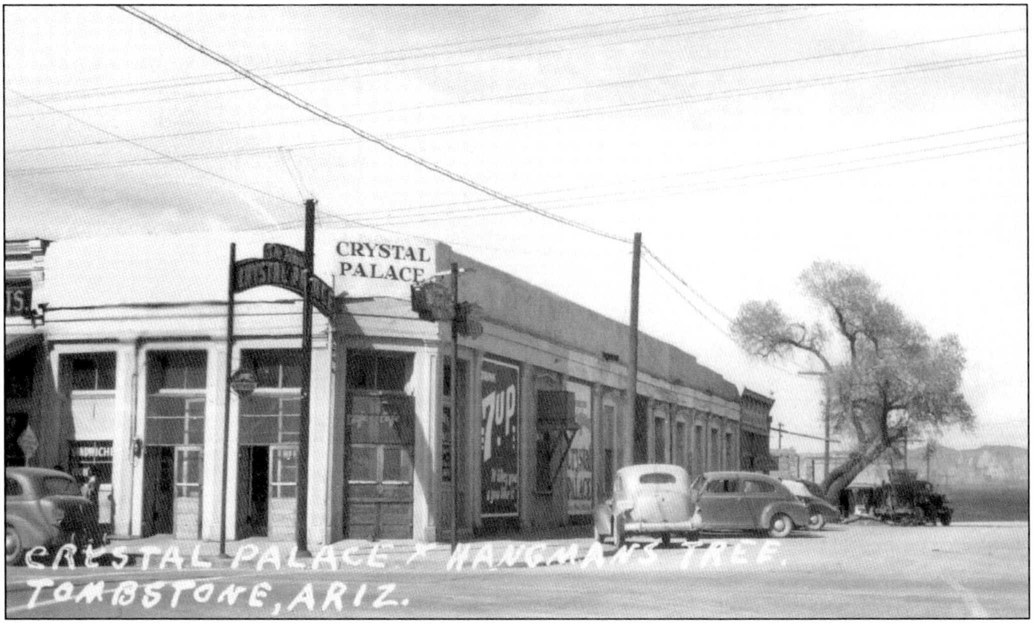

In 1880, the Tribolet brothers and Bernhardt Wehrfritz opened the Golden Eagle Brewery. They offered a free lunch of pig's feet and Limburger cheese, among other things. The brewery was also called the Fredricksburg Lager Beer Depot at one time. It burned in the 1882 fire, and when Wehrfritz rebuilt, he opened his establishment as the Crystal Palace Saloon. (Courtesy of Don Taylor.)

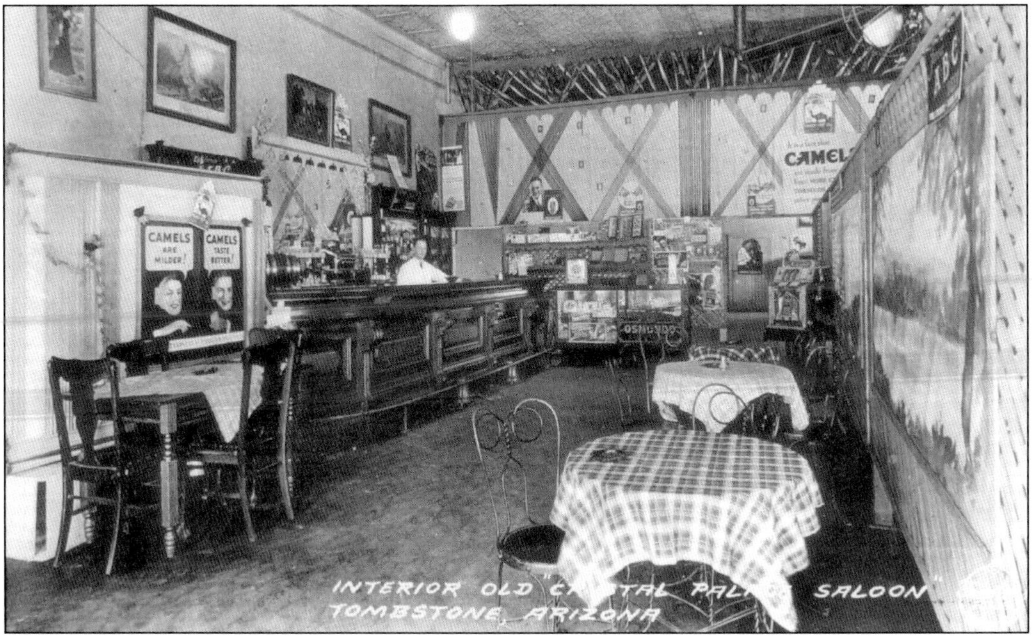

This photograph shows the interior of the Crystal Palace. After Prohibition, the saloon reopened as the Crystal Palace Saloon, and in the 1960s it was restored to its former 1882 glory. It remains the most popular saloon in Tombstone today. (Courtesy of Don Taylor.)

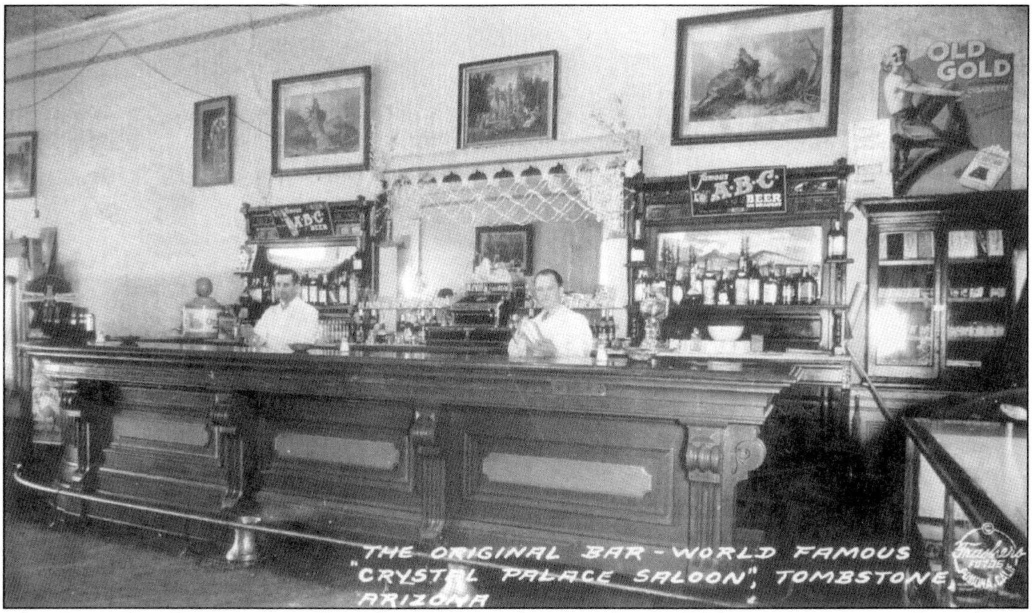

The Crystal Palace reopened in the 1920s without its beautiful bar. It appears to have been removed during Prohibition and disappeared. In the early 1960s, an effort was made to rebuild the old bar, still beautiful long after most the inhabitants had moved away. Today the Crystal Palace still slakes the thirst of many customers. (Courtesy of Nancy Lewis Sosa.)

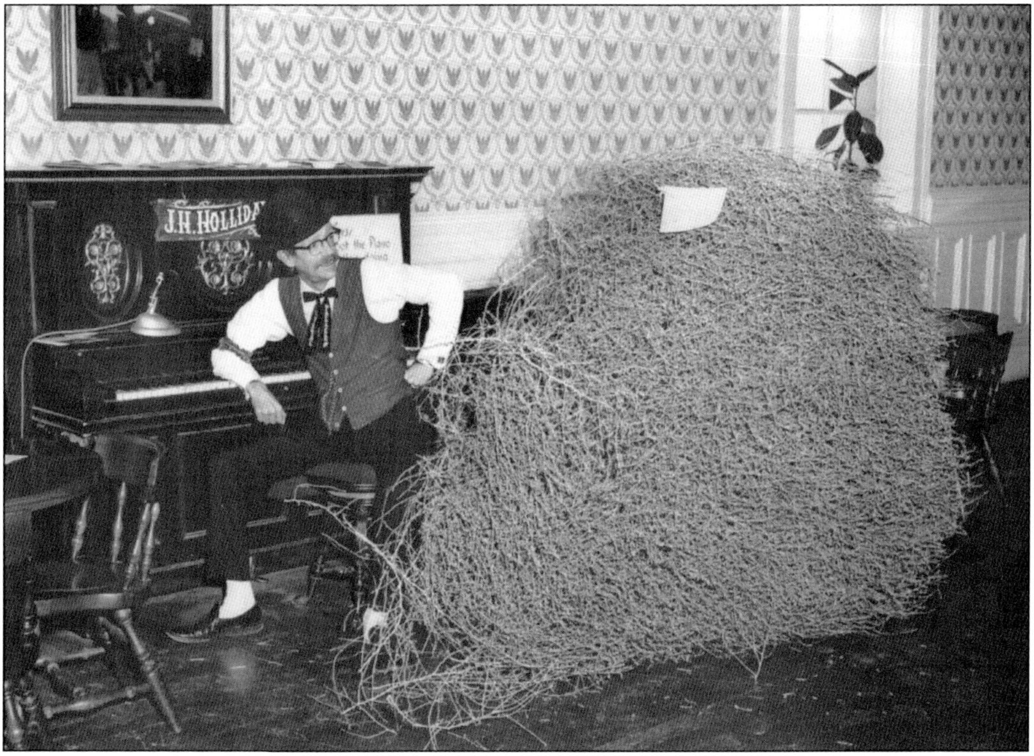

Denver Smith, an erstwhile Tombstone piano player, probably at the Crystal Palace, is very surprised at the large tumbleweed that blew in from the street. (Courtesy of Don Taylor.)

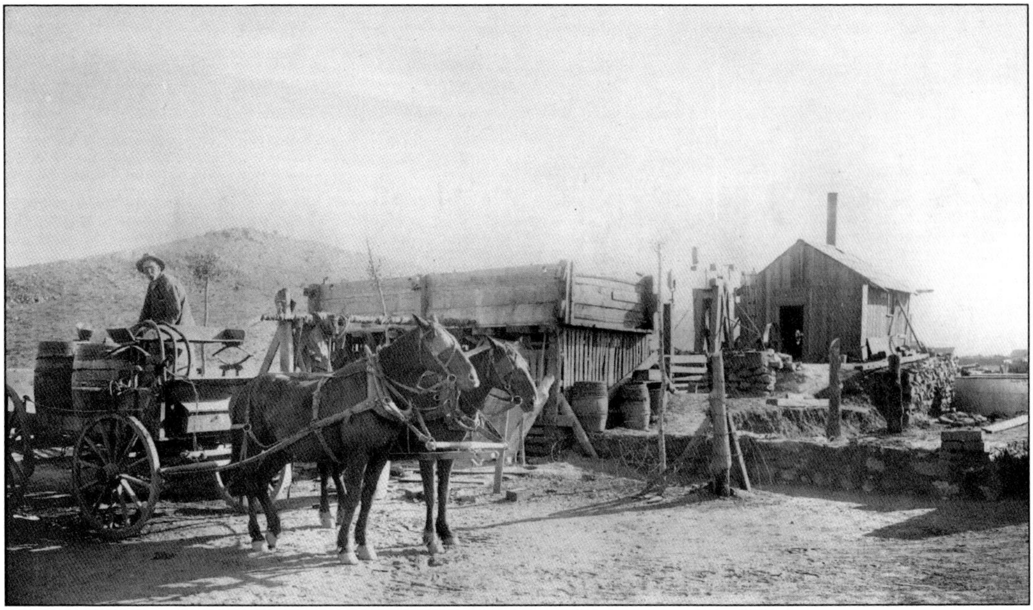

This water wagon was owned and operated by Jim Harper and Owen Williams of Pearce, Arizona. They also owned a well due east of town and sold water to the local inhabitants. Note the pump house and walking beam. (Courtesy of Hayden Arizona Collection, Tempe, Arizona.)

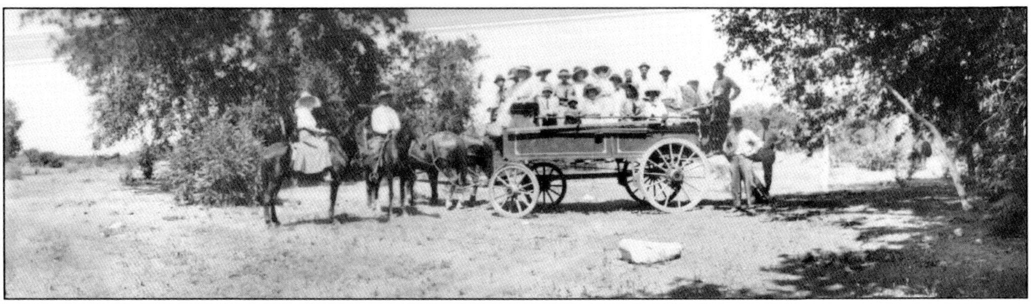

Here people gather to ride into Tombstone in a wagon to celebrate Helldorado Days. (Courtesy of Arizona State Archives, Phoenix, Arizona.)

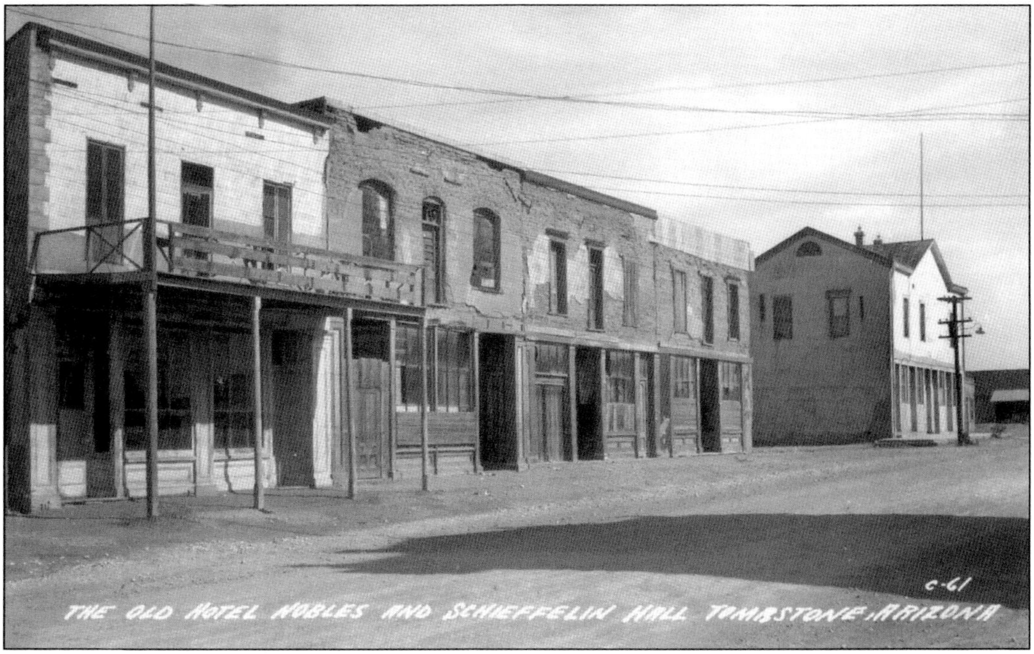

Today Highway 80 runs by Schieffelin Hall, at far right, and Tombstone's main business district. Also pictured here is the Hotel Nobles, at far left, next to the Tombstone Epitaph Building. (Courtesy of Arizona Historical Society, Tucson, Arizona.)

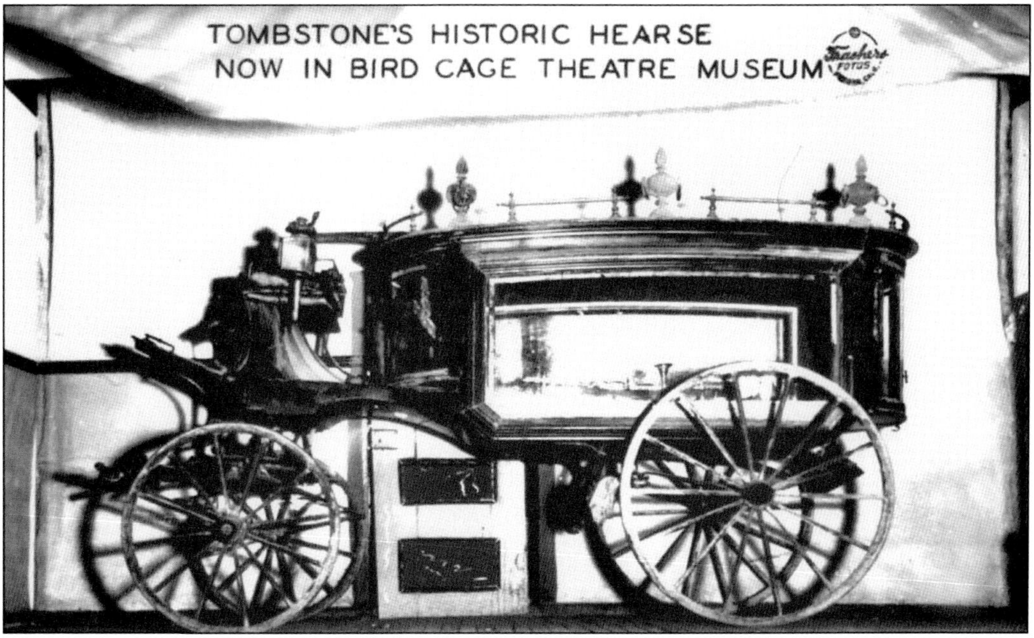

Tombstone's historic hearse, drawn by six white horses, would have carried the deceased to Boot Hill Cemetery. (Courtesy of Arizona Historical Society, Tucson, Arizona.)

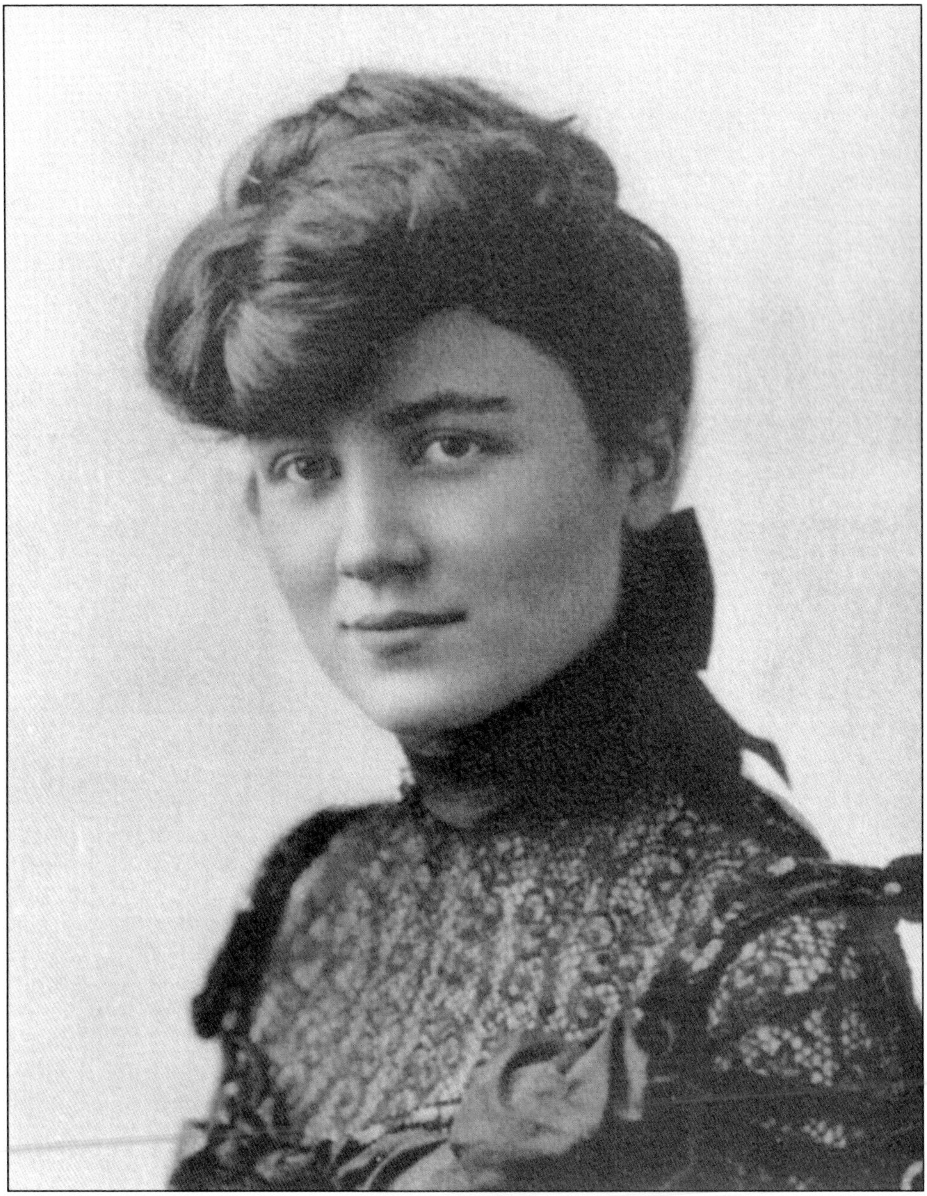

Apache Indians in the Arizona Territory named Juanita Lynch. Juanita's father, Albert G. Smith, a graduate of DePauw University in 1870, and her mother, Sarah Anna Parks, had moved to the Tombstone area for Albert's health. They had three small boys and another child on the way. This was still wild territory, and the Apaches had a habit of getting rid of settlers. Several Apache Indians stopped by the small house the day the child was born. When they were invited in to eat, they noticed the new baby girl with a fringe of red hair and asked if they could name her. Her surprised parents said yes. The Apaches suggested the Spanish name Juanita. After Alfred died, Sarah Smith moved her family to Hutchinson, Kansas, where her mother lived. Alfred's wife never remarried, but his daughter Juanita married a Kansan whose brother helped turn the Arizona Territory into a state. Her brother-in-law was Charles Lynch, an executive with the copper mine in Jerome, who also dealt in Jerome real estate. (Courtesy of Juanita's granddaughter, Barbara Lacy.)

Nellie Cashman, born in County Cork, Ireland, was known in Tombstone as the miner's angel. During her Tombstone years, Nellie made a living from her restaurant and a hotel; she also bought and sold a number of profitable mine properties. It was said no one ever left her establishment hungry but woe to the person who dared to criticize her cooking. She later became ill in Alaska but made it to Victoria where she entered a hospital, which she had helped found with the Sisters of St. Anne. When Nellie died on January 4, 1925, a number of prominent newspapers from New York to San Francisco found her newsworthy. She has her own postage stamp with this portrait and a Tombstone scene in the background. (Courtesy of Arizona Historical Society, Tucson, Arizona.)

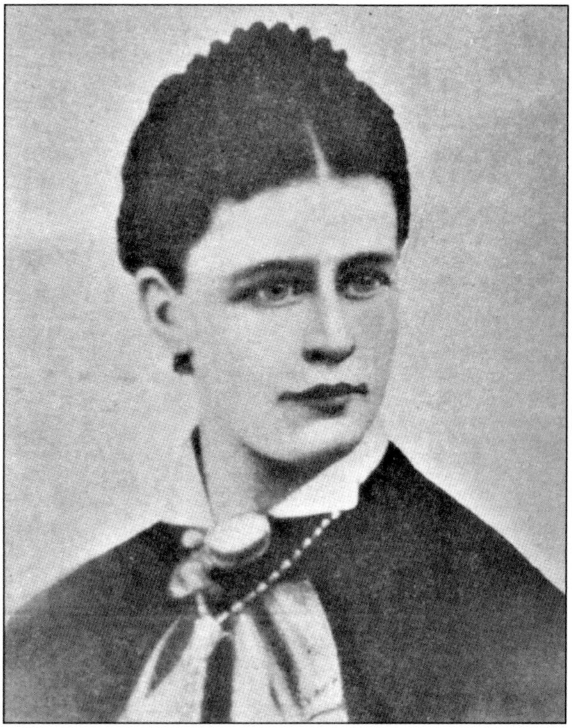

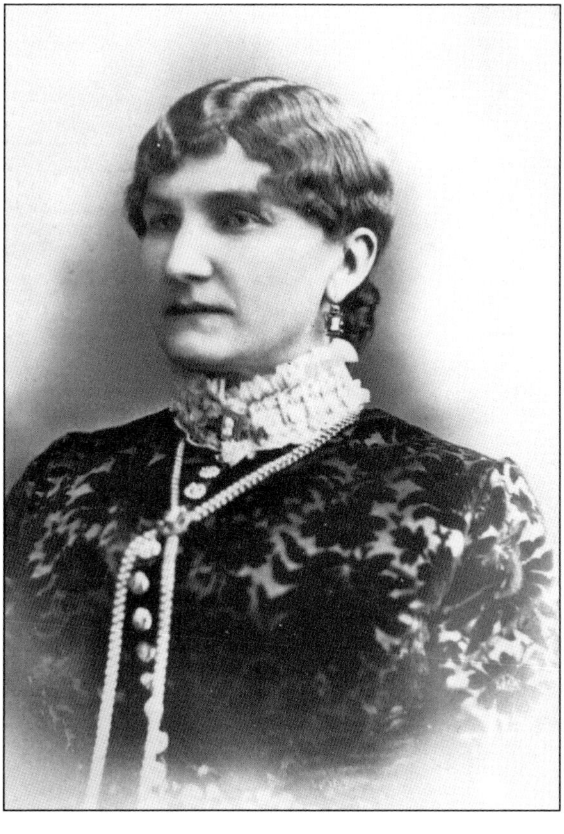

Celia Ann "Mattie" Blaylock (1850–July 3, 1888) was the second romance of Wyatt Earp. Mattie, born in Wisconsin and raised in Fairfax, Iowa, ran away from home at the age of 16 and worked as a prostitute in Dodge City where she may have met Wyatt in 1873. They probably never married, but in the 1880 United States Census, she is listed as Wyatt's wife. In Tombstone, she became addicted to laudanum (opium). When Wyatt became infatuated with Josephine Marcus, there were several severe altercations. When it became obvious that Wyatt had no more interest in her, Mattie went to Pinal City where she worked as a prostitute. On July 3, 1888, she took a lethal dose of laudanum with alcohol. Her death was officially ruled as a suicide. She is buried in the cemetery at Pinal City, now a ghost town. (Courtesy of Macia-Devere family.)

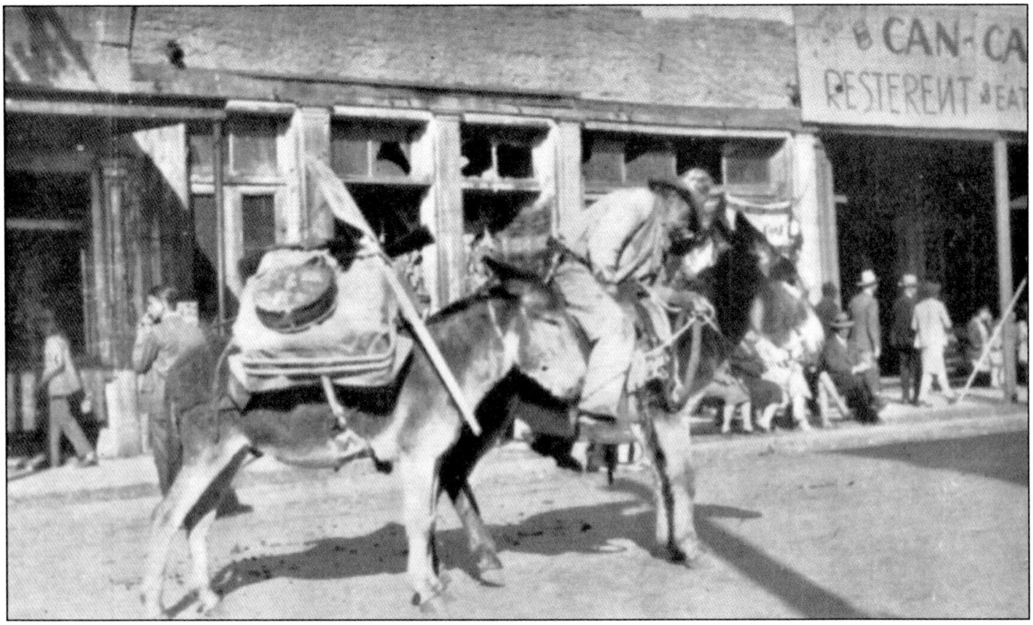

Many a time a burro or horse wandered into town carrying a dead man. Here, however, the burro and prospector are a part of the Helldorado Days parade. The townsfolk do not look too concerned about the burro's load. (Courtesy of Arizona Historical Society, Tucson, Arizona.)

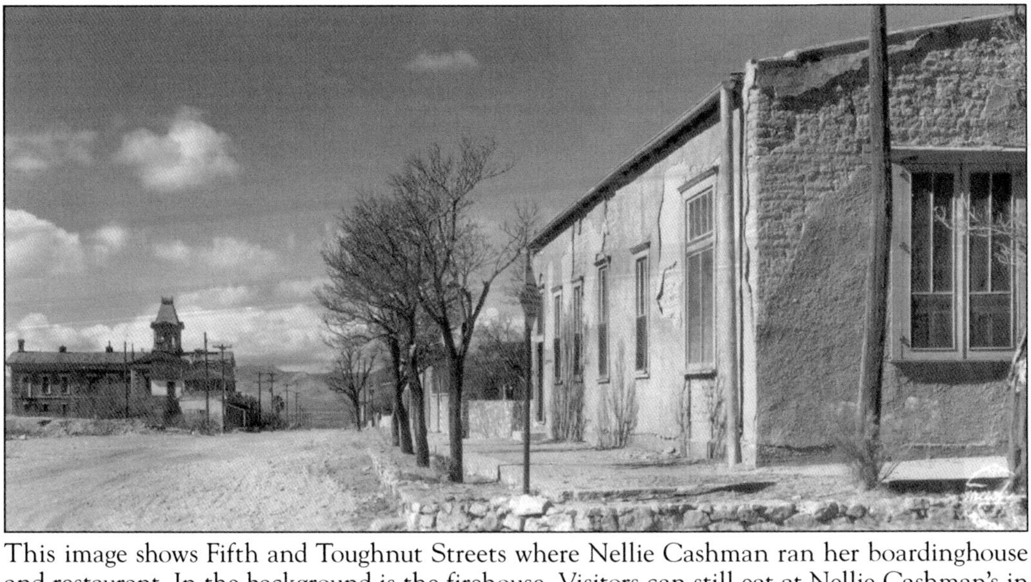

This image shows Fifth and Toughnut Streets where Nellie Cashman ran her boardinghouse and restaurant. In the background is the firehouse. Visitors can still eat at Nellie Cashman's in Tombstone. (Courtesy of Arizona Historical Society, Tucson, Arizona.)

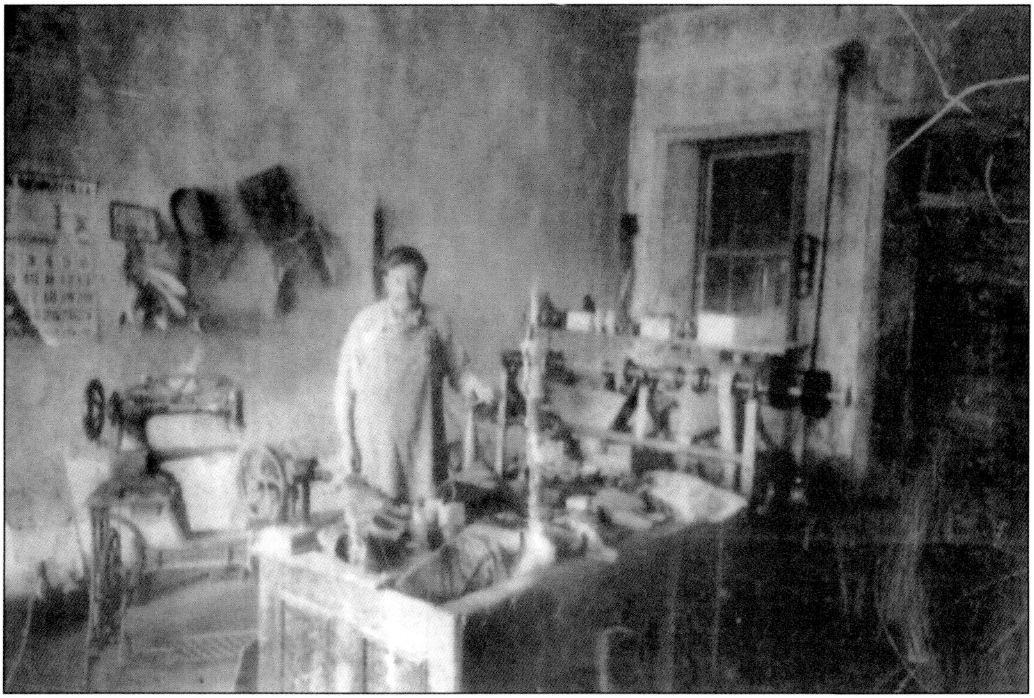

Mr. Ramirez made certain that Tombstone residents were properly shod with both new footwear and repaired boots and shoes. (Courtesy of Charles and Betty Escapule.)

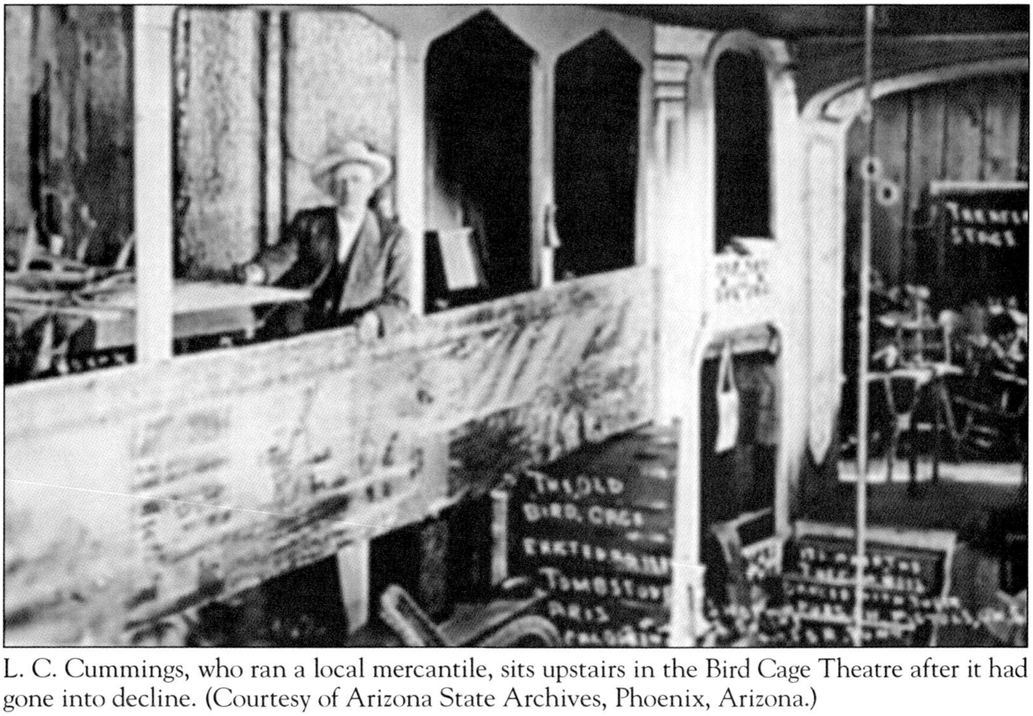

L. C. Cummings, who ran a local mercantile, sits upstairs in the Bird Cage Theatre after it had gone into decline. (Courtesy of Arizona State Archives, Phoenix, Arizona.)

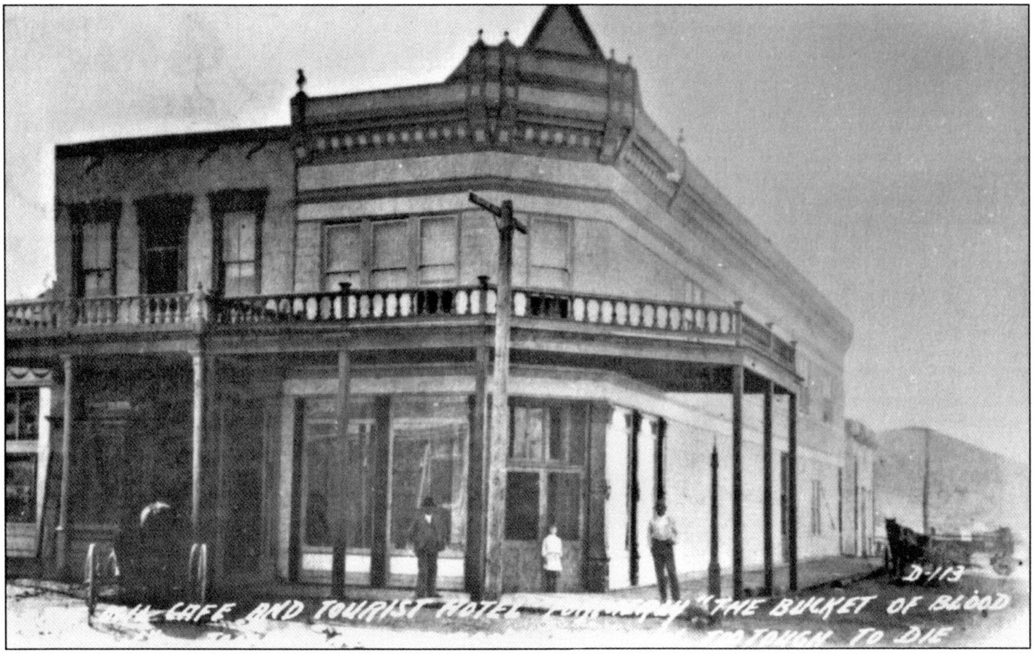

The Owl Café and Tourist Hotel had a bar known as the Bucket of Blood. (Courtesy of Arizona Historical Society, Tucson, Arizona.)

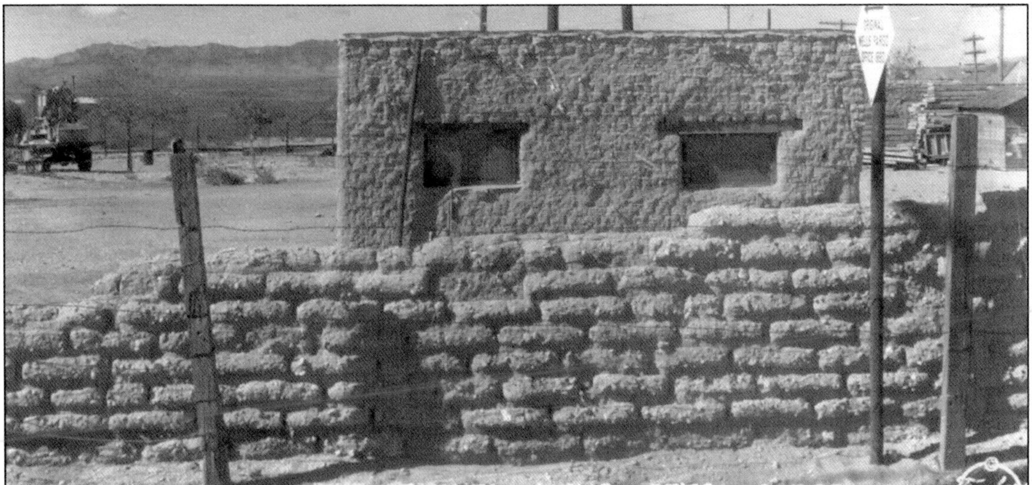

All that is left of Wells Fargo's Tombstone station is crumbling adobe bricks. In March 1881, Wells Fargo was the center of a holdup. The trouble between the Earps and the Clanton and McLaury boys may have grown out of the robbery of the Benson stage. On March 15, 1881, the stage with a Wells, Fargo & Company express left Tombstone for Benson. Bud Philpot drove, and Bob Paul served as Wells, Fargo & Company messenger and rode shotgun. At 7:30 p.m., the order to halt was given along with two shots. One shot killed Philpot and the other perforated the cushion upon which Paul was sitting. Paul emptied his gun, returning shot for shot, but without effect. The horses kept running, and the robbers kept shooting, in all firing some 20 bullets at the stage with passengers. The robbers killed one man who rode on top. Paul managed to stop the team, gather up the lines, and drove rapidly to Benson, where he telegraphed the news to Tombstone. (Courtesy of Don Taylor.)

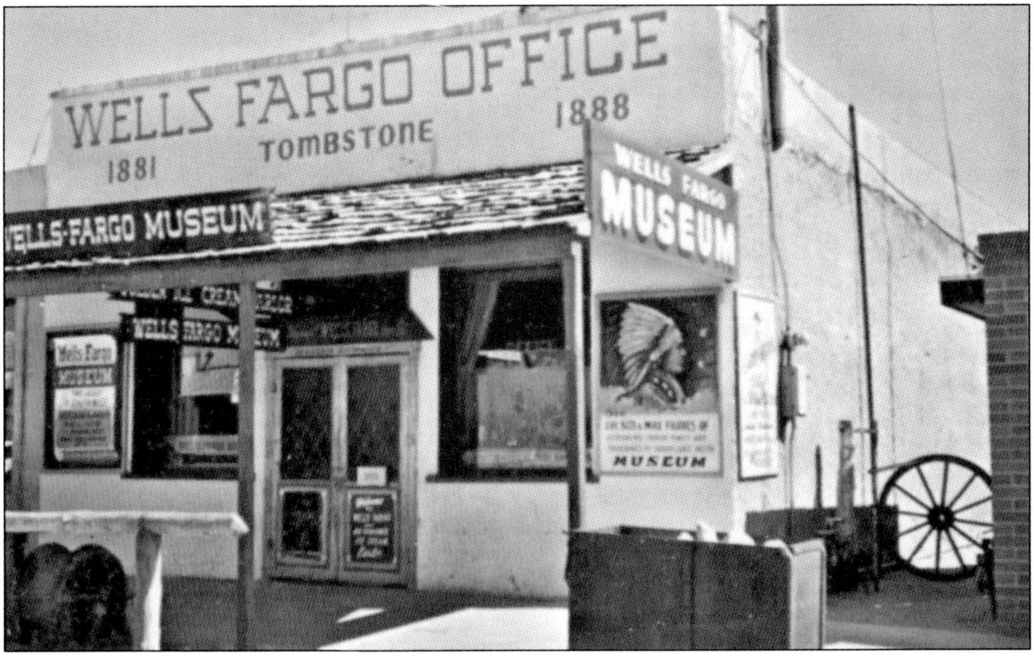

To continue the Wells Fargo story, Agent Williams of Wells, Fargo & Company and the Earp brothers prepared to hunt for the robbers. At 8:30 that same evening, Doc Holliday rode up to a saloon in Charleston, 10 miles from the scene of the attempted robbery, and asked for Billy Clanton. On being told that he was not there, Holliday started for Tombstone. Around 10:00 p.m., he rode up to a saloon on a back street in Tombstone and called for a big drink of whiskey, which he drank at a gulp, without dismounting. At midnight the agent and the Earp brothers, with Holliday, left town to meet Bob Paul. It was too dark to follow a trail, but the next morning they found three masks made of hay rope and about 20 large-size rifle cartridges. They followed a trail for about three weeks without catching anyone except a supposed accomplice who escaped from the jail. (Courtesy of Don Taylor.)

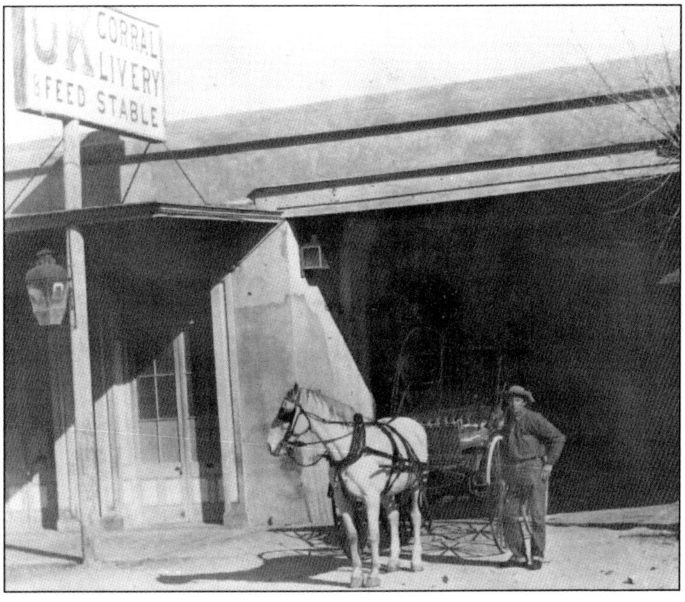

The O. K. livery stable served Tombstone travelers for several years. Before the 19th century, hotels had livery stables. Facilities at a livery yard normally included a loose box or stable and access to grass for the horses to graze. They also provided horses for those who did not have their own. Long after the infamous fight at the O. K. Corral (which did not actually take place at the O. K. Corral) was over, it still served many travelers as a livery stable. (Courtesy of Arizona Historical Society, Tucson, Arizona.)

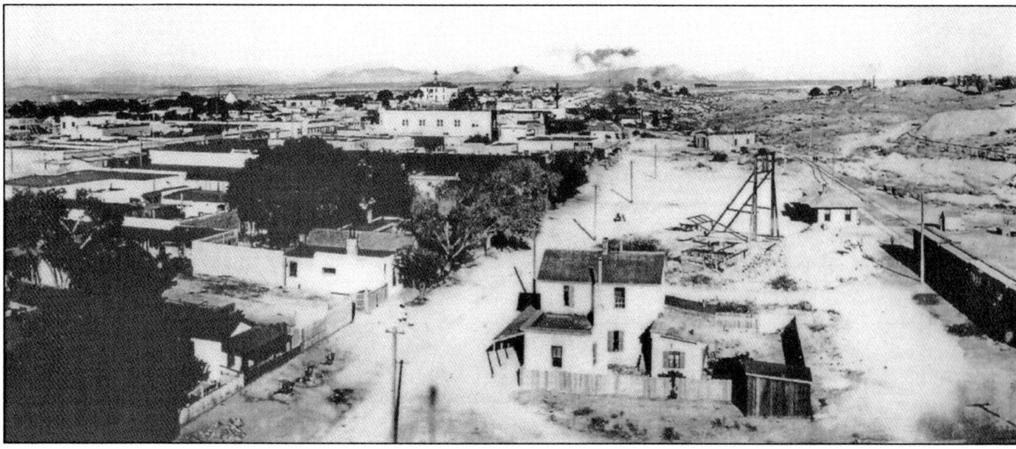

This is Tombstone in its heyday. One can see smelter smoke in the distance and a mine entrance at the center of the picture. Fueled by mineral wealth, Tombstone had a population of 1,000 by 1881, along with refrigeration for ice cream and later ice-skating, running water, a telegraph, and limited telephone service. Capitalists moved in from the eastern United States, and mining was carried out by European immigrants. Laundry, construction, restaurants, and hotels were staffed by Chinese and other immigrants. (Courtesy of Arizona Historical Society, Tucson, Arizona.)

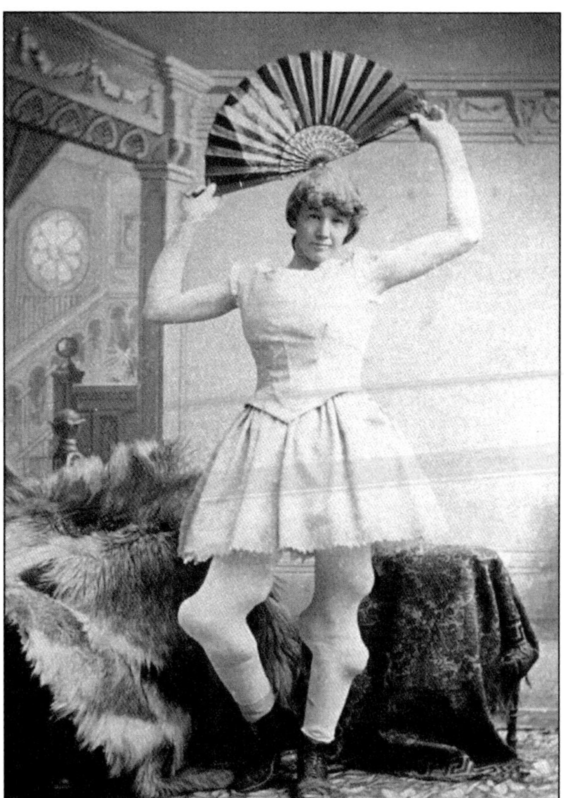

David Waters is dressed for a masquerade ball. Entertainment in early Tombstone could be outrageous with clientele and entertainers mingling with each other. The entertainers provided comic skits, ribald ballads, and women who impersonated men and vice versa. David Waters and Will Curlew provided some of the most popular entertainment. (Courtesy of Arizona Historical Society, Tucson, Arizona.)

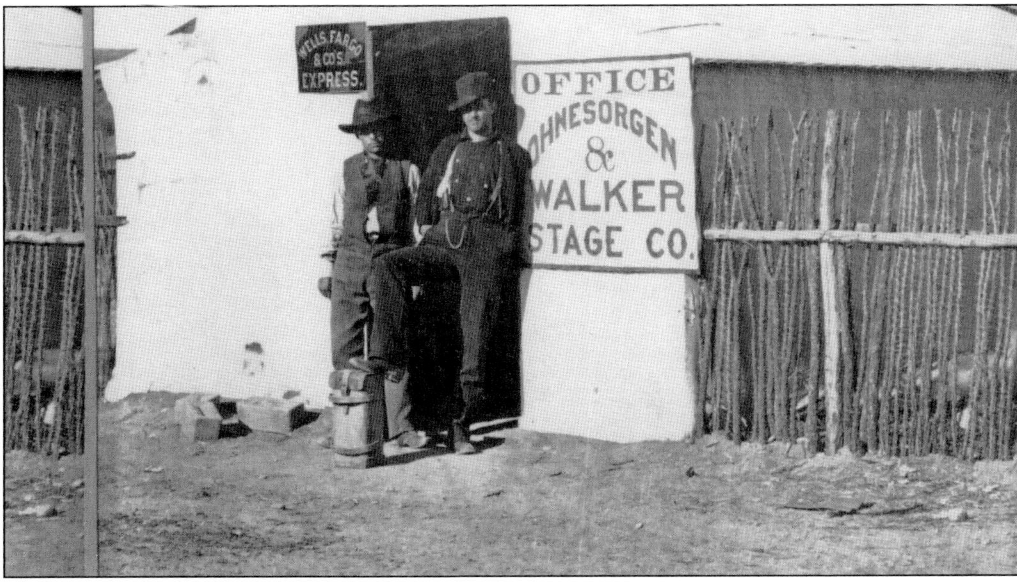

William Ohnesorgen was born in Germany and in 1853 came to America, where he settled in San Antonio. As an adult, William came to Tombstone and opened a stage business, which prospered for about a year. However, others had the same idea and there was soon a glut in the stagecoach market. He got out of the stagecoach business and prospered in ranching, which included cattle and sheep. He also served as a justice of the peace in Benson, Arizona. (Courtesy of Arizona Historical Society, Tucson, Arizona.)

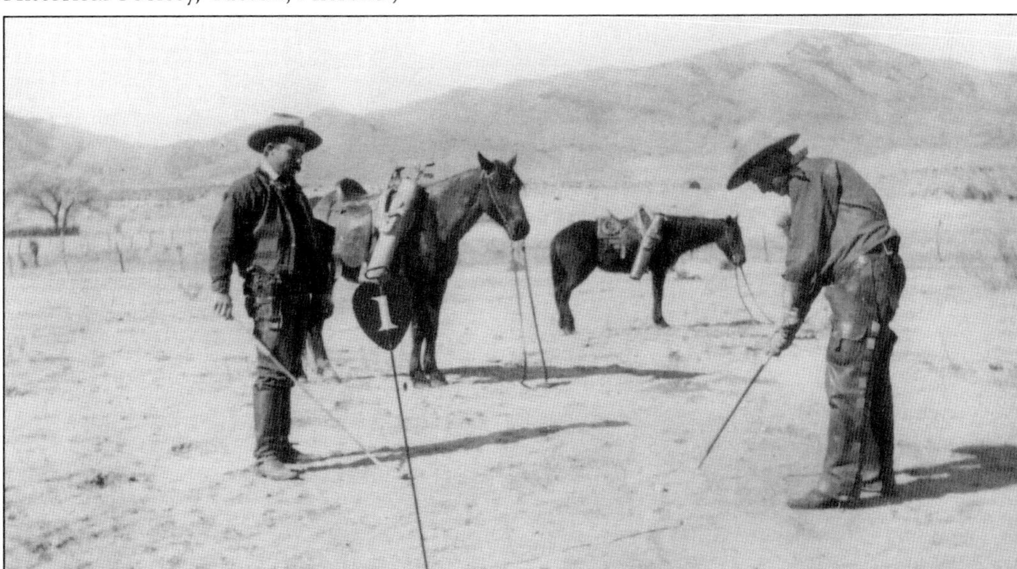

Amos Wien and Ed Smith constructed a three-hole golf course near Russellville, which some unkind souls claimed was nothing more than a glorified sand trap. They purchased their golf clubs through the Montgomery Ward catalog and trained their horses to stand still when they dropped the rein (so they would not wander off while they were playing). Both men worked as miners, ranchers, and lawmen in Cochise County. Wien was also a truant officer and would parade kids who were staying out of school through the streets of Benson. Smith ran a saloon in Charleston. (Author's collection.)

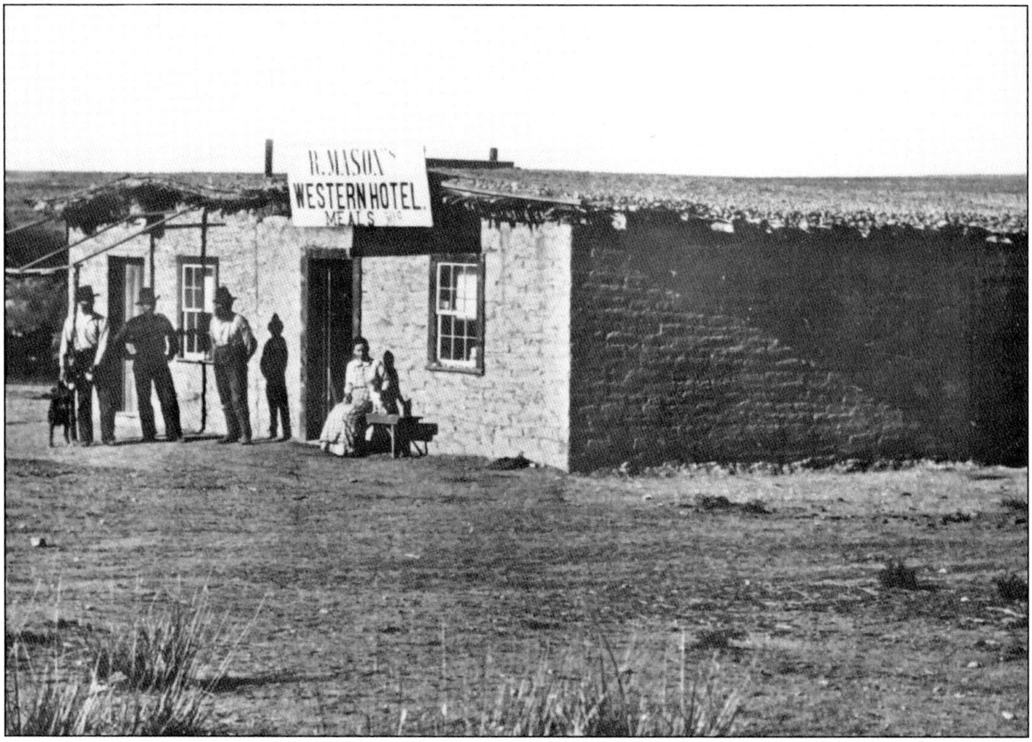

Very little is known of J. R. Mason, the proprietor of the Western Hotel in Contention. He was shot and instantly killed at Fairbank on May 19, 1884, by William Humphries, presumably the result of an old feud. (Courtesy of Arizona Historical Society, Tucson, Arizona.)

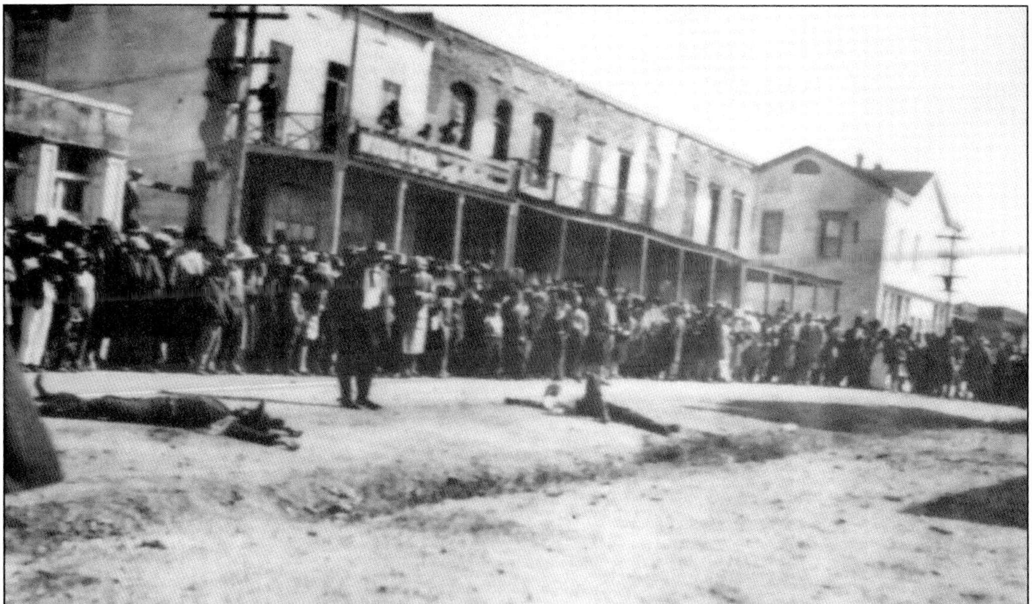

The crowd is enjoying a mock gunfight in front of the Nobles Hotel on Fifth Street, probably part of a Helldorado Days weekend. (Courtesy of Arizona Historical Society, Tucson, Arizona.)

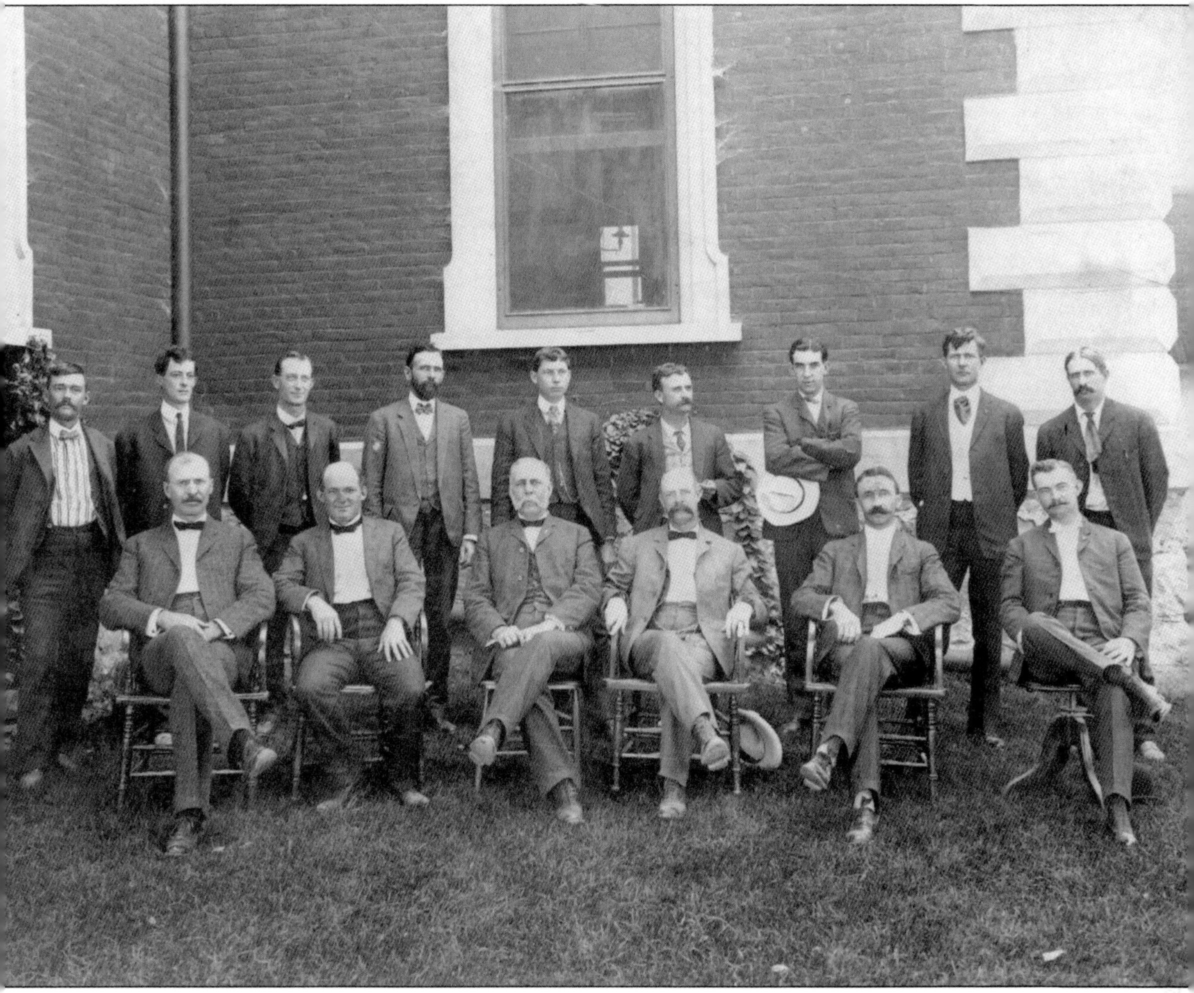

Pictured here are Cochise County officials in 1905. They include B. J. O'Reilly, Fletcher Doan, John J. Brown, Philip Wilcox, Allie Howe, Tom Flannigan, C. A. Taylor, William Riggs, Stewart Hunt, John Walker, Frank Goodbody, and Tom Flannigan. (Courtesy of Arizona State Archives, Phoenix, Arizona.)

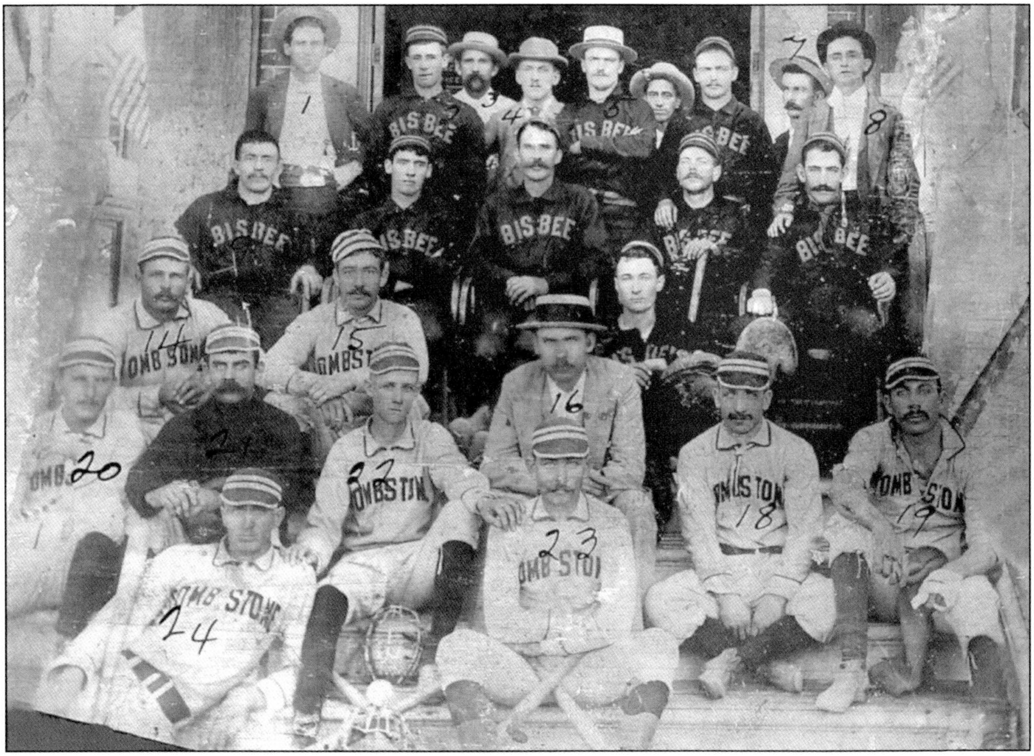

The 1895 Tombstone baseball team was coached by Bob Crouch, also known as "Sandy Bob" (center). He was the proprietor of the Arizona Mail and Stage Line with its office at 406 Allen Street under the Occidental Hotel. He made $50 a day and bought a ranch outside of town. Crouch died in Mexico on September 10, 1898. (Courtesy of Arizona State Archives, Phoenix, Arizona.)

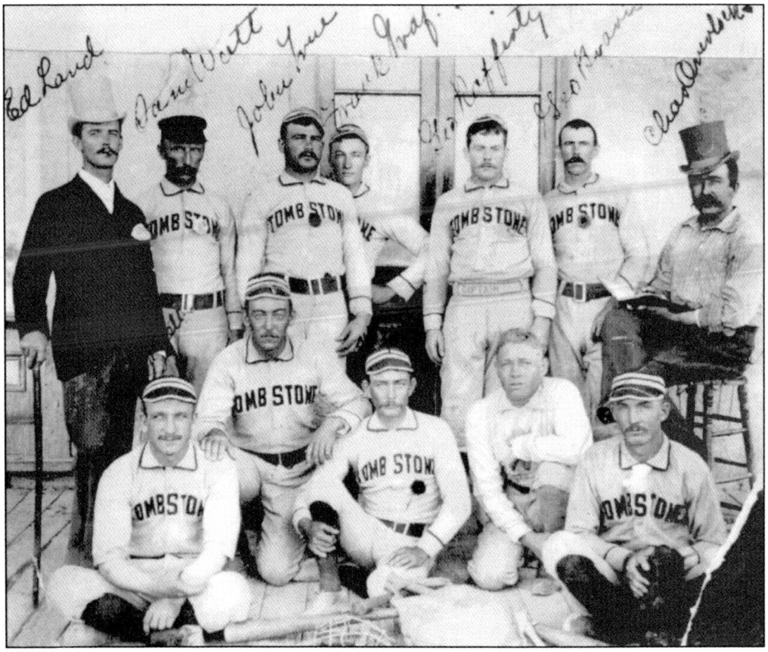

From its inception, Tombstone was fiercely proud of its baseball teams. When one team wanted to play on Sunday, the Reverend Endicott Peabody gave permission for them to do so in the afternoon, just so long as they attended services in the morning. Then Peabody would join them. (Courtesy of Arizona State Archives, Phoenix, Arizona.)

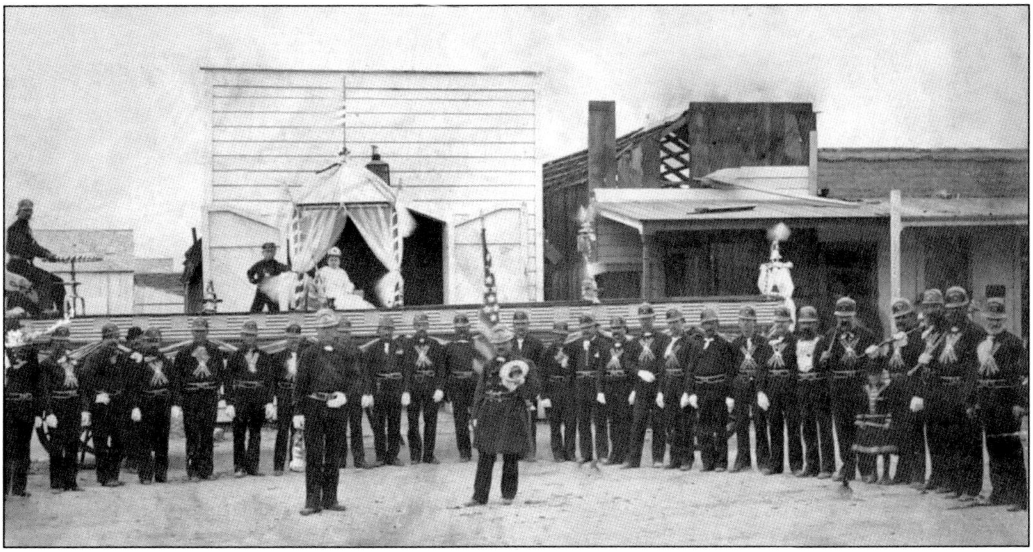

The Tombstone Volunteer Fire Department is in formation in 1883. In the center foreground is Frank "Fatty" Ryan. Fatty, born in Ireland, appeared in Tombstone in 1884. He became a town constable and served as a fire chief. He was also part owner in the Exchange Saloon. The *Weekly Orb* reported that Fatty cashed in his checks on December 11, 1898. (Courtesy of Arizona State Archives, Phoenix, Arizona.)

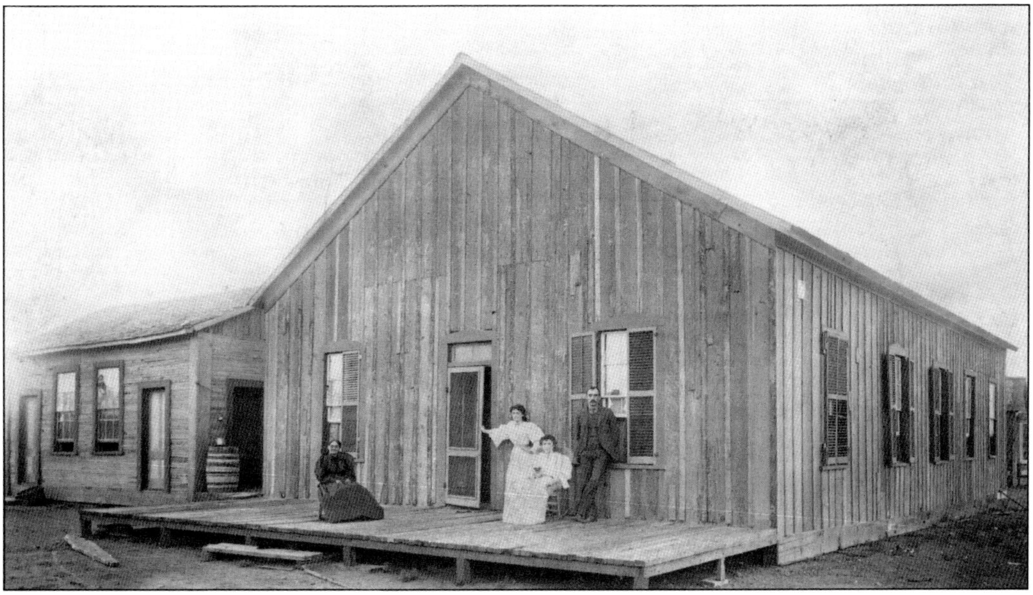

Pictured here is a boardinghouse in Pearce, Arizona Territory, in 1876. The man standing is Frank Barnett. (Courtesy of Arizona Historical Society, Tucson, Arizona.)

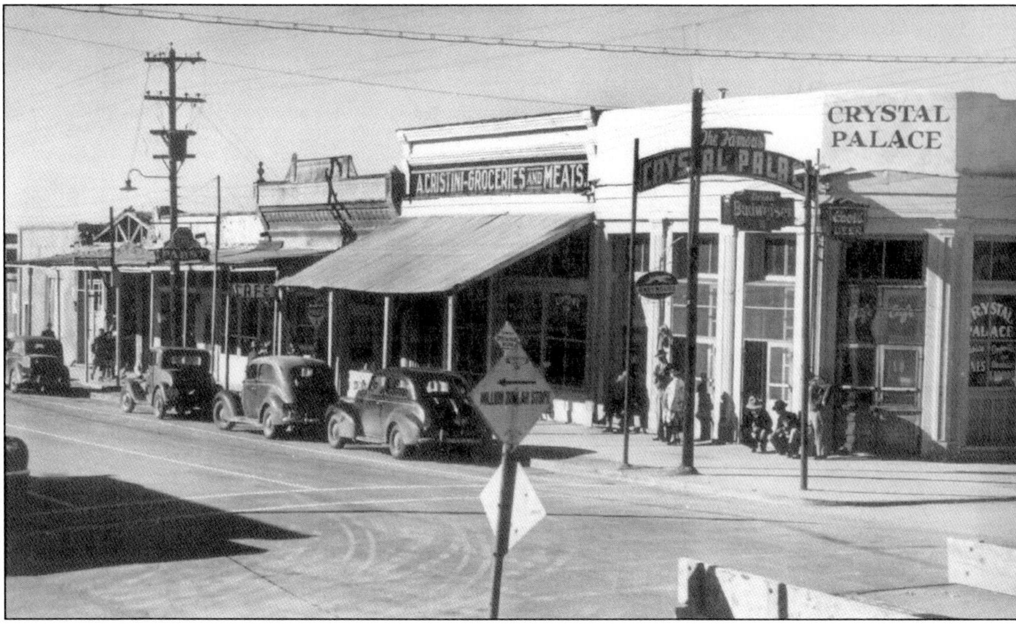

Tombstone changed, but the Crystal Palace remained and was in the hub of the town's business center. (Author's collection.)

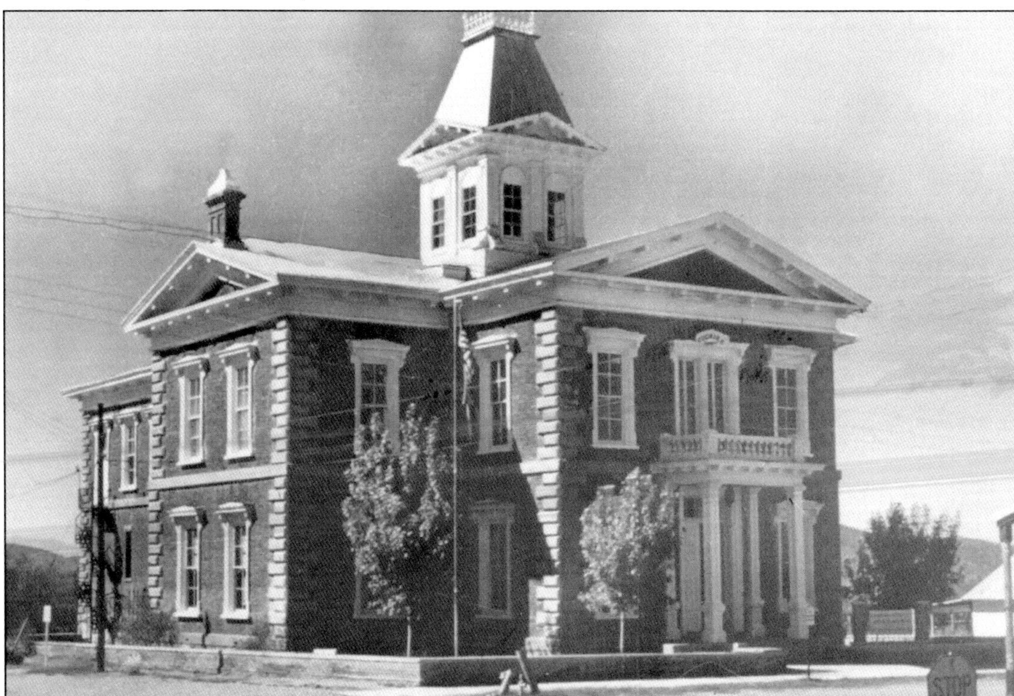

The courthouse in Tombstone is one of the jewels in the crown of the Arizona State Parks. On August 11, 1882, the cornerstone was laid in a pleasing ceremony with eloquent speeches. The prayer by a venerable bishop and the mementos deposited in the courthouse made the event a memorable occasion. The official Cochise County Court House moved to Bisbee in 1929. (Courtesy of Arizona Historical Society, Tucson, Arizona.)

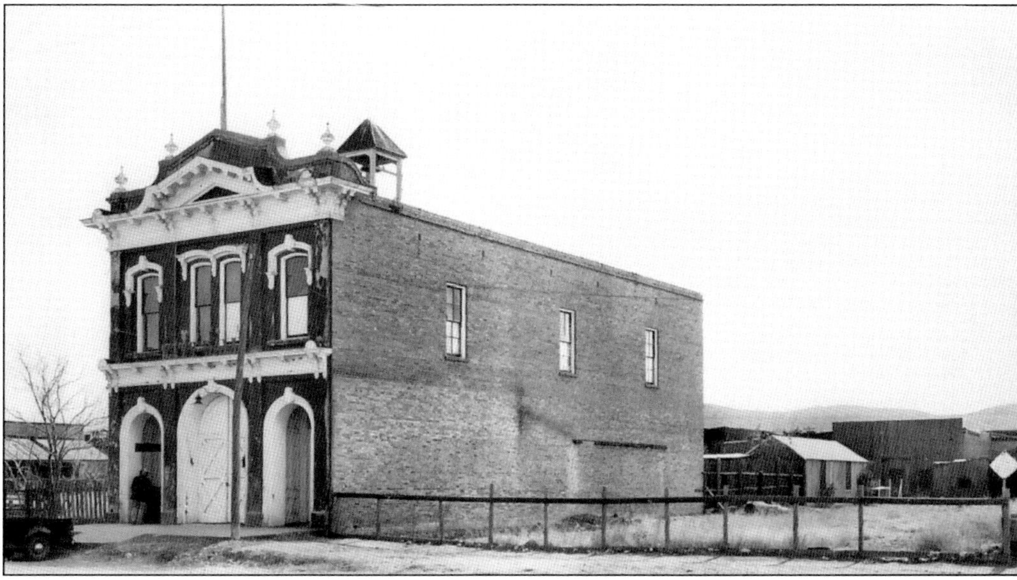

Another of Tombstone's architectural gems is the 1881 city hall. Tombstone was originally located in Pima County. However, it was now the county seat of newly created Cochise County and home to those who were in charge of preserving the peace of the town and the surrounding area. (Author's collection.)

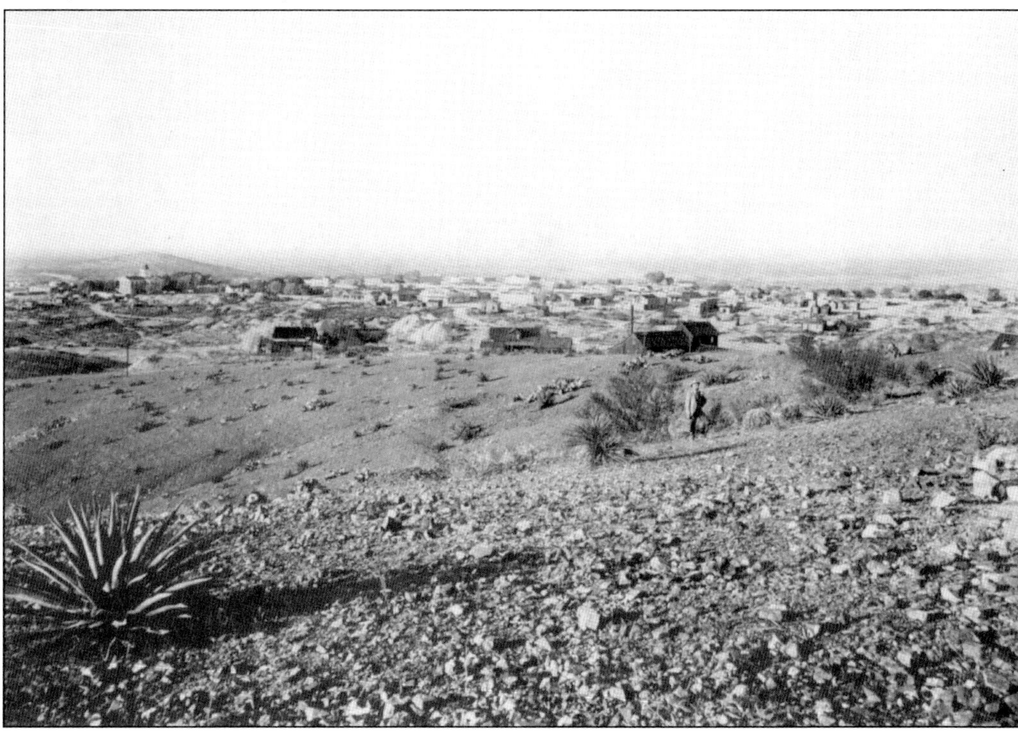

When the word spread about Ed Schieffelin's silver strike, prospectors, cowboys, homesteaders, lawyers, speculators, gunmen, and businesspeople descended on an area known locally as Goose Flats. In 1879, a town site was laid out on the nearest level spot to the mines and named Tombstone after Ed Schieffelin's first mining claim. (Courtesy of Arizona Historical Society, Tucson, Arizona.)

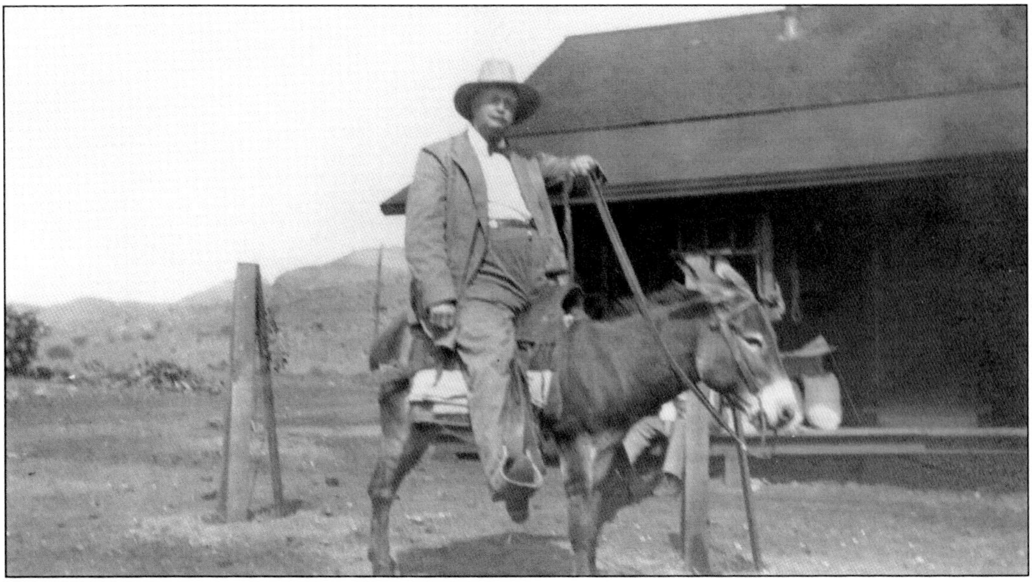

A prospector, known only as "Pop" Harmer, and his burro pause to have their picture taken. (Courtesy of Arizona Historical Society, Tucson, Arizona.)

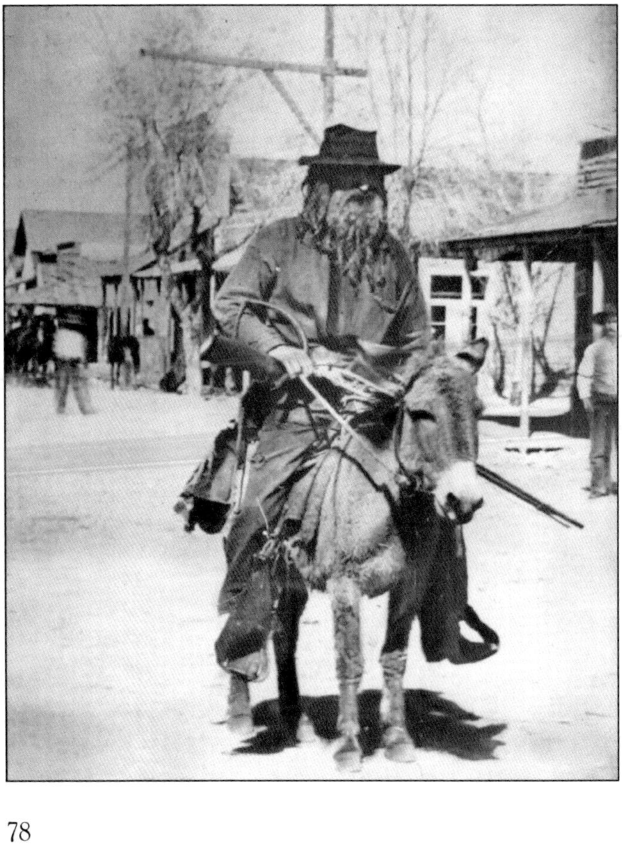

A prospector meanders down the streets of Tombstone with his burro. (Courtesy of Viji Winters.)

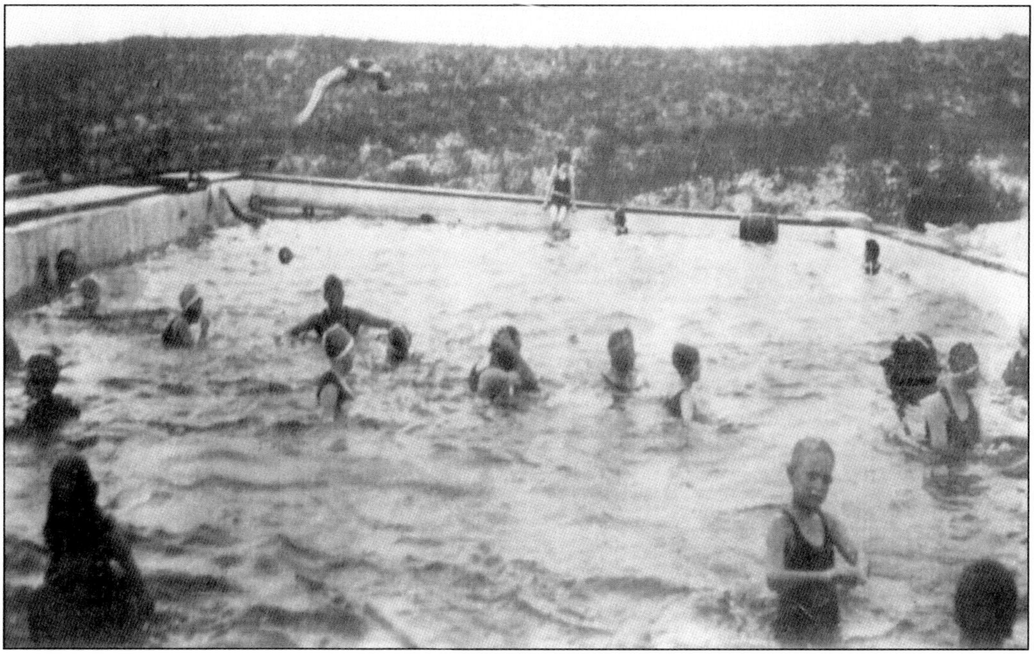

Established in 1883, the Tombstone Municipal Swimming Pool is the oldest continuously used swimming pool in the Southwest. On May 19, a partnership was established between A. J. Mitchell and C. N. Pring to manage the swimming baths at the north end of Fifth Street. Within a few months, the partnership was dissolved, and Pring assumed the responsibility for the baths. In 1885, L. W. Blinn took over and opened the baths under the management of his lumber company. In 1924, there was a call to establish a public swimming pool, and by 1929 the management of the Tombstone Municipal Swimming Pool came under the City of Tombstone. For many years, the pool was segregated with blacks and Mexicans swimming only on certain days. This cement swimming pool turned 124 years old in 2007. (Courtesy of Nancy Lewis Sosa.)

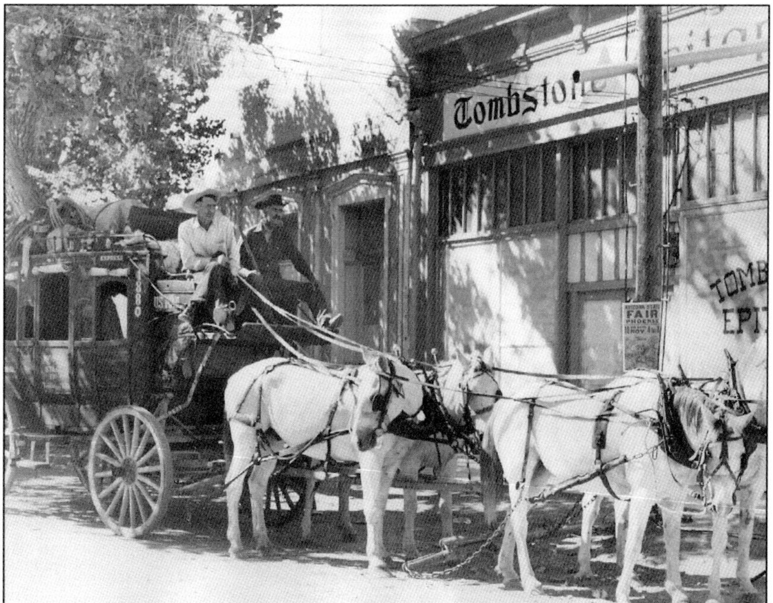

The Modoc stagecoach stops in front of the Nobles Hotel, which is next door to the *Tombstone Epitaph*. (Courtesy of Arizona Historical Society, Tucson, Arizona.)

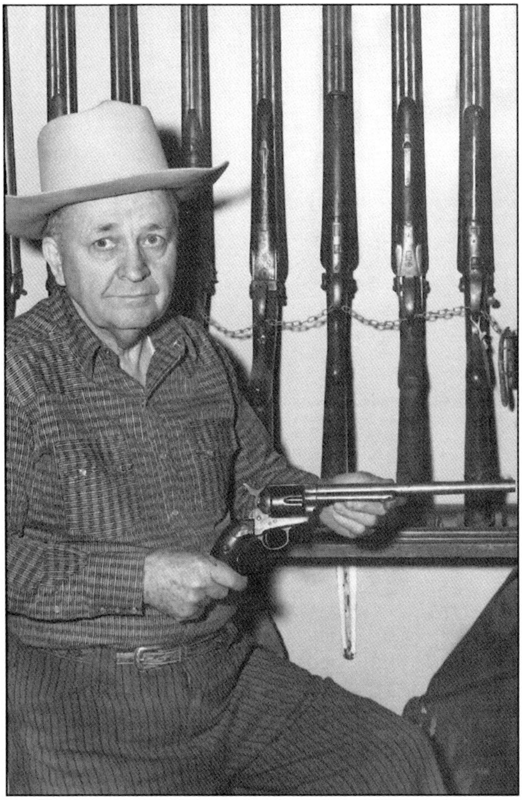

Floyd Laughrin is pictured with an original Buntline, acquired by the Wells Fargo Museum in Tombstone in 1965. The Buntline Peacemaker, produced by Colt before World War II, had a very long barrel. It took its name from the dime novelist E. Z. C. Judson, who wrote under the pen name Ned Buntline. (Courtesy of Arizona Historical Society, Tucson, Arizona.)

In 1906, the Tombstone Grammar School at Ninth and Fremont Streets encompassed all grades. (Courtesy of Viji Winters.)

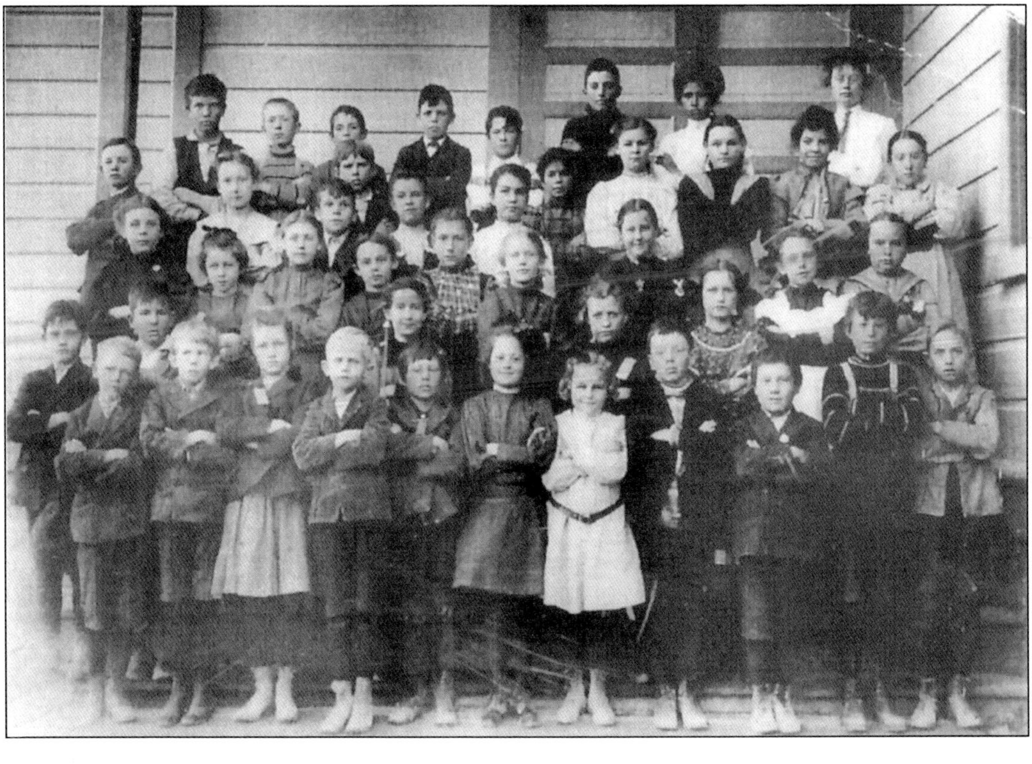

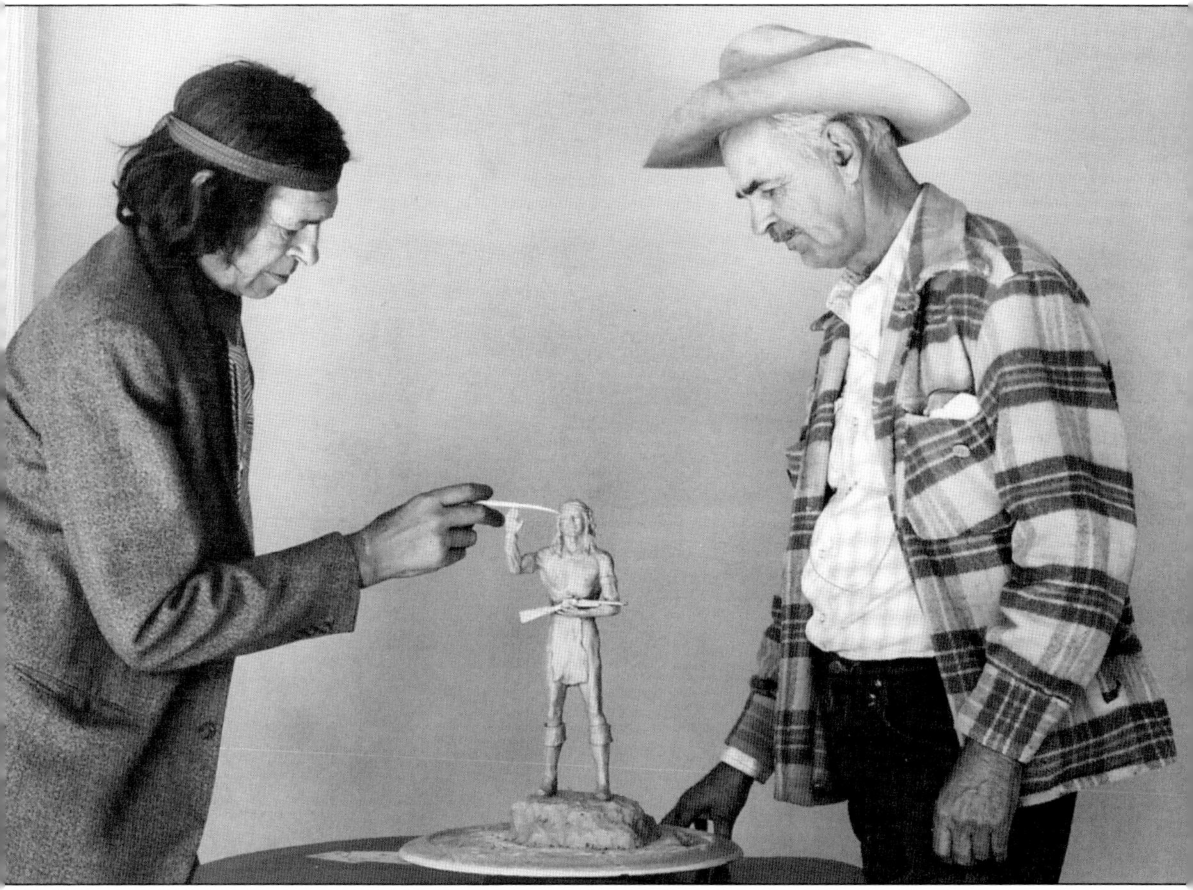

Nino Cochise received his Social Security checks under that name and claimed to be descendant of Cochise. Cochise (*c.* 1815–1874), chief of the Chiricahua Apaches in Arizona, was friendly with the whites until 1861, when some of his relatives were hanged by U.S. soldiers for a crime they claimed they did not commit. The incident was one of many that touched off the Apache wars. Cochise's friendship with Thomas Jeffords, a U.S. Army scout and Indian agent, was the key to peace. In 1872, Gen. Oliver Otis Howard, the Native American commissioner, took Jeffords with him to Cochise's stronghold. As a result, Cochise agreed to live on a reservation. After Cochise's death, his people were removed to another reservation. Cochise County in Arizona is named for him. (Courtesy of Viji Winters.)

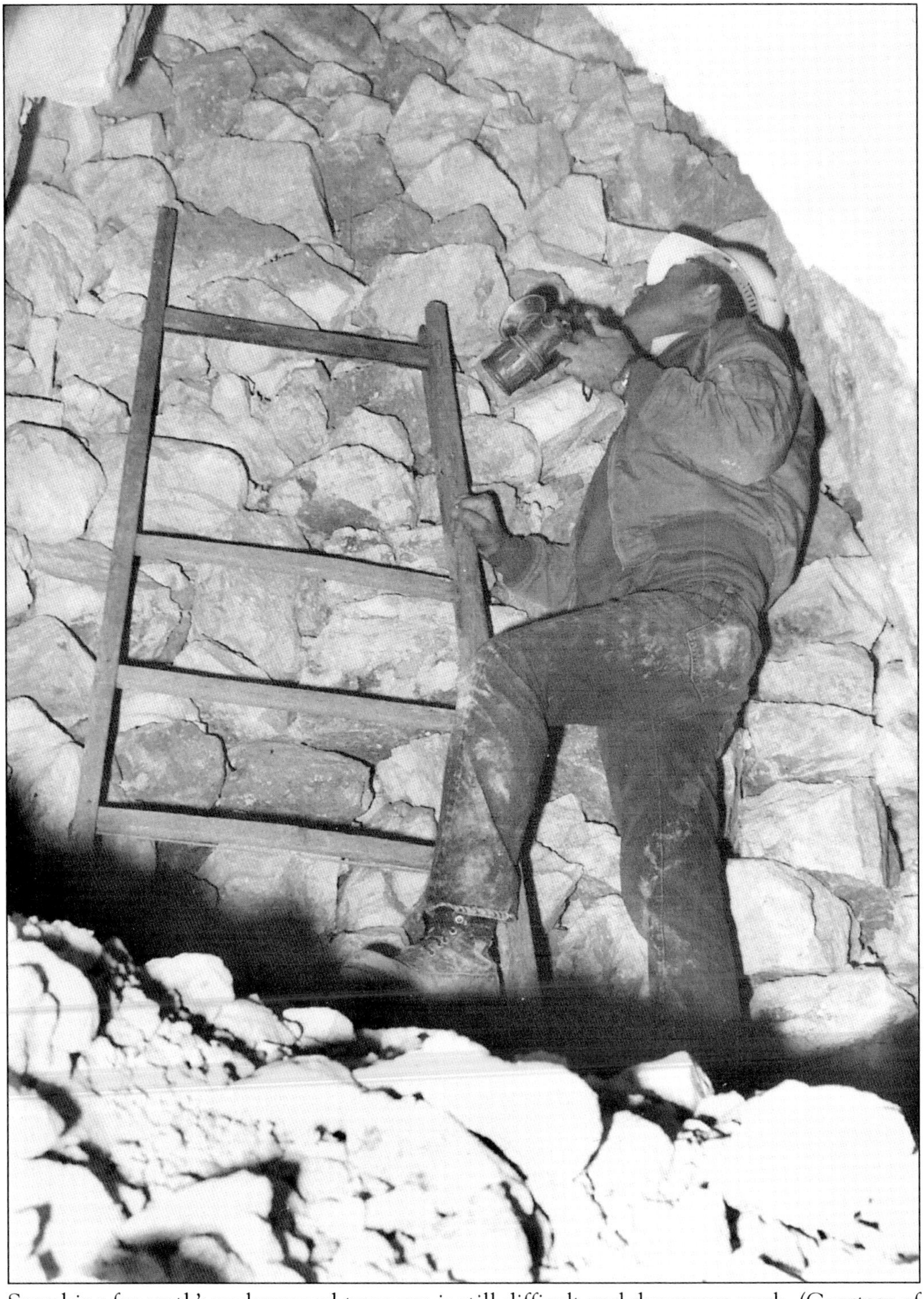

Searching for earth's underground treasures is still difficult and dangerous work. (Courtesy of Viji Winters.)

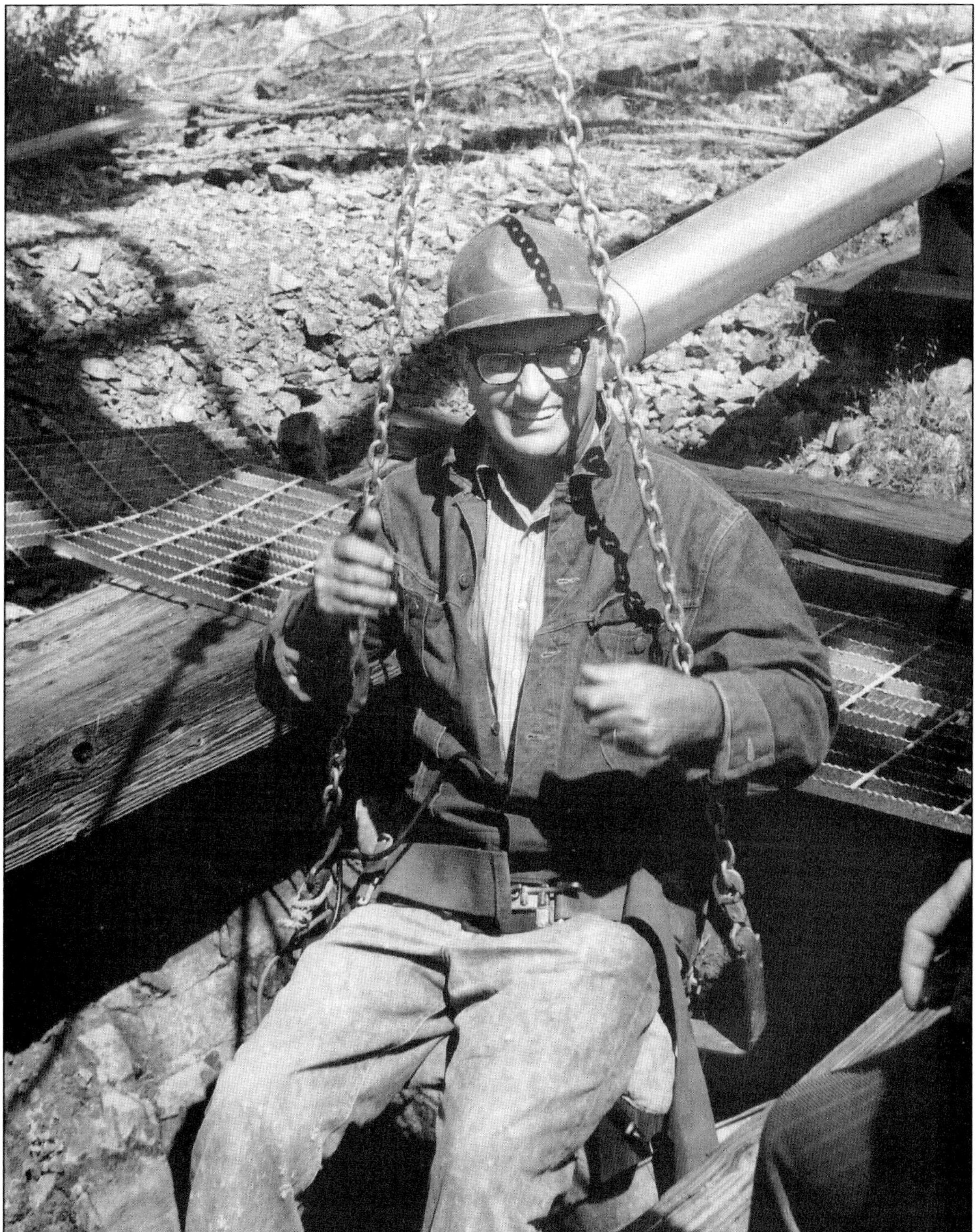

Wayne Winter is being lowered into his mine. In 1964, an important period of transition for the *Tombstone Epitaph* began when Detroit, Michigan, investors, headed by attorney Harold O. Love, purchased the *Epitaph* along with other Tombstone landmarks, including the O. K. Corral, the Crystal Palace, and Schieffelin Hall. For the next decade, the *Epitaph* was capably edited by Wayne Winters, who had both mining and newspaper experience. (Courtesy of Viji Winters.)

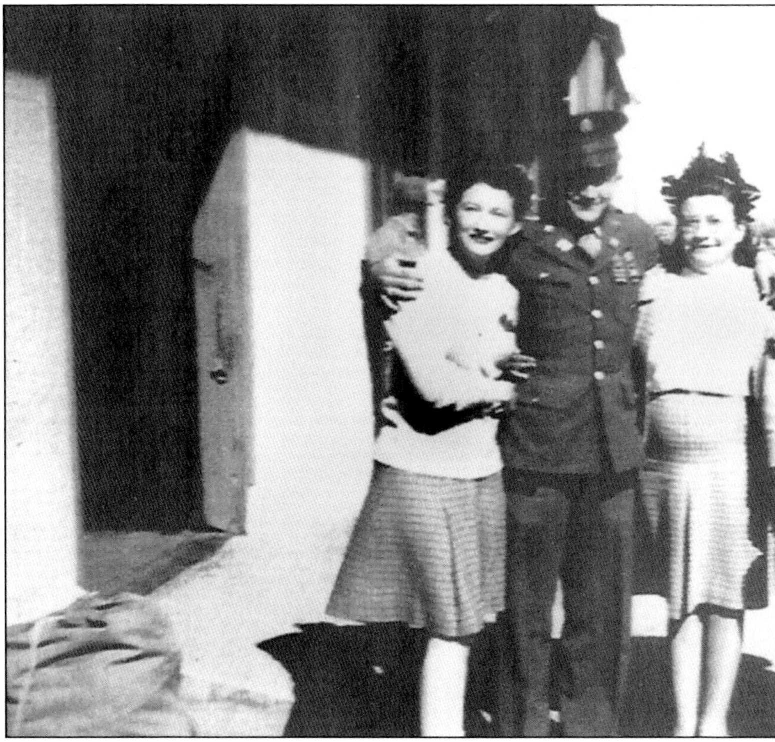

The Main family was one of the early ranching families around Tombstone. Pictured here are, from left to right, Marjorie, Wallace, and Ann Main. Wallace was home on furlough. (Courtesy of Charles and Betty Escapule and Viji Winters.)

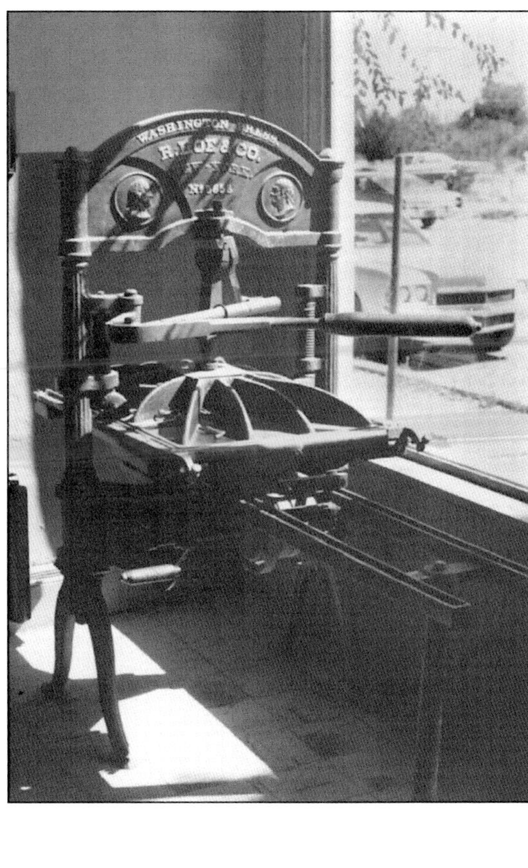

Pictured is an old printing press that was collected by Wayne Winters, which he got into working order. (Courtesy of Viji Winters.)

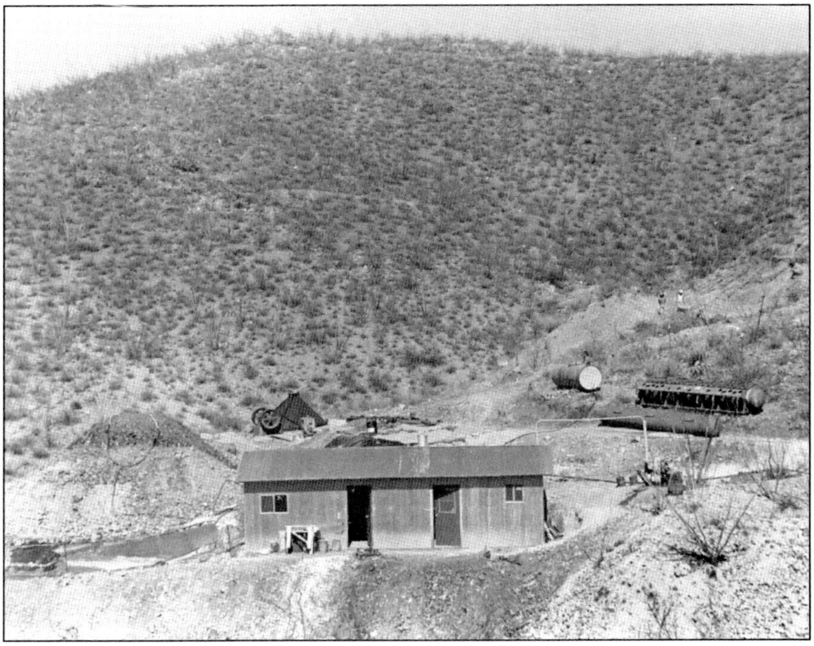

Seen here are old mine workings near Charleston. (Courtesy of Viji Winters.)

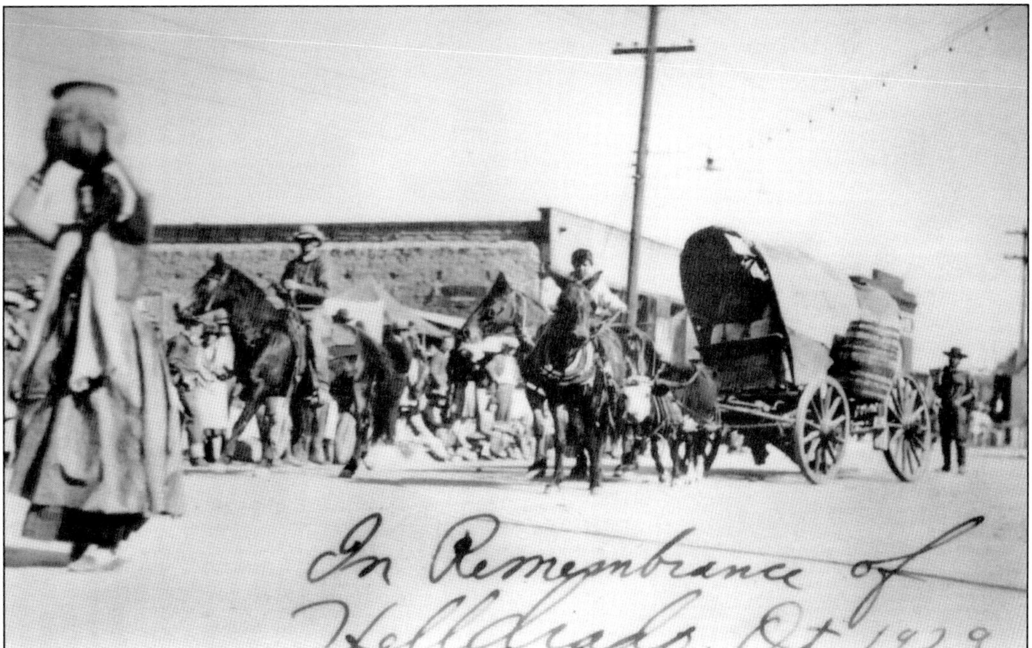

Pictured is the first Helldorado Days parade. The first Helldorado, Tombstone's oldest celebration, was first held from October 24–27, 1929. Many of the old-timers were disappointed and claimed that the reenactments did not tell the real history of Tombstone. William Kelly, editor of the *Tombstone Epitaph* newspaper, conceived the idea. This was at a time when Tombstone was about to lose its position as the county seat, and Kelly thought an influx of interest would stave off the loss. It did not. (Courtesy of Viji Winters.)

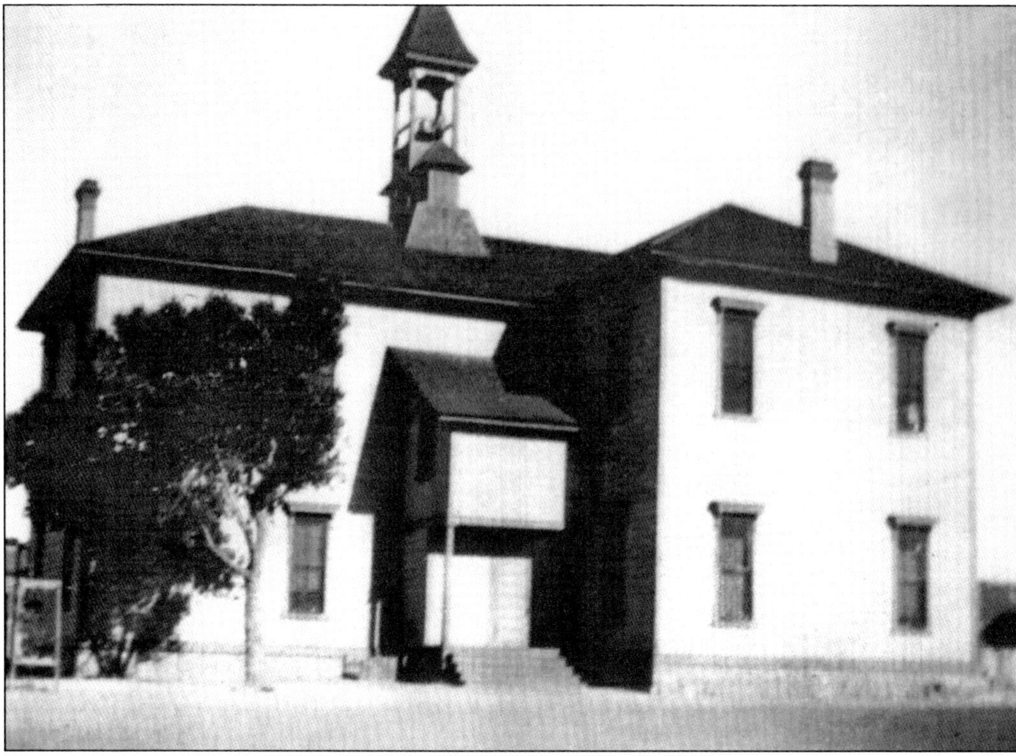

This handsome two-story building is the Tombstone public school around 1890. (Courtesy of Viji Winters.)

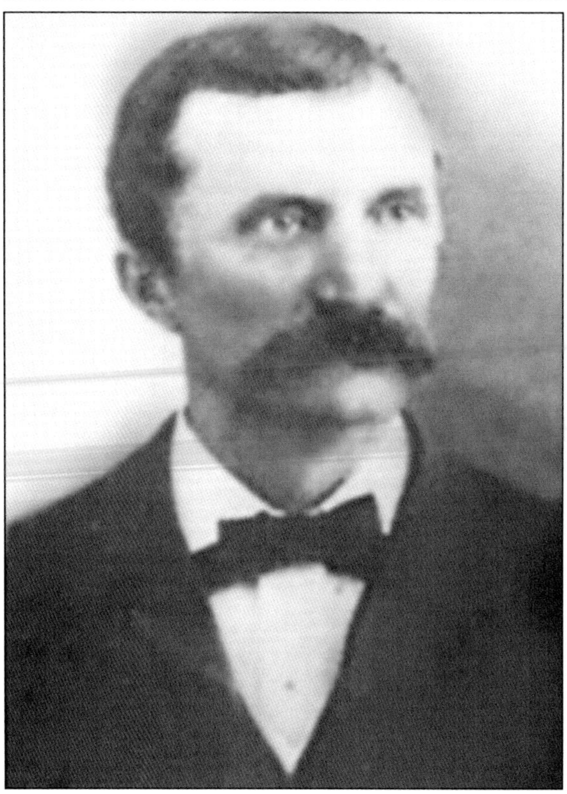

Elliott Larkin Ferguson (also known as Pete Spence or Peters Spencer) was an all-around bad Texas egg. He was a cattle rustler, murderer fugitive from Texas justice, and train robber. He was finally turned in to Cochise County authorities by his wife. Ferguson left Arizona and became a deputy sheriff and constable in New Mexico after marrying into the Clantons. He died of pneumonia near Globe, Arizona, on January 30, 1914, and is buried in Globe's Pioneer Cemetery. (Courtesy of Viji Winters.)

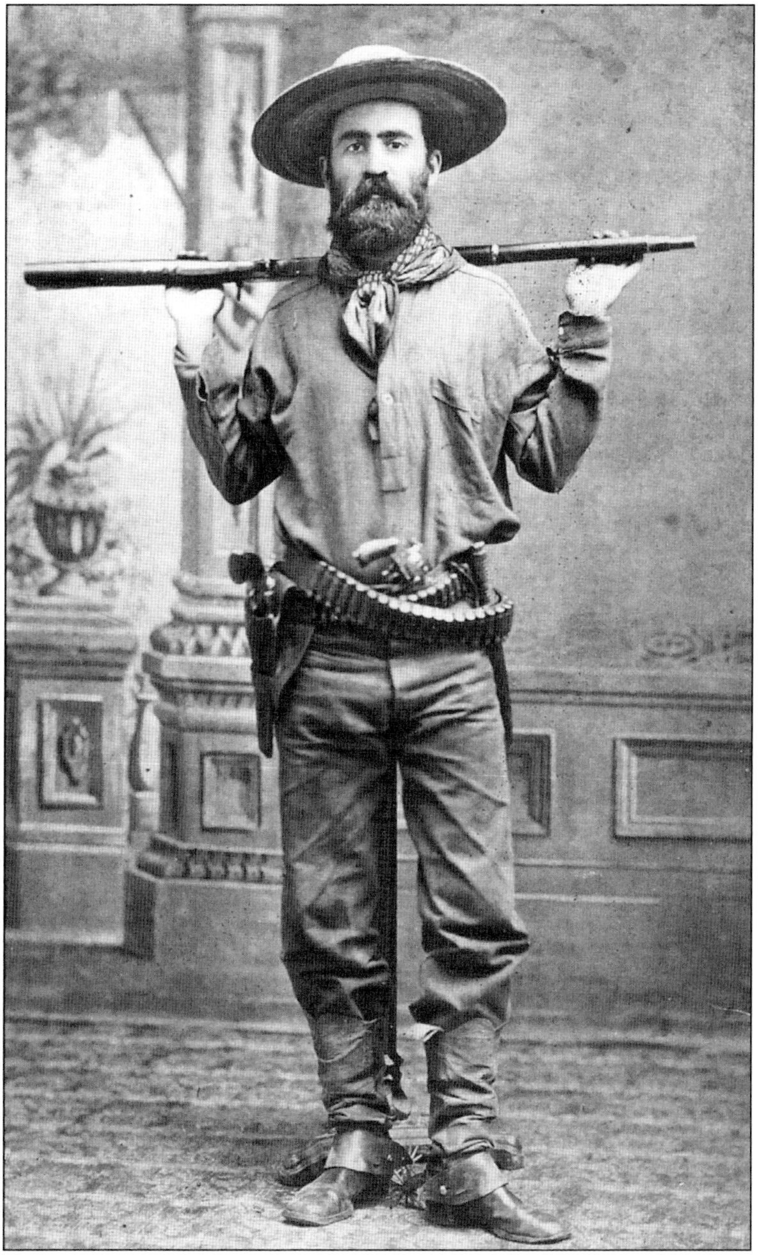

George Whitwell Parsons (August 26, 1850–January 5, 1933) was a licensed attorney turned banker and a real tenderfoot before arriving in Tombstone. His diary is one of the best accounts of Tombstone during the Wyatt Earp era. Parsons was born in Washington, D.C., but he sought his fortune elsewhere. He salvaged shipwrecks off the coast of Florida around 1874. In California, he worked as a bank clerk for three years and then moved to Tombstone, Arizona, where he became associated with John Clum, the mayor and editor of the *Tombstone Epitaph*. He had begun writing his diaries in 1869 and became a member of the Committee of Vigilance in Tombstone, an organization of local citizens in support of law and order. Parsons was, in 1885, the first librarian for the Tombstone Library. Parsons died in Los Angeles and was buried in Evergreen Cemetery. (Courtesy of Viji Winters.)

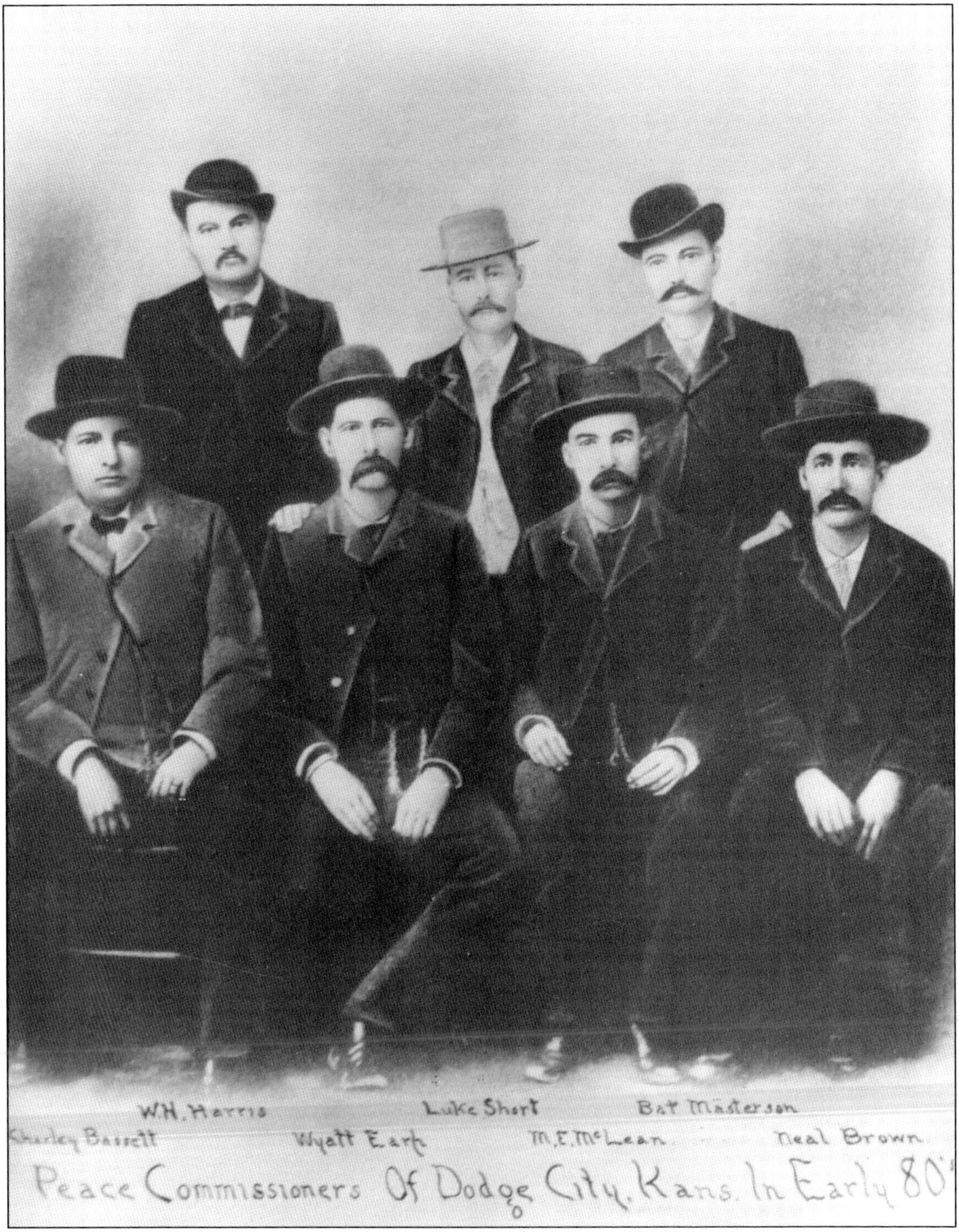

Pictured here in June 1883 is the Dodge City Peace Commission. From left to right are (seated) Charley Bassett, Wyatt Earp, Frank McLean, and Neal Brown; (standing) W. H. Harris, Luke Short, and Bat Masterson. Whiskey and wild cowboys gave Dodge City a bad reputation, and these were the men that were supposed to clean up the town. (Courtesy of Viji Winters.)

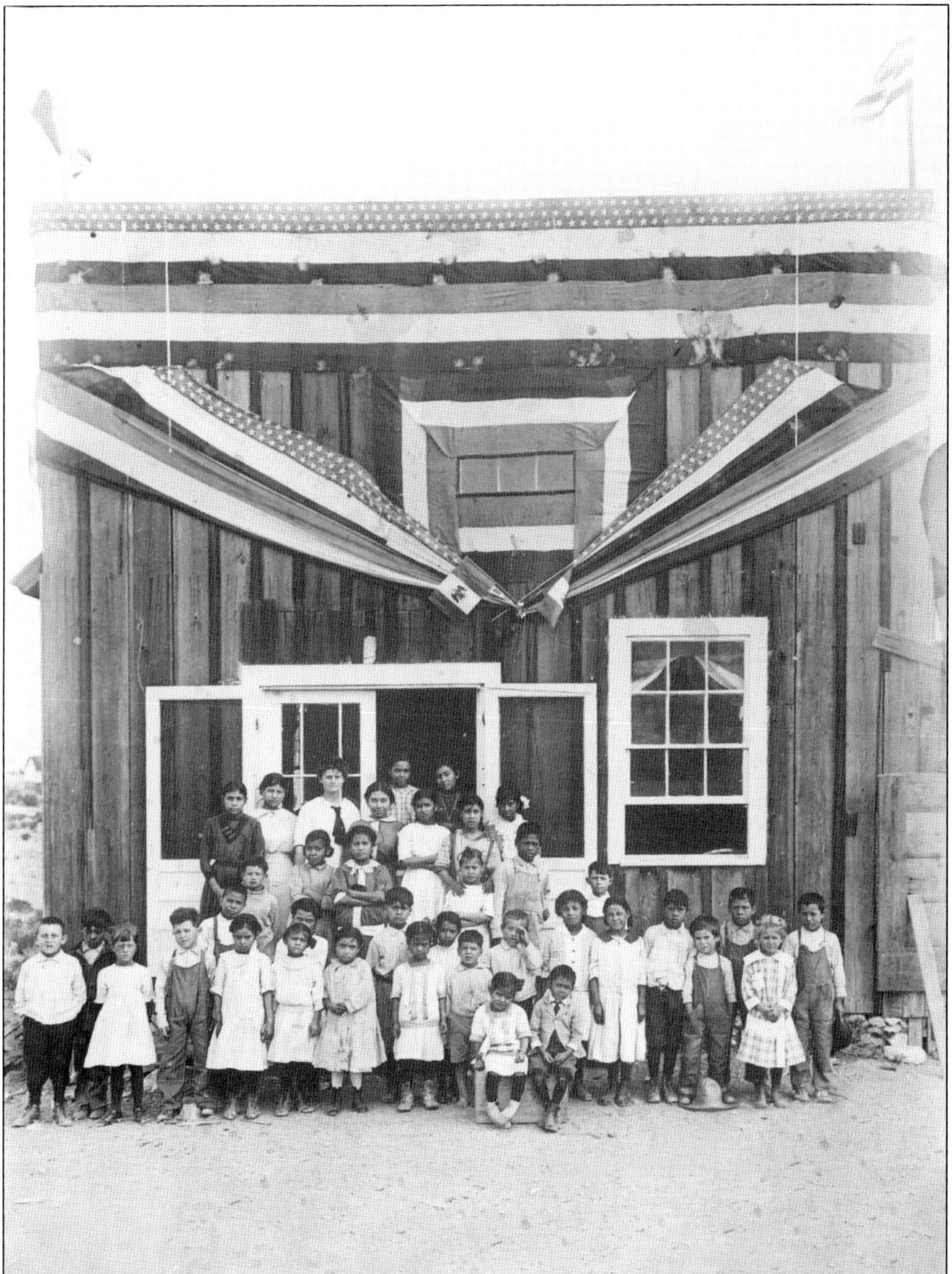

The Charleston School was nothing if not patriotic, decorating the entire school in the red, white, and blue before having their picture taken. (Courtesy of Arizona Historical Society, Tucson, Arizona.)

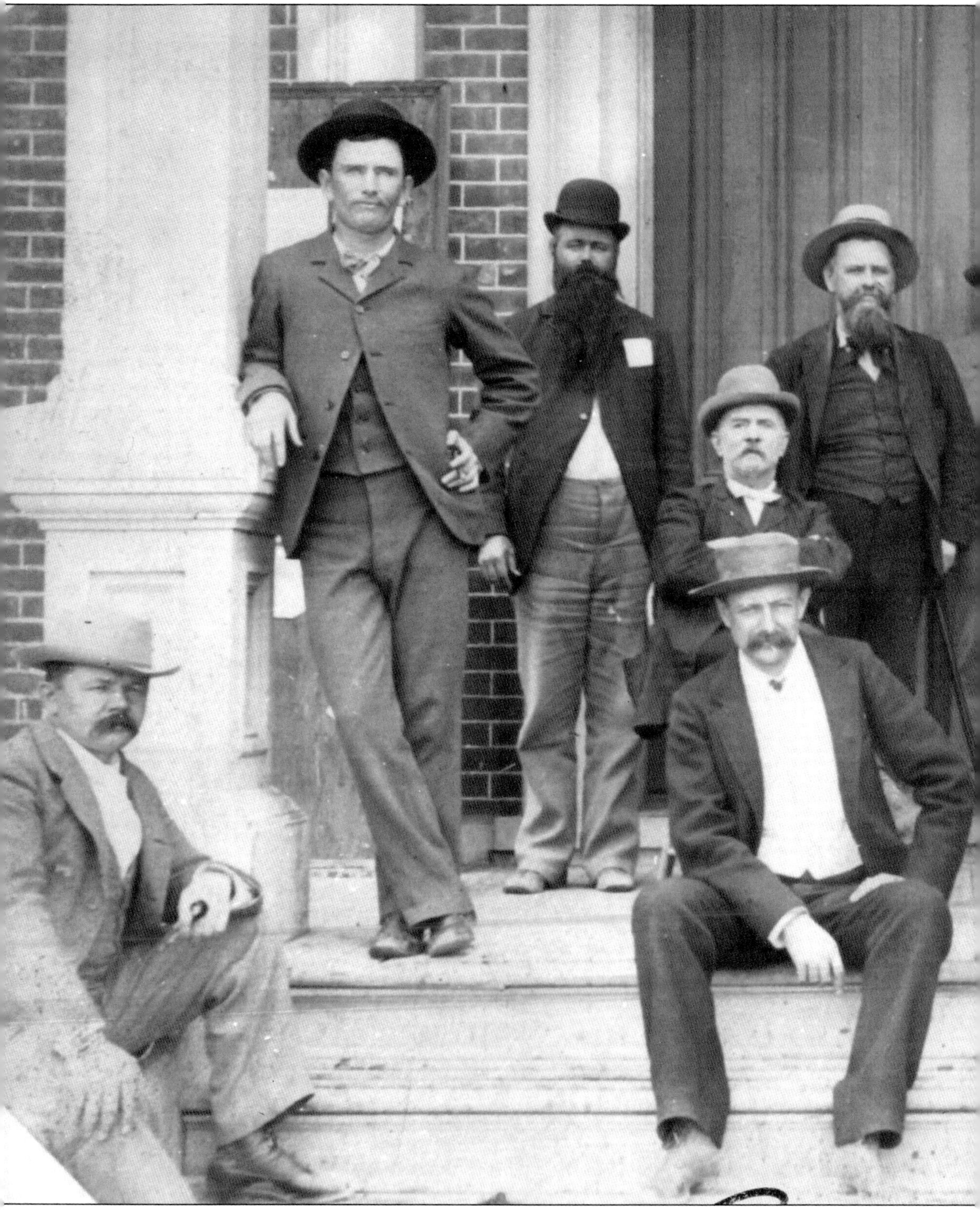

Early tombstone officials are, from left to right, (seated) D. H. Wardwell, unidentified, attorney W. C. Steahle, county treasurer M. D. Scribner, A. W. Wentworth, and W. D. Monmonier; (standing) deputy sheriff Billy Bradley, county attorney George Washington Swain, unidentified clerk, clerk

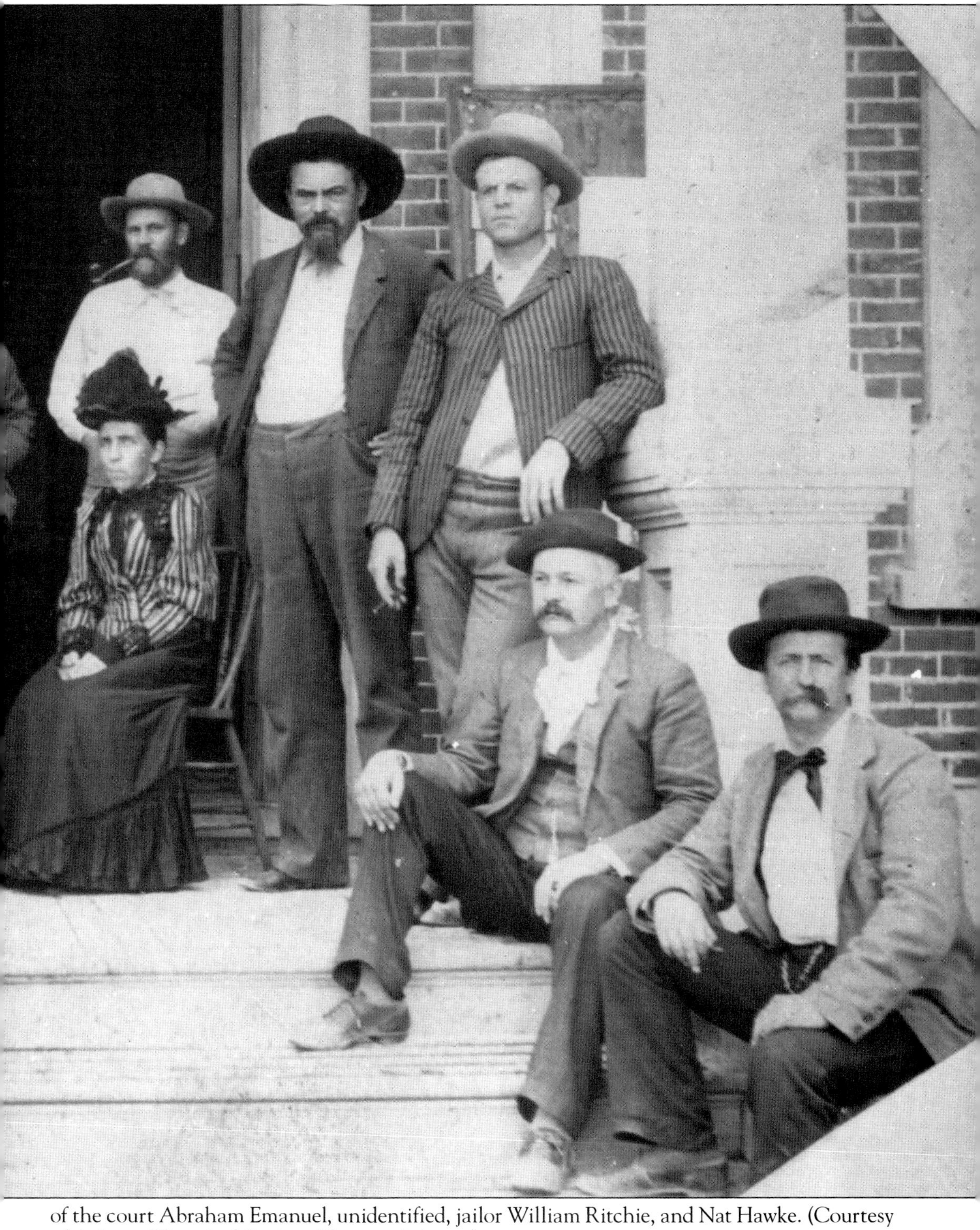

of the court Abraham Emanuel, unidentified, jailor William Ritchie, and Nat Hawke. (Courtesy of Arizona Historical Society, Tucson, Arizona.)

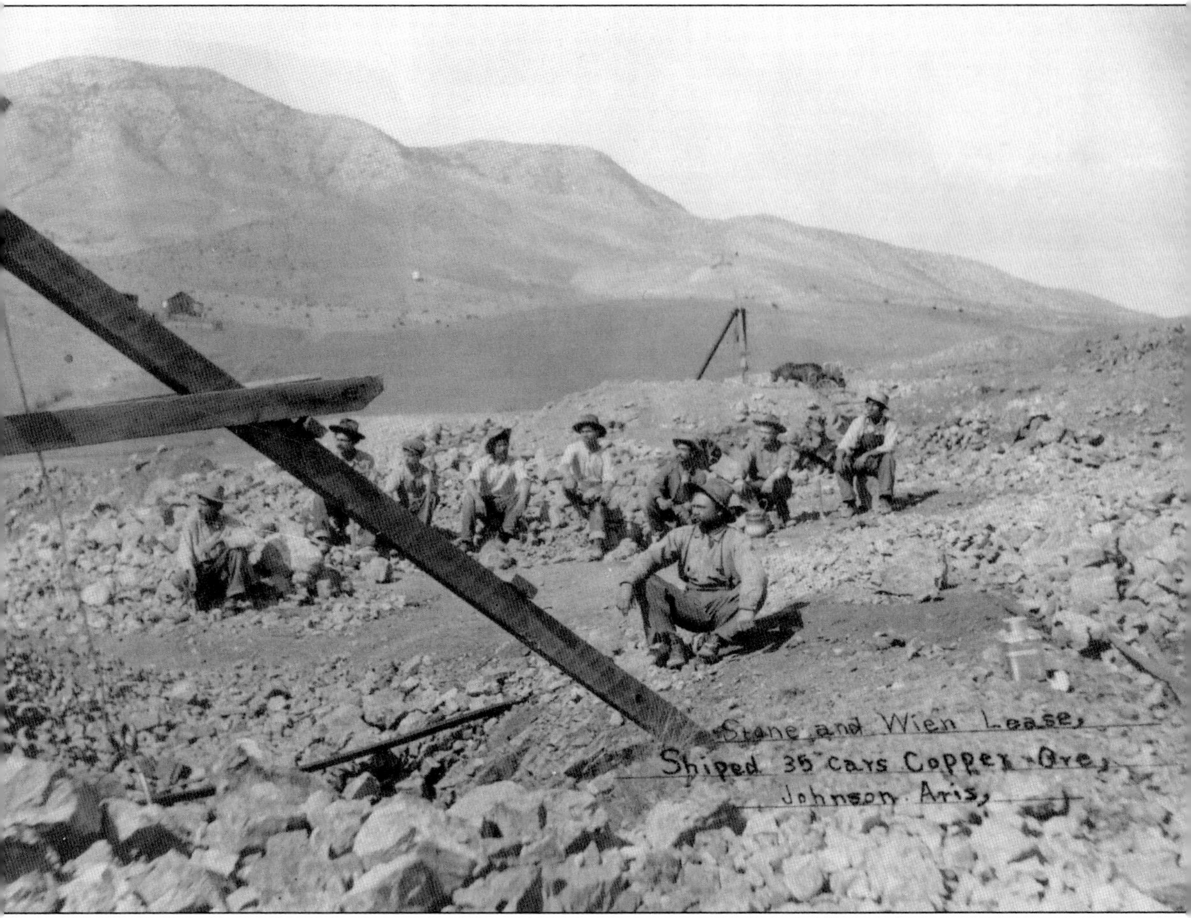

Earnest Escapule is the mine foreman in the foreground. This mine near Johnson, Arizona, is proud to have shipped out 35 cars of copper ore. (Courtesy of Arizona Historical Society, Tucson, Arizona.)

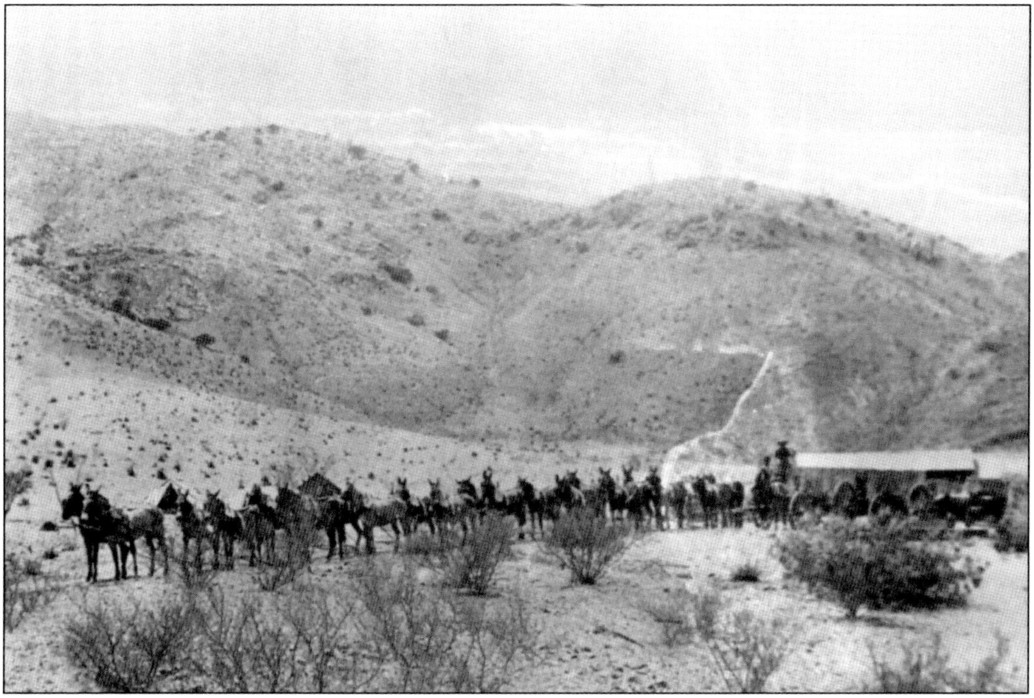

A long mule train is heading out of the Tombstone hills, probably with supplies to Tombstone and to pick up ore. (Courtesy of Viji Winters.)

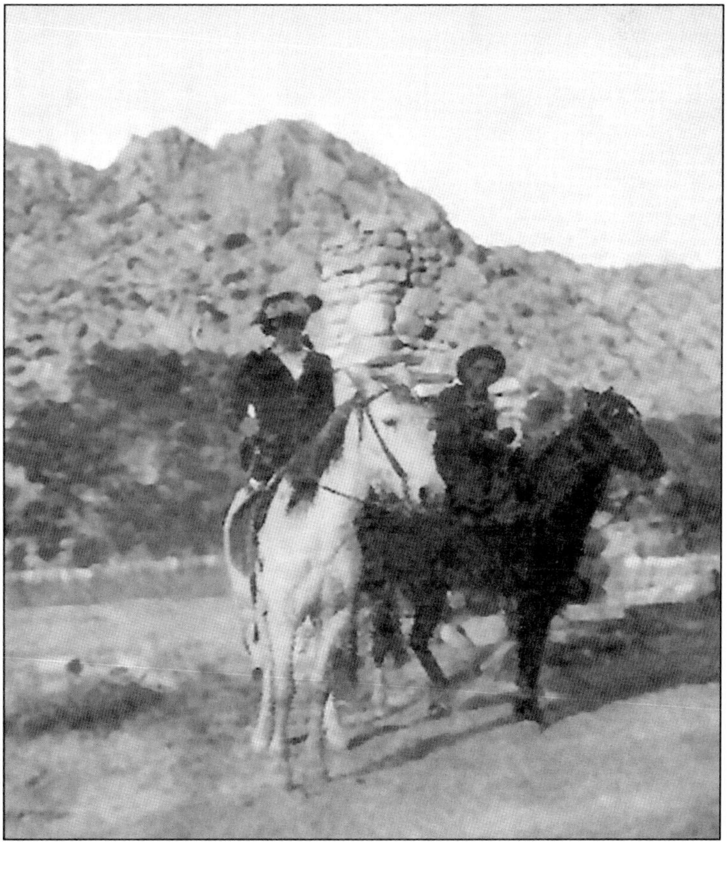

Unidentified riders are pictured near the Garfield monument, erected as a memorial to Pres. James A. Garfield. Black members of the 9th and 10th U.S. Cavalries, also known as Buffalo Soldiers, constructed the monument during the Indian Wars of the 1880s. (Courtesy of Chiricahua National Monument, Arizona.)

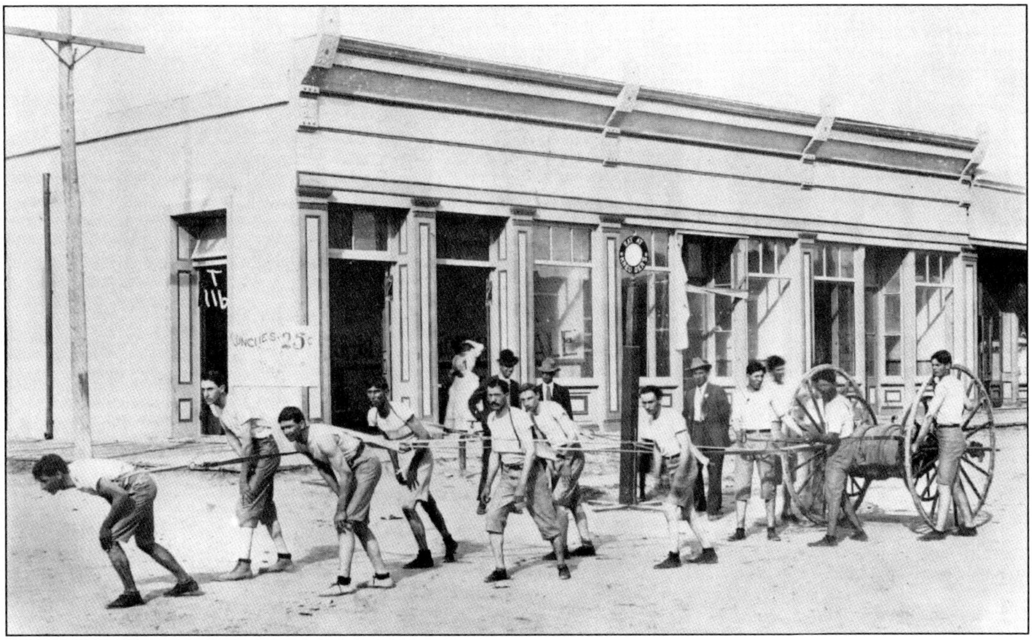

Competition in various contests was fierce among Arizona's early towns. Here the Tucson Volunteer Fire Department is serving as human mules and pulling the Tombstone fire engine. (Courtesy of Viji Winters.)

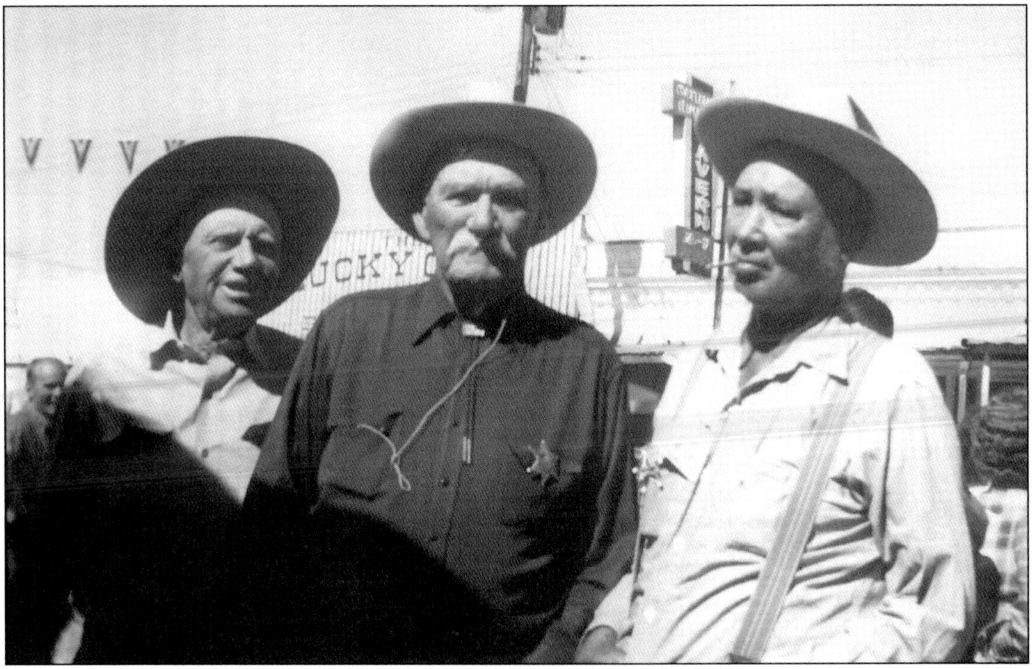

Pictured here are, from left to right, John Escapule Jr., deputy Fred Bennett, and Ben Sala. The Escapule family has long been involved in mining and ranching in the Tombstone area. John Sr., a Basque, immigrated to the United States in 1876 from France. After working in California and Texas for a while, he settled in Charleston, where he worked as a mill man. His sons and grandsons would follow in his footsteps as miners and ranchers. (Courtesy of Betty and Charles Escapule.)

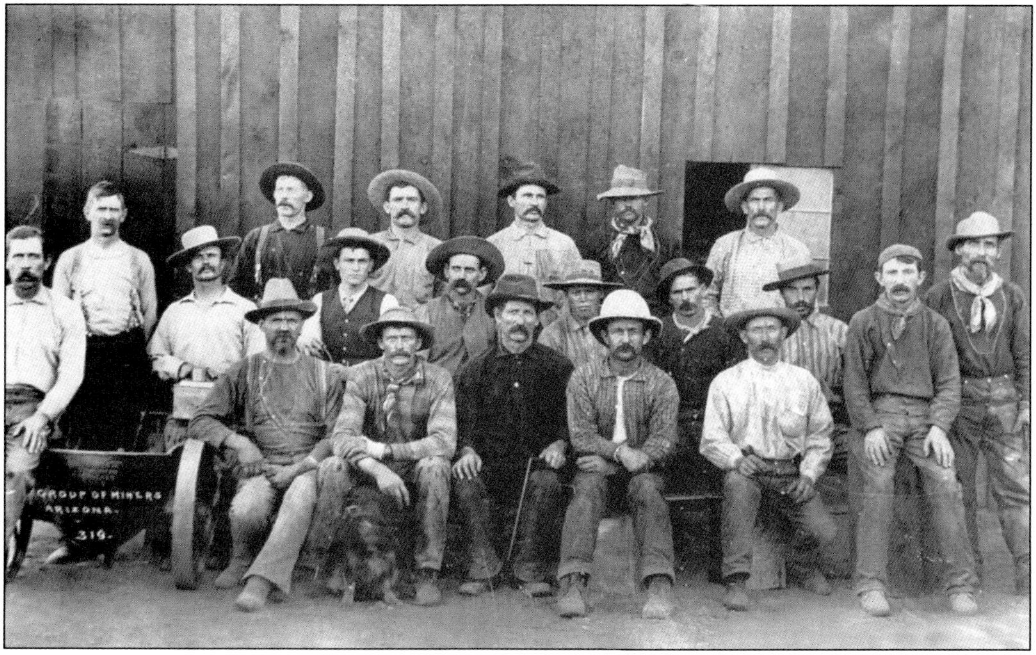

The picture is simply labeled, "A group of miners." This is unfortunate because by looking at their faces, each man surely would have an interesting story to tell. This is fairly early in mining history because only one man is wearing a hard hat. (Courtesy of Viji Winters.)

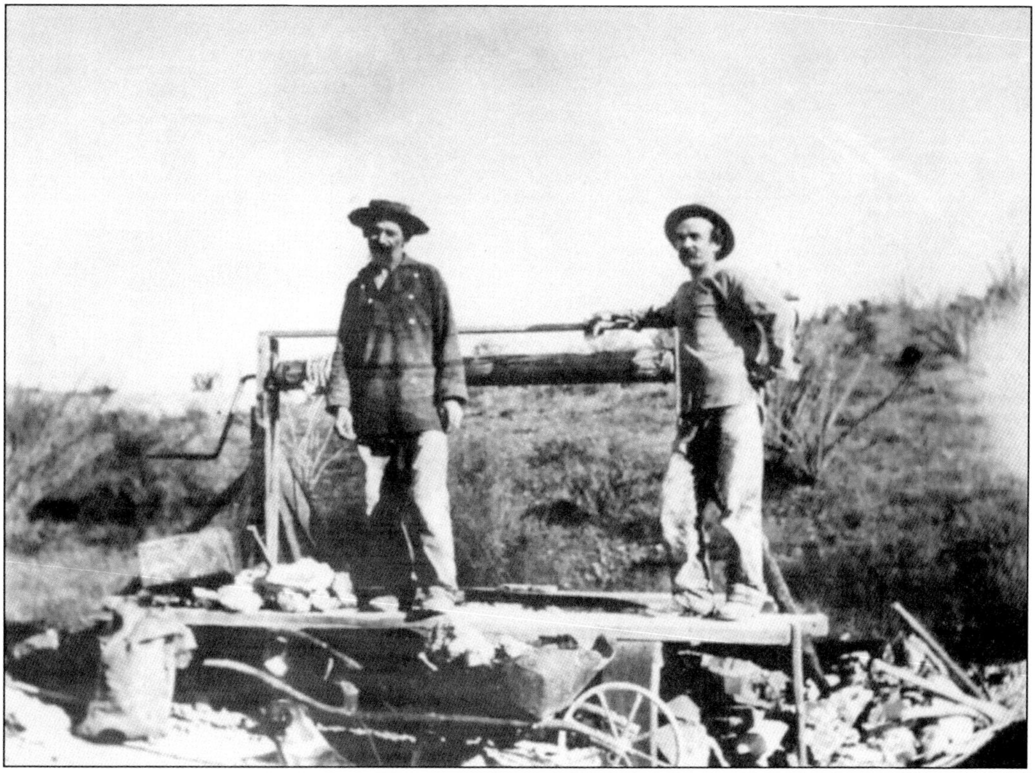

These men are about to install underground mining equipment. (Courtesy of Viji Winters.)

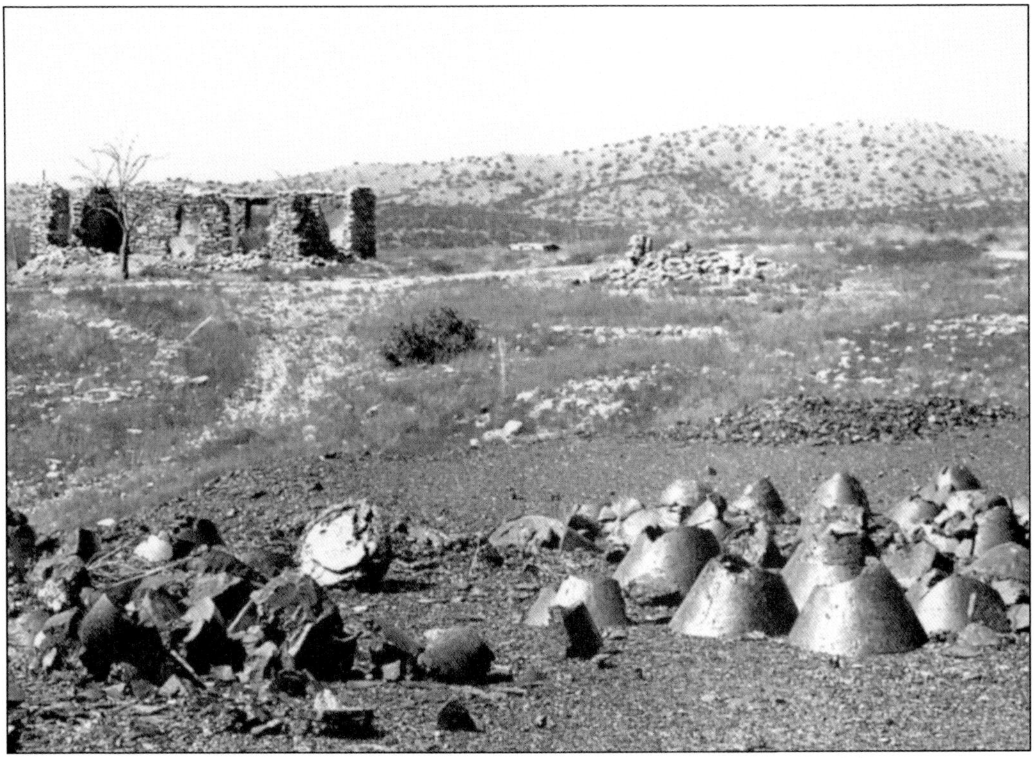

The Escapule family was responsible for developing a system that could be used by one person to extract silver in 3-pound silver ingots, as seen here. (Courtesy of Charles and Betty Escapule.)

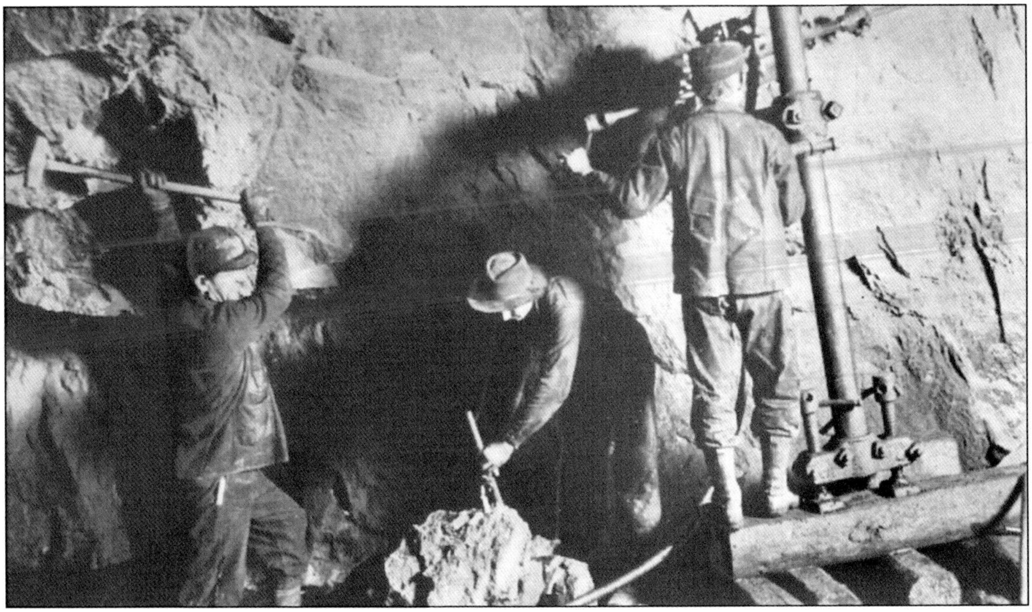

There is still no substitute for hard, backbreaking work to extract the underground ore. (Courtesy of Charles and Betty Escapule.)

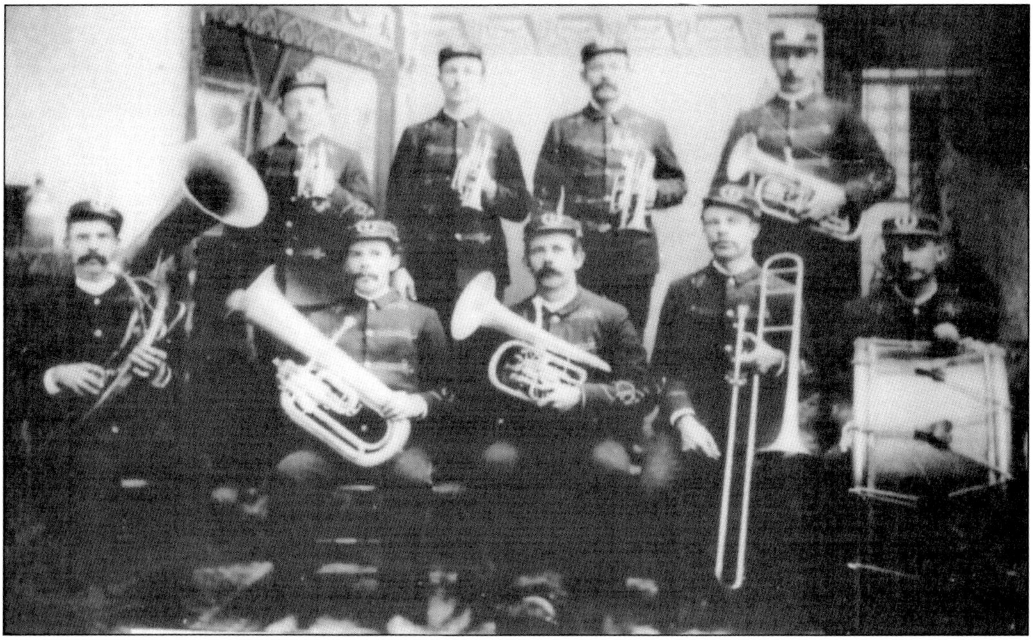

The Tombstone Volunteer Fire Department formed their own band and acquired very handsome uniforms. (Courtesy of Charles and Betty Escapule.)

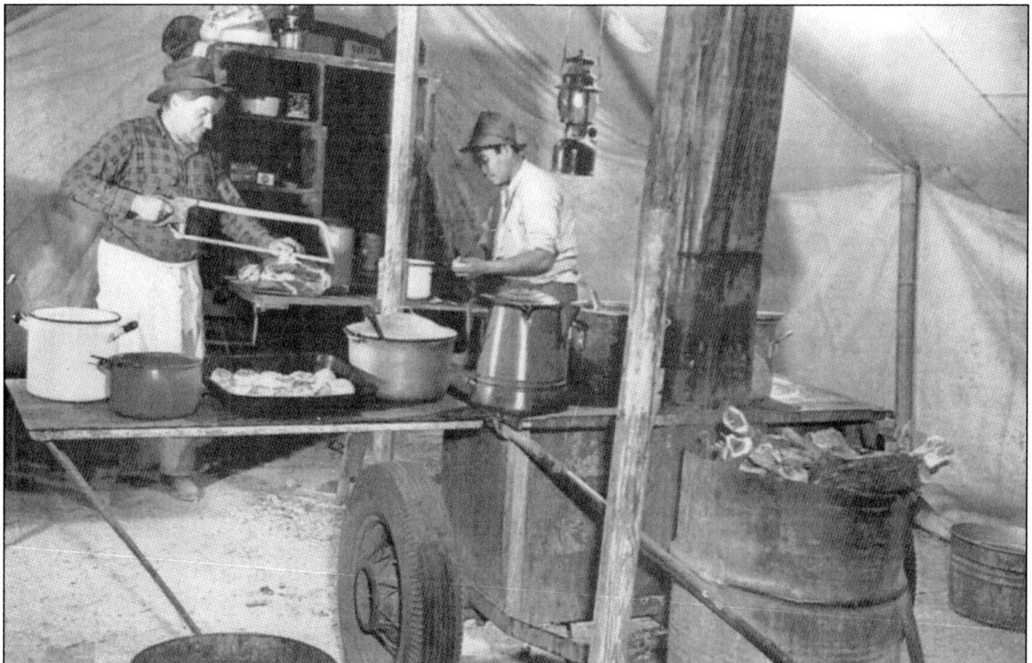

On the roundup, Clyde Allen is cutting meat for supper and Flunky is peeling potatoes. The stove hooked on behind the truck when they moved camp, and the table folded over the stove. The washtubs on the ground are the dishpans. (Courtesy of Charles and Betty Escapule.)

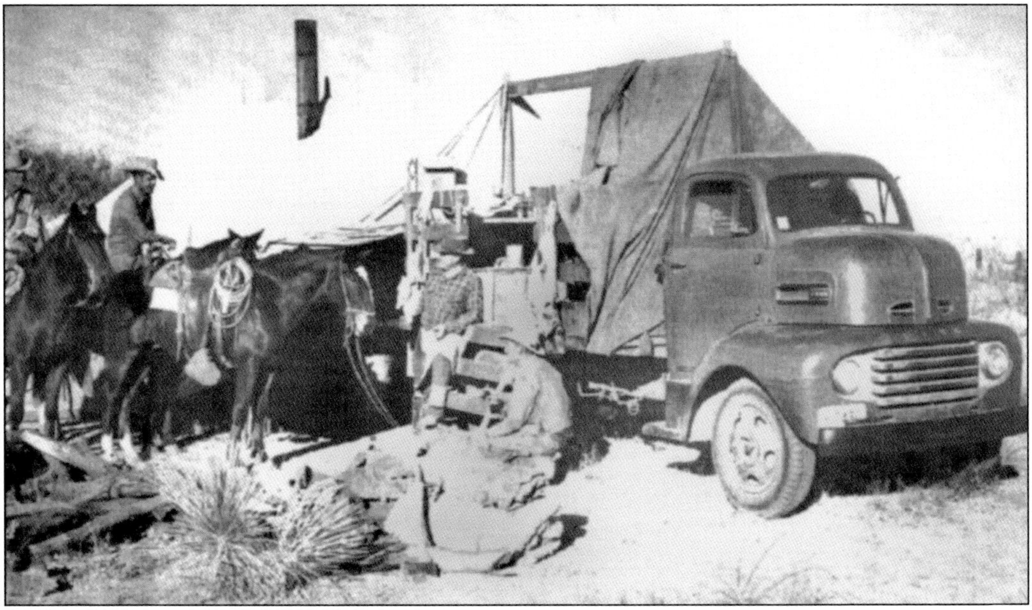

Seen with the cowboys' chuck wagon are, from left to right, Leo McKinney, general manager of the Boquilas Land and Grant Company (now managed by the Bureau of Land Management); Joe Kitchen, foreman; Clyde Allen, cook; and Betty Foster Escapule's father, Sam, holding his horse Doc. (Courtesy of Charles and Betty Escapule.)

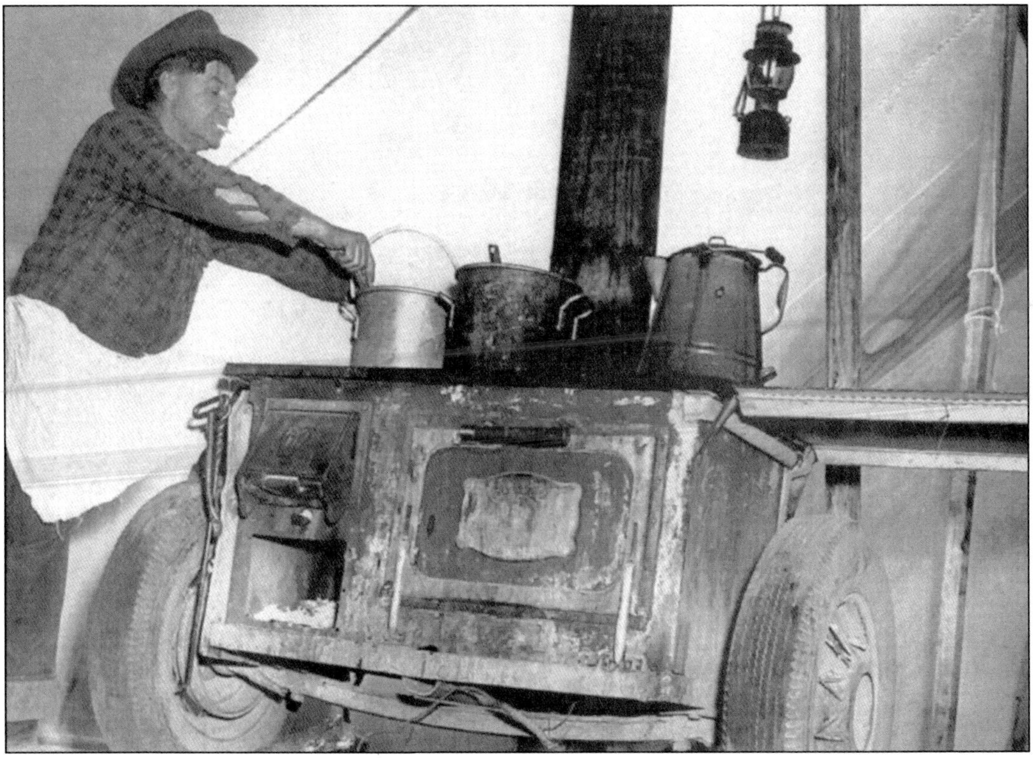

Clyde Allen is cooking supper for the cowboys on the stove on wheels, which is now in the home of Charles and Betty Escapule. (Courtesy of Charles and Betty Escapule.)

Charles Escapule is demonstrating the width of the ore body underground in the family's mine. (Courtesy of Charles and Betty Escapule.)

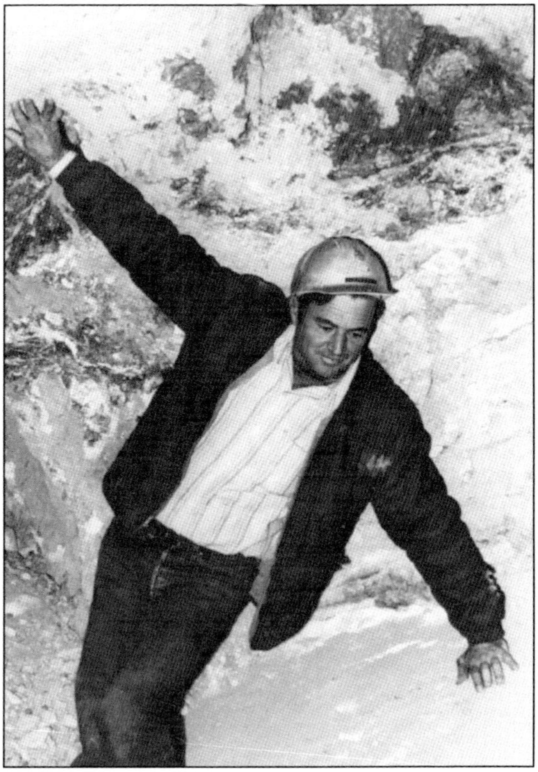

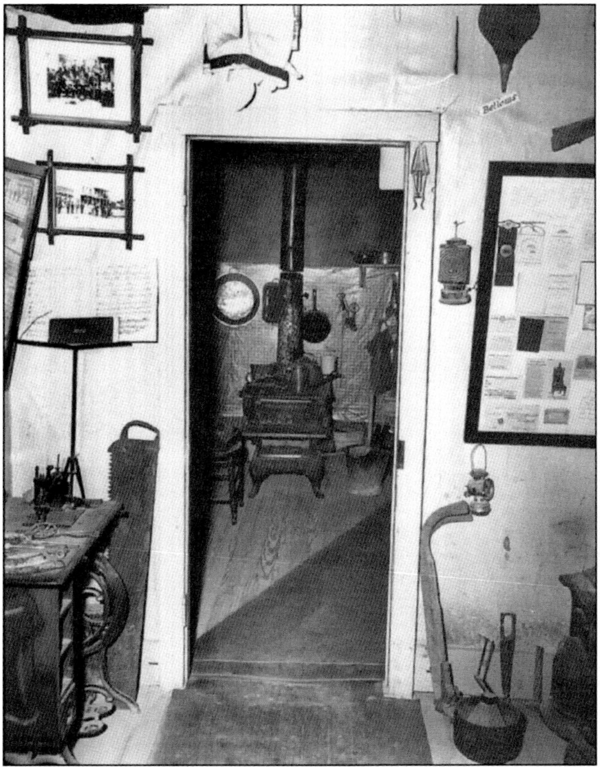

Pictured here is the interior of a miner's camp. (Courtesy of Charles and Betty Escapule.)

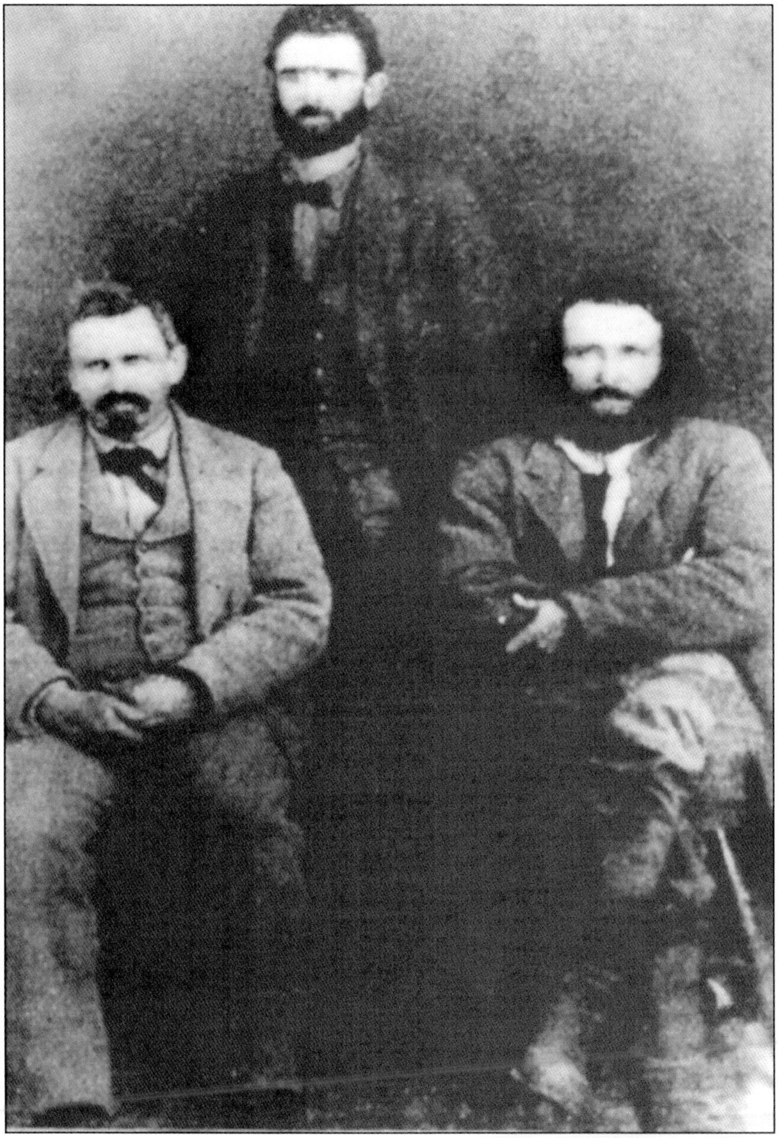

Seen here in 1878 are, from left to right, Richard Gird, Al Gird, and Ed Schieffelin. Col. James H. McClintock described Schieffelin as "about the queerest specimen of humanity ever seen in Tucson. His clothing was worn and covered with patches of deerskins, corduroy and flannel, and his old slouch hat too, was so pieced with rabbit skin that very little of the original felt remained. Although only 29 years of age he looked at least forty. His black hair hung down below his shoulders, and his full beard, a tangle of knots, was almost as long and he appeared to be a fur-bearing animal." Col. James McClintock, born in Sacramento, California, on February 23, 1864, was educated in California and later graduated from Arizona State University at Tempe. He taught school for several years. He arrived in Arizona Territory by train in June 1879. He lived in Phoenix, joining his brother Charles, who was publishing the *Phoenix Herald*. McClintock took part in the first Republican organization in Phoenix. He later wrote for several papers in Phoenix, Prescott, Globe, Tempe, and Tucson. At age 22, he served as a justice of the peace in Tempe. He became a colonel while serving in the Spanish-American War. All his life he was interested in preserving the history of Arizona. (Courtesy Arizona Historical Society, Tucson, Arizona.)

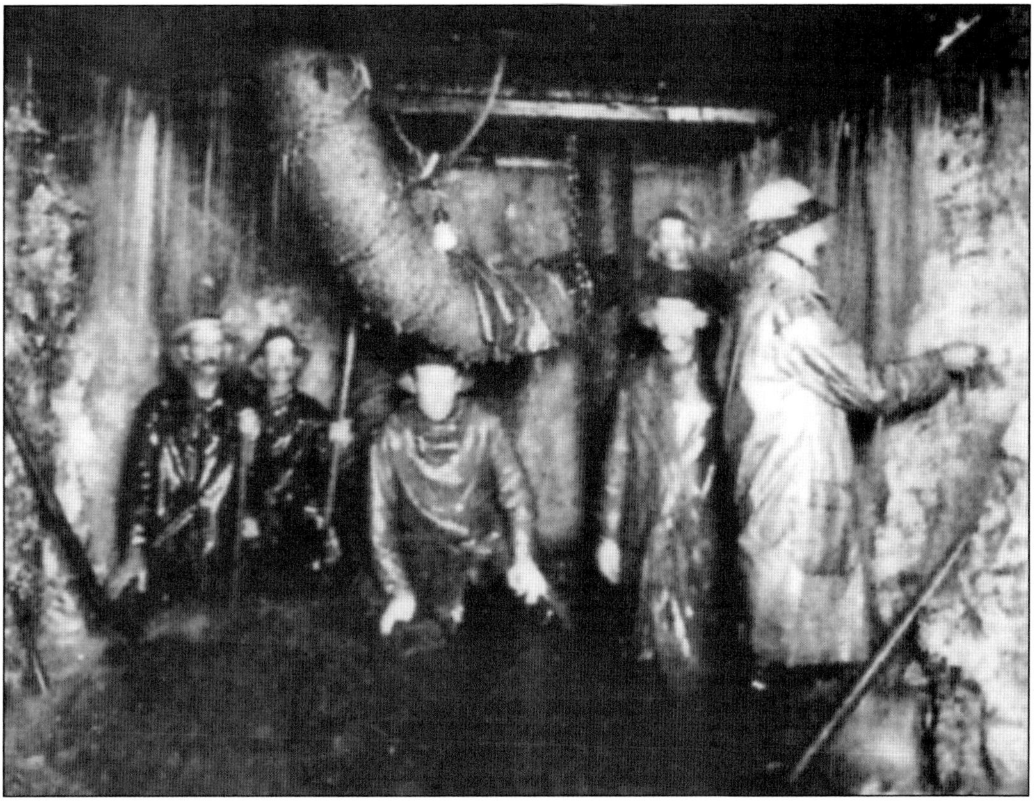

Around 1900, miners were still trying to bring out silver, but the water was already flooding most of the underground mines. Here water is streaming in from all sides. (Courtesy of Charles and Betty Escapule.)

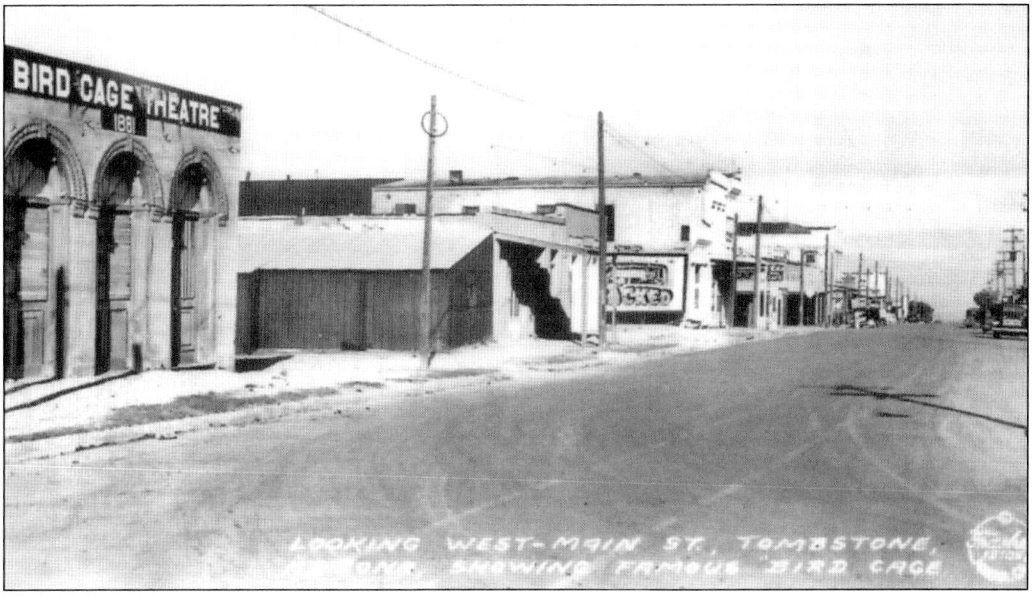

By the 1930s, Tombstone had almost become a ghost town. However, it was still the "Town Too Tough to Die," even though it was in bad disrepair. (Courtesy of Viji Winters.)

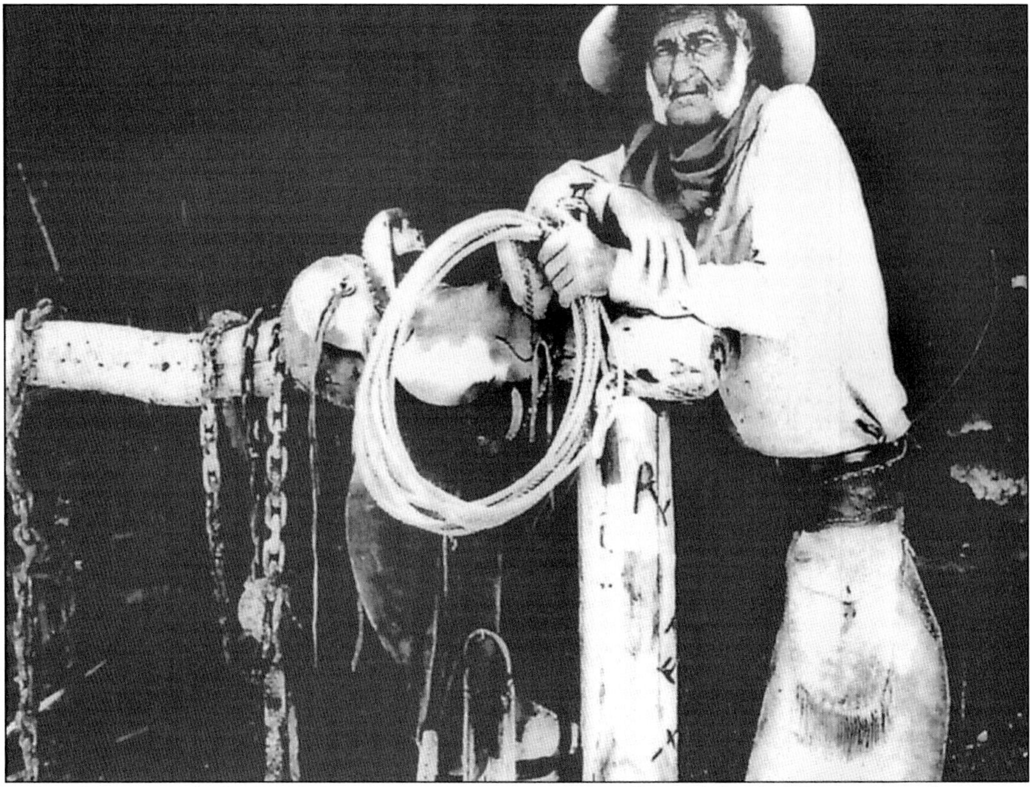

Sid Wilson is ready for a riding performance. He poses with a saddle that he used in the movie *Stars and Stripes*. He had also been a performer with Buffalo Bill's Wild West Show. (Courtesy of Viji Winters.)

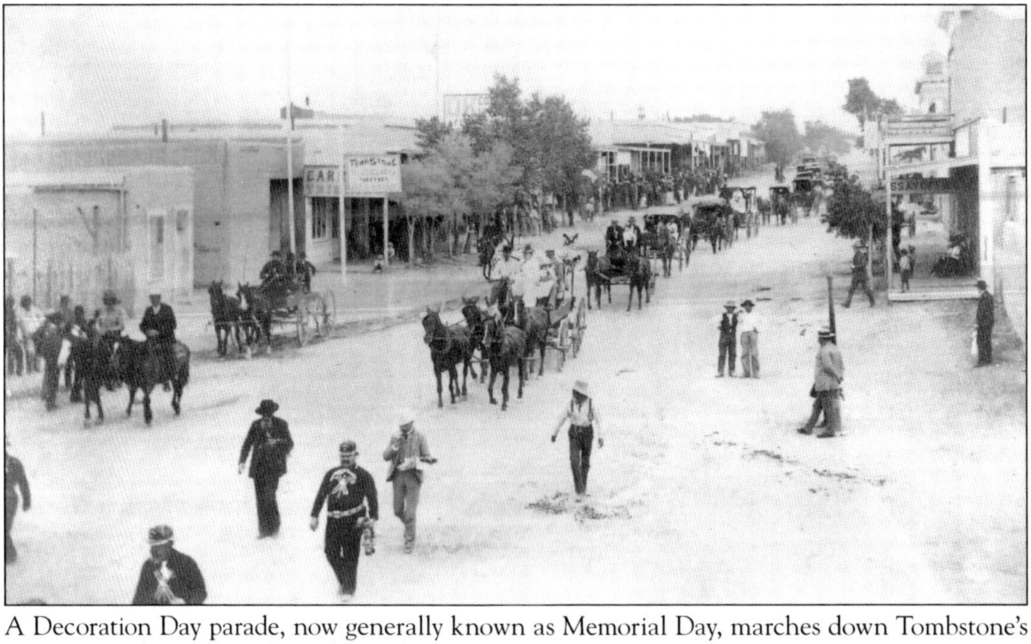

A Decoration Day parade, now generally known as Memorial Day, marches down Tombstone's main street. (Courtesy of Charles and Betty Escapule.)

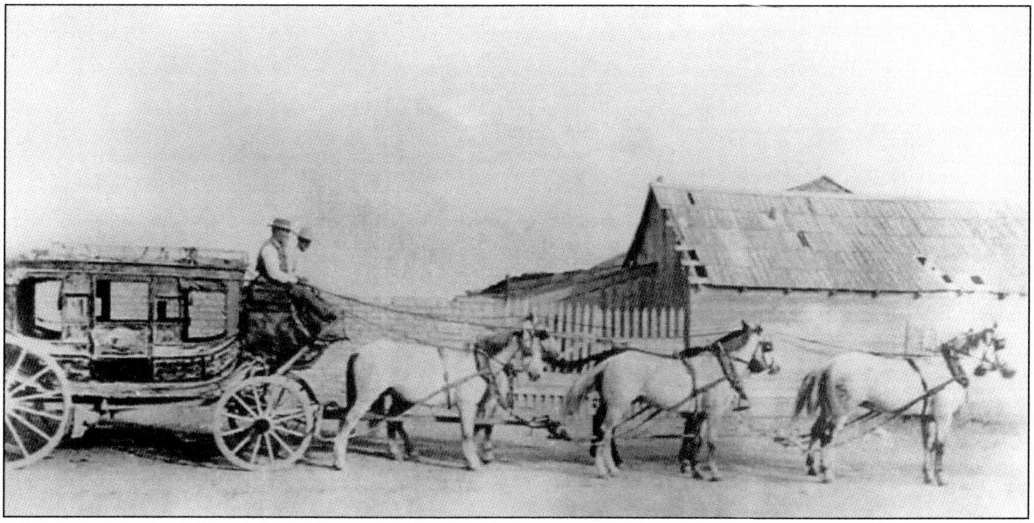

This is a view of the old Modoc hearse, which escorted the bereaved and the departed to Boot Hill Cemetery. (Courtesy of Don Taylor.)

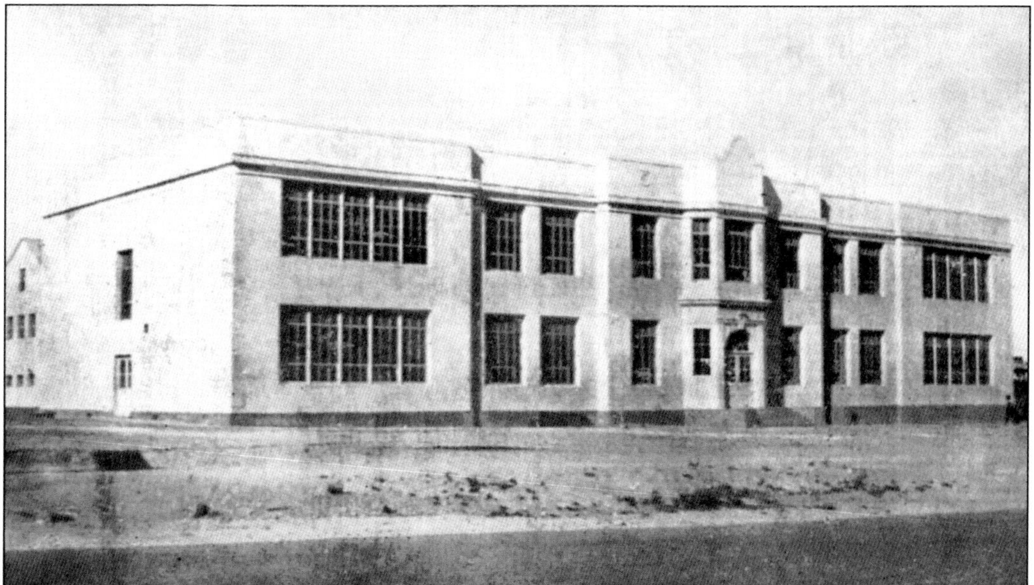

Pictured is the old Union High School, which saw many young Tombstone residents pass on to another level of education. (Courtesy of Nancy Lewis Sosa.)

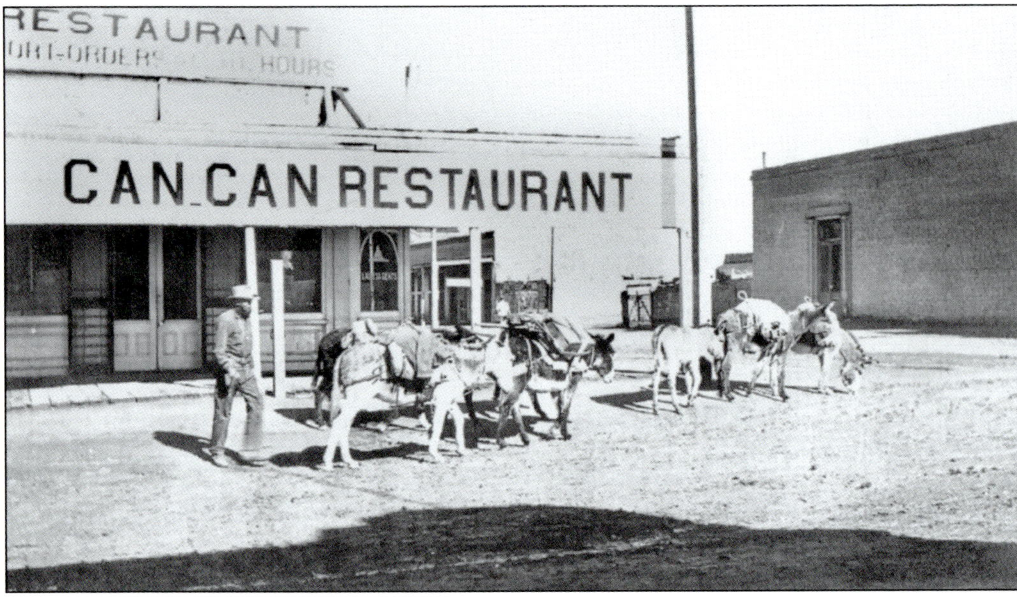

This is a marvelous view of a prospector and his burros passing by the Can Can Restaurant. (Courtesy of Don Taylor.)

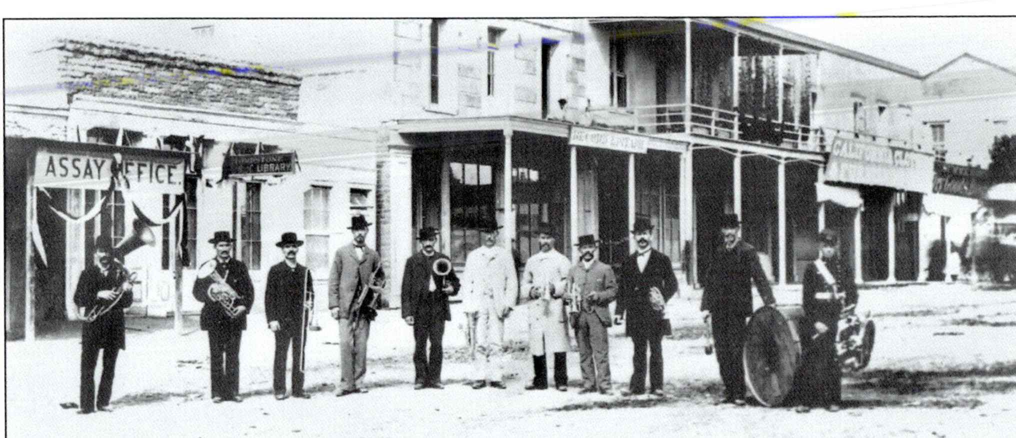

Another Tombstone band assembles for a portrait in front of the Tombstone Assay Office and the Nobles Hotel. (Courtesy of Nancy Lewis Sosa.)

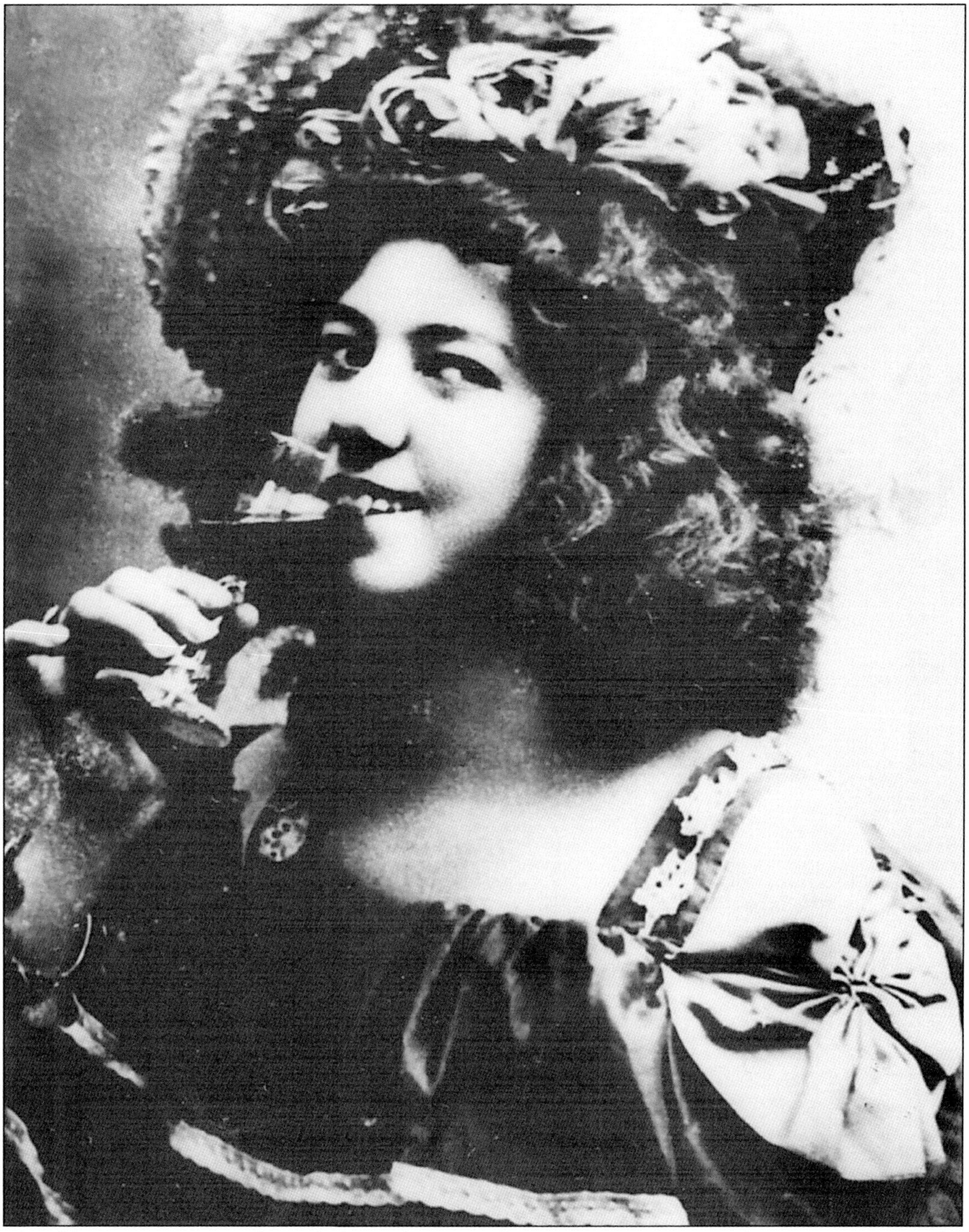

Klondike Kate prospected in Alaska and eventually made her way to Tombstone. Women in the early days of mining were few and far between. Klondike Kate was reputed to be smart and tough. (Courtesy of Viji Winters.)

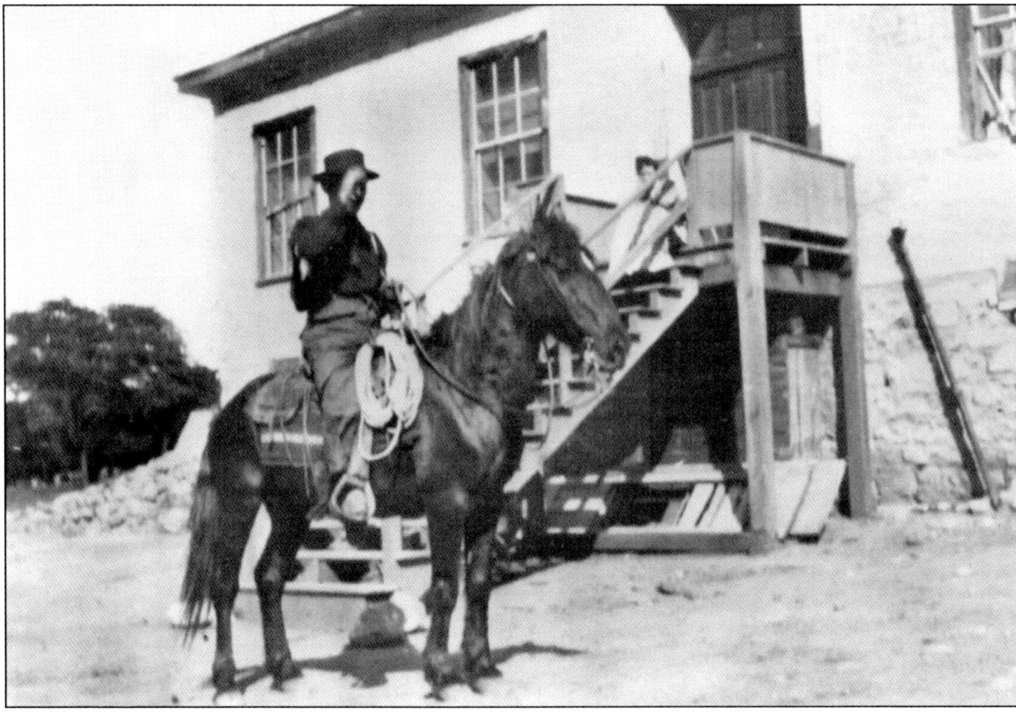

Soldiers from nearby Fort Huachuca frequently visited Tombstone. (Courtesy of Fort Huachuca.)

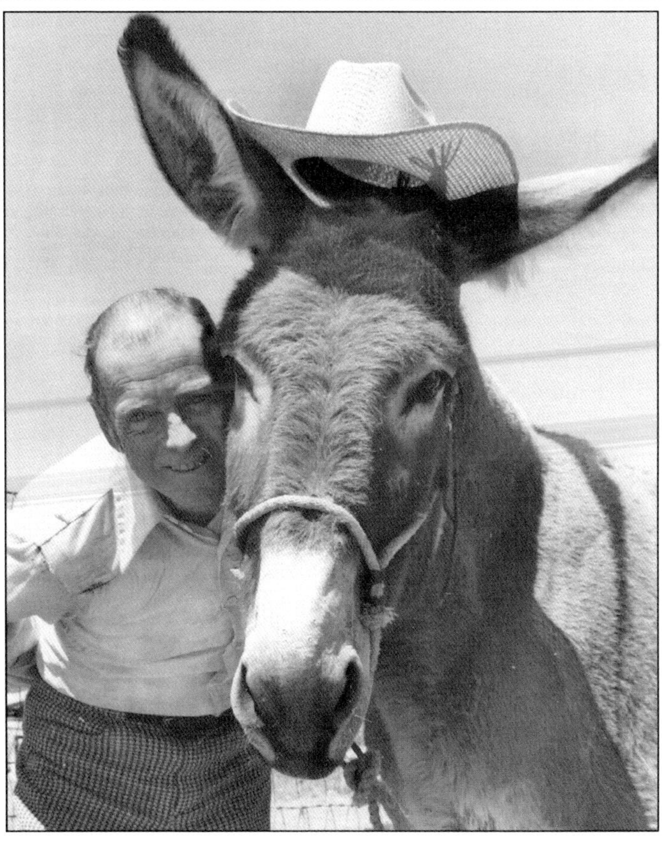

Wayne Winters and a friend pose for a picture before searching the hills for their fortunes. (Courtesy of Viji Winters.)

Seen here is an early mining office. (Courtesy of Viji Winters.)

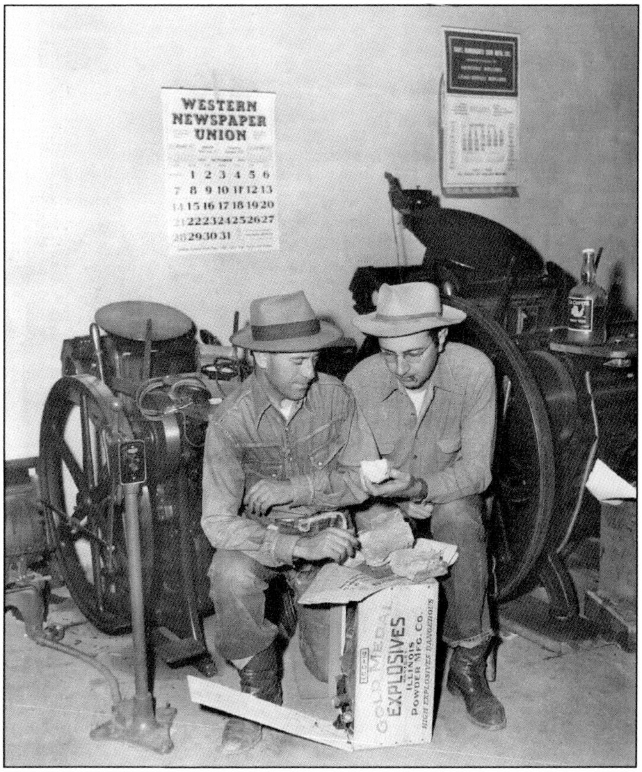

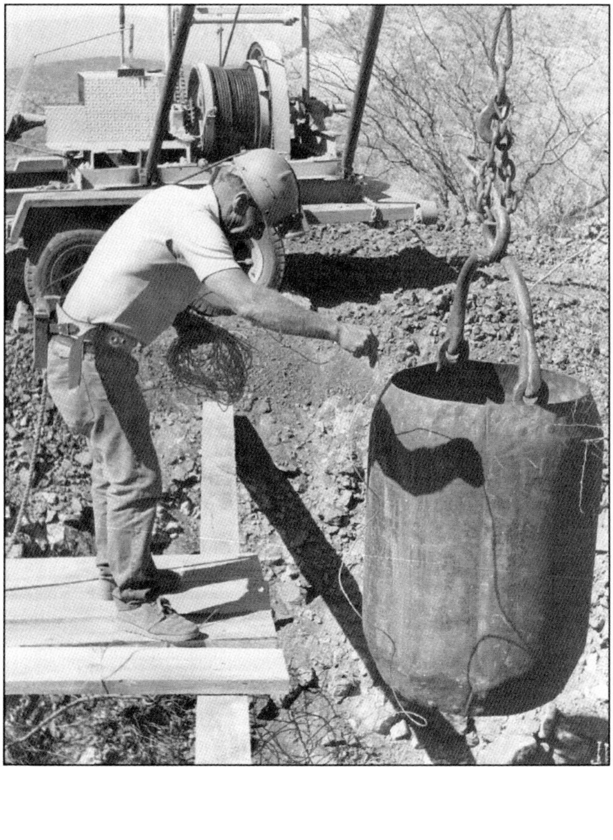

Here a miner lowers an ore bucket into one of the Tombstone area mines. (Courtesy of Viji Winters.)

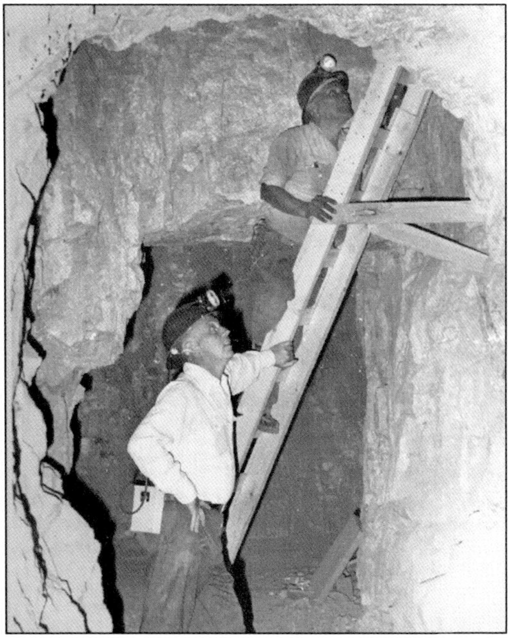

Miners are climbing on underground ladders. Mining, especially underground, was and still can be a dangerous business. (Courtesy of Viji Winters.)

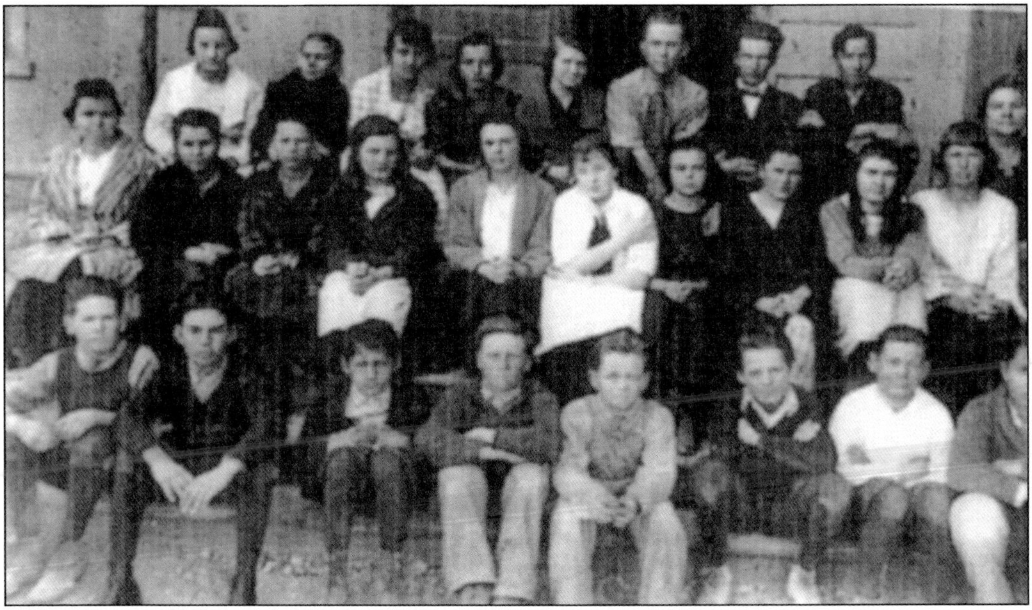

These students at Tombstone's Walcott School, pictured from left to right, are (first row) Bill Fowler, Art Stannegar, Dannie Hughes, Louis John Escapule, Louis Igo, Theos Bernard, Harry Eskermarr, Monty Reed; (second row) Bertha Brant, Charlotte Lockwood, Mattie Reed, Dorothy Krebs, Joan Sparks, Carol Launders, Katherine Bravin, Beatrice Frederick, Helen Reeves, Mildred Elliott, and Miss Brady (teacher); (third row) Elizabeth Thurman, Lucille Bennett, Dorothy Thurman, Lena Giacoletti, Elva Rushin, Dick Lamb, Dick Struthers, and Jeff Clark. The school was named after Frank Newton Walcott, who was a longtime trustee of the school, a Tombstone justice of the peace, and ran a department store on Allen Street. In 1917, he went hunting in the Chiricahuas and accidentally shot and killed himself. It was said that his funeral was one of the largest in Tombstone. He is buried in the Allen Street cemetery. (Courtesy of Charles and Betty Escapule.)

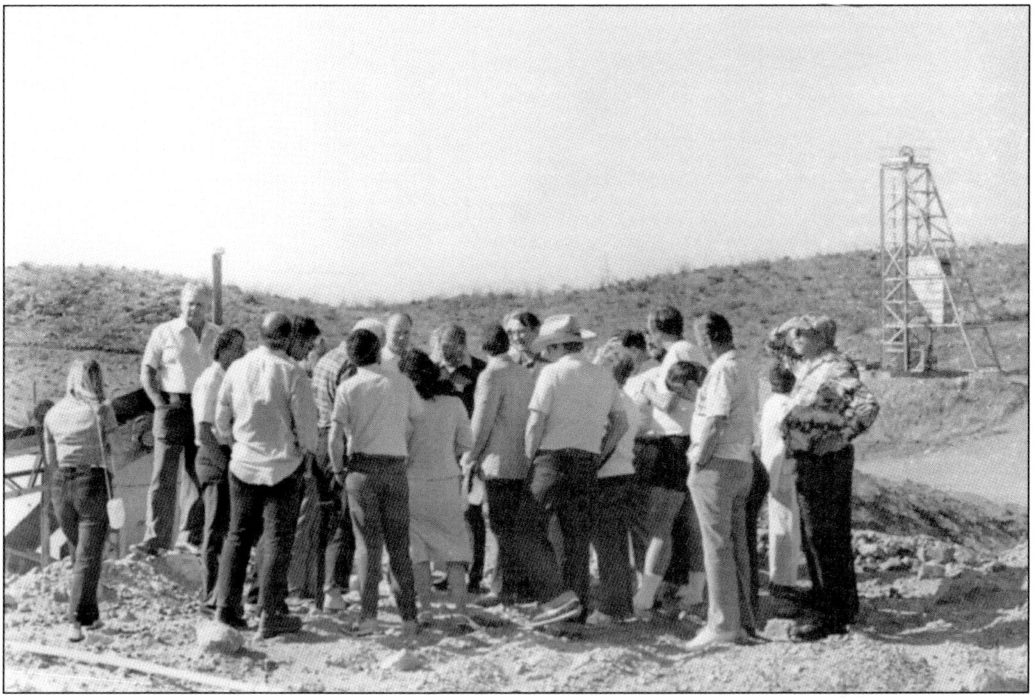

Miners and their families gather for the opening of the Nicolas Gambasino project, a gold and silver mining operation near Tombstone. (Courtesy of Viji Winters.)

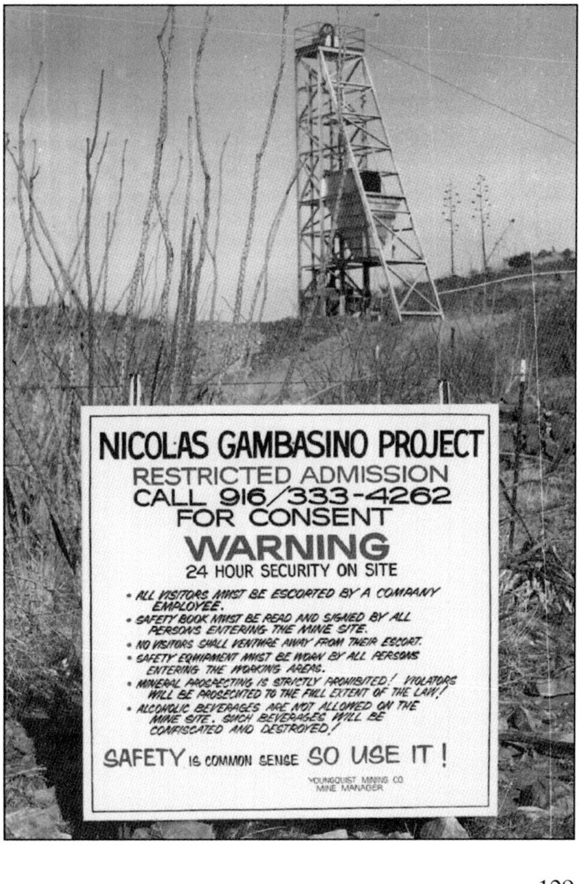

Pictured here is one of the restricted admittance signs for the Nicolas Gambasino project. One of the favorite signs hung at the mining project read, "Trespassers will be shot; Survivors will be prosecuted." (Courtesy of Viji Winters.)

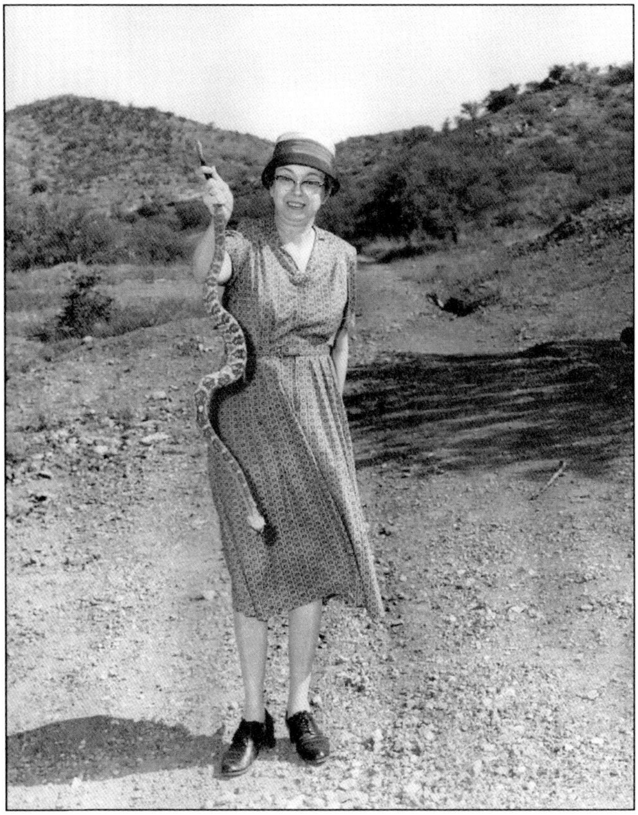

Wayne Winters's sister demonstrates how to handle a large snake. (Courtesy of Viji Winters.)

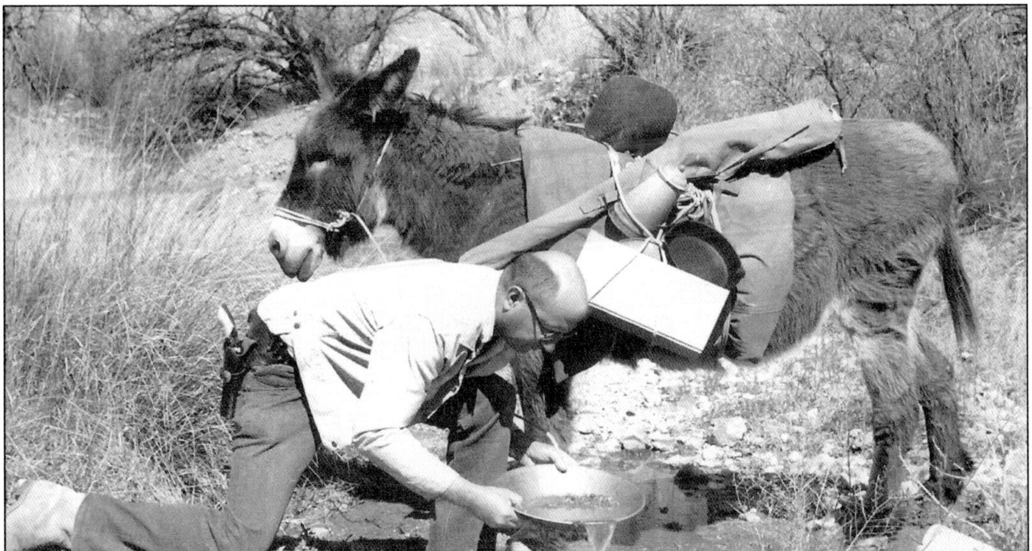

Wayne Winters pans for gold while his best friend waits patiently nearby. (Courtesy of Viji Winters.)

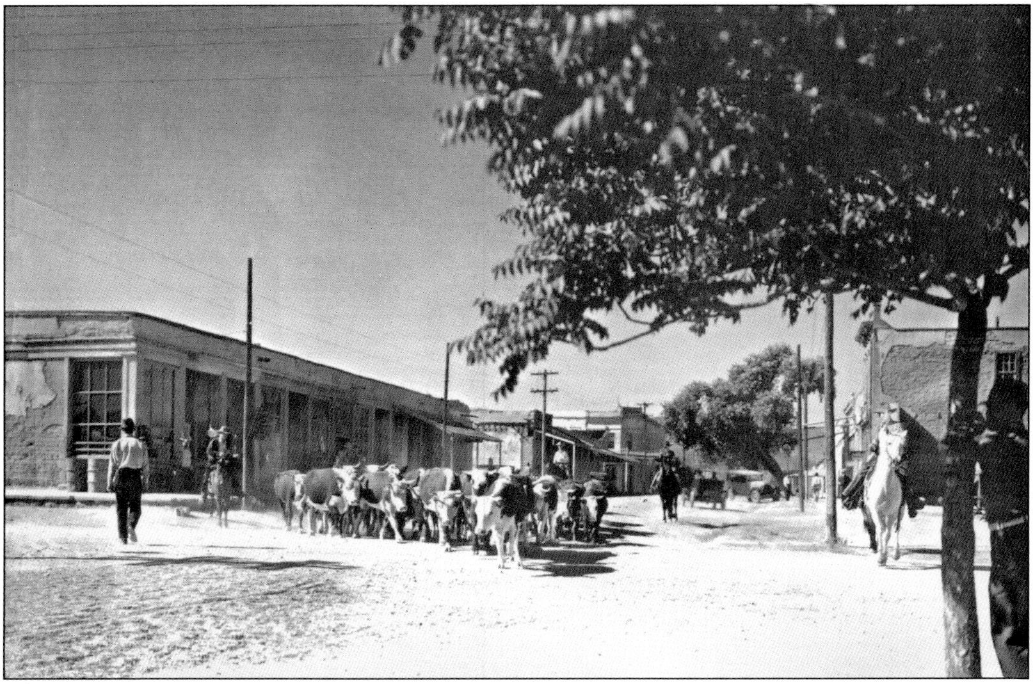

In the 1930s, longhorn cattle were herded down Tombstone's main street. (Courtesy of Linda D'Ambrose.)

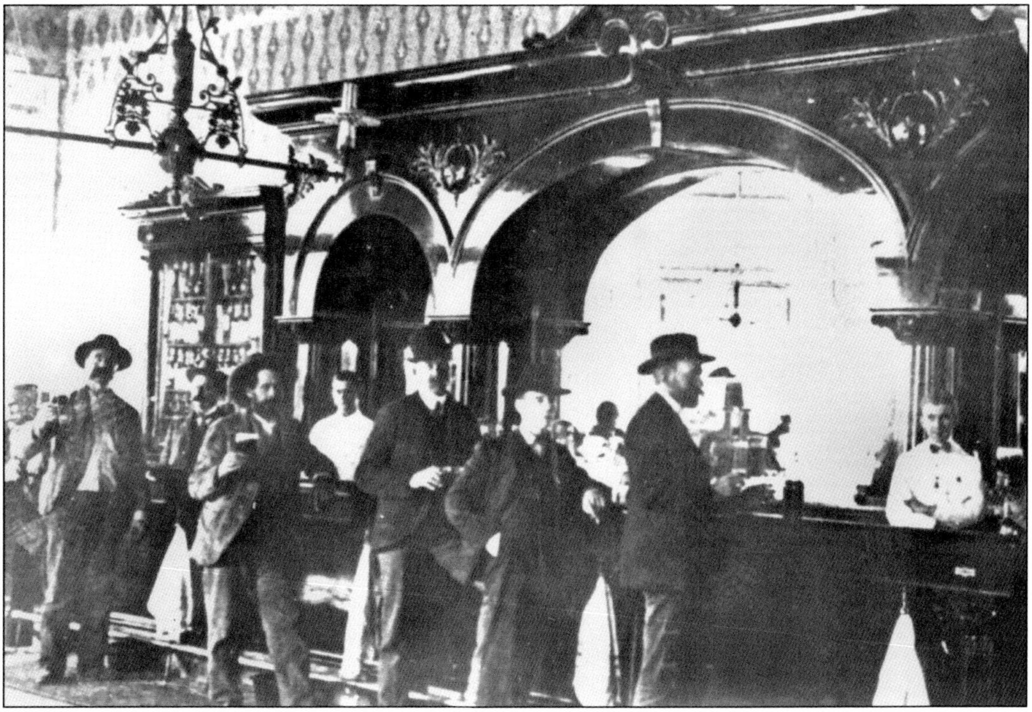

In the 1930s, the Works Progress Administration (WPA) sent photographers to Tombstone to document its remaining buildings. Pictured here is the famous Crystal Palace. (Courtesy of Library of Congress.)

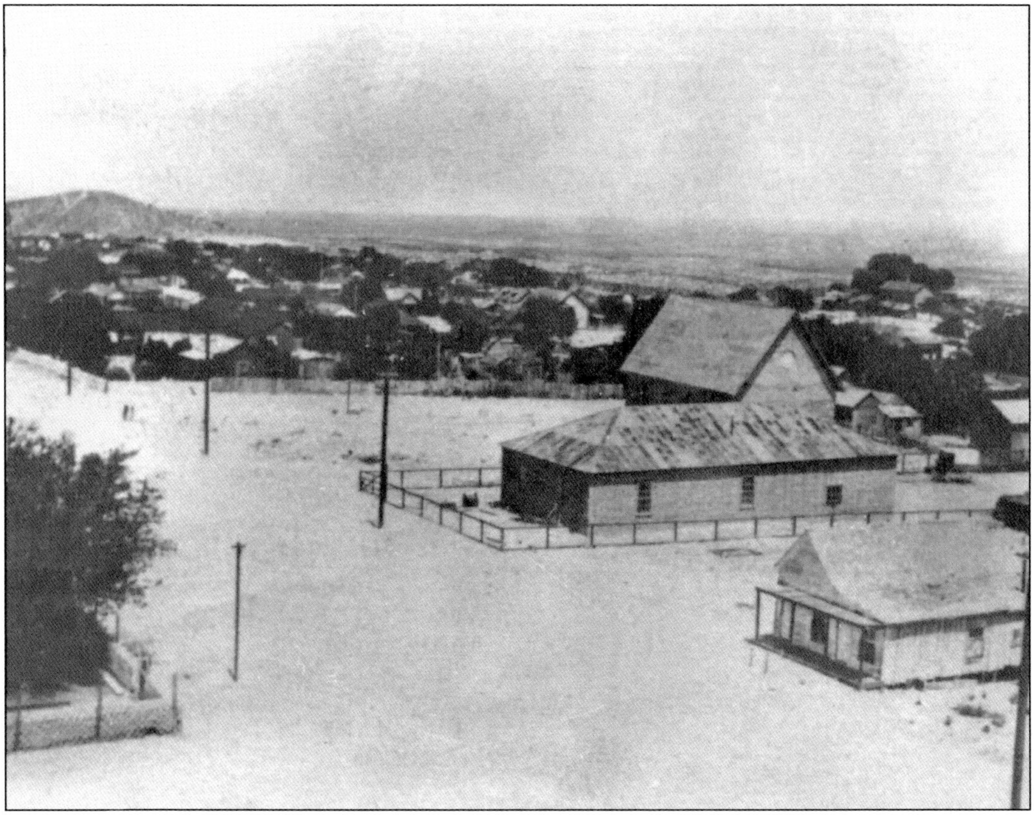

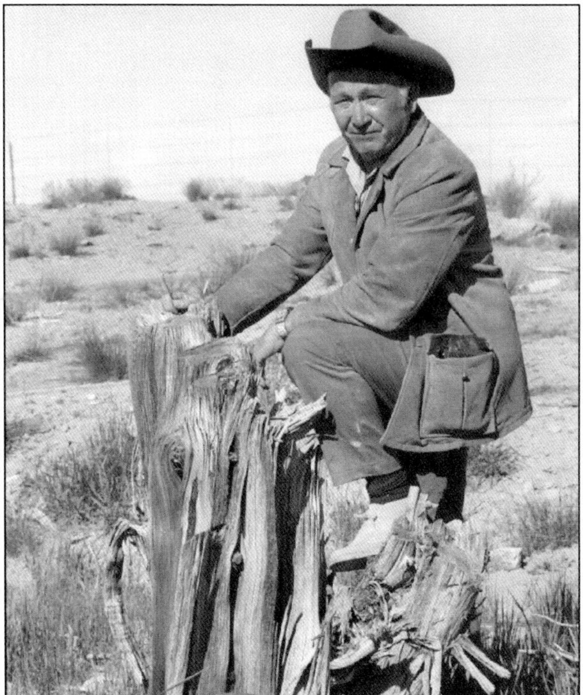

This is an early 1900s view of Tombstone. (Courtesy of Viji Winters.)

Hale Tognoni was a mining engineer and a mining attorney who loved to search the mines in California, Nevada, and Arizona—especially the Tombstone area. (Courtesy of Viji Winters.)

Wayne Winters, for many years the editor of the *Tombstone Epitaph*, is pictured here with old issues of the newspaper and an old printing press. (Courtesy of Viji Winters.)

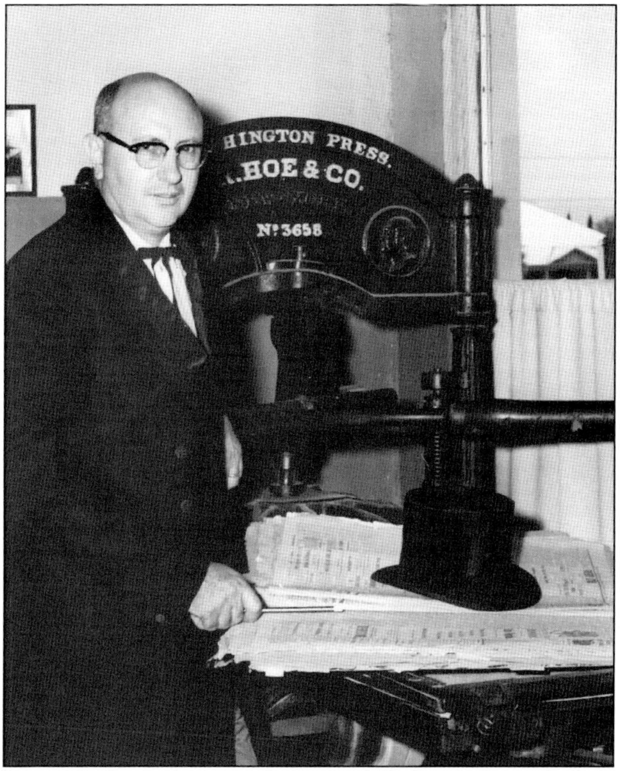

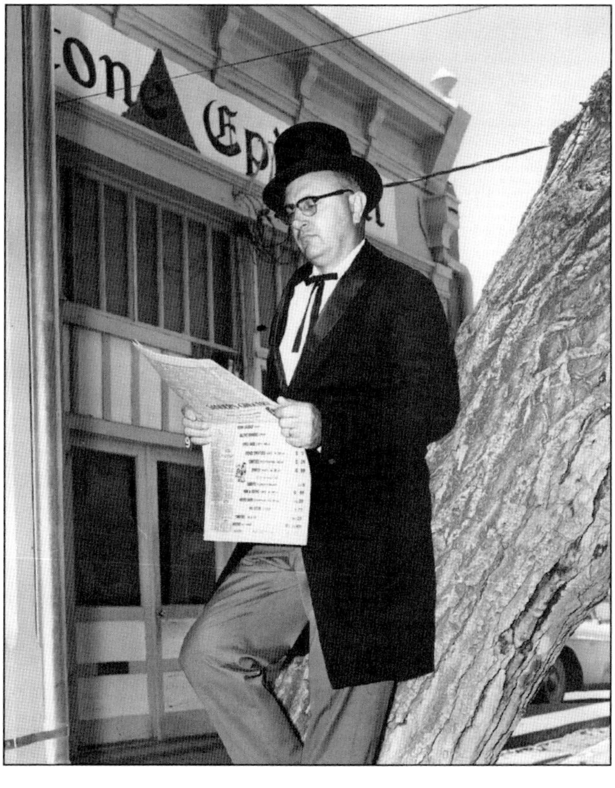

Wayne Winters was both a miner and a newspaperman with a deep appreciation of Tombstone's history. (Courtesy of Viji Winters.)

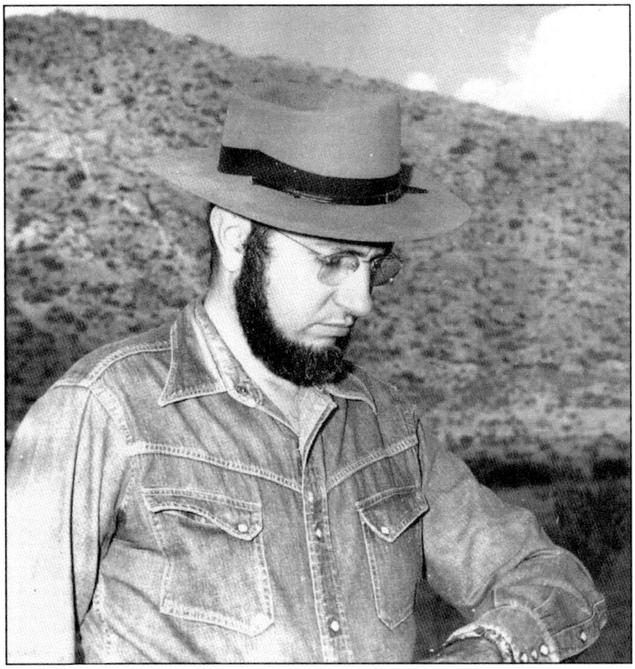

Wayne Winters, editor of the *Tombstone Epitaph*, was also the author and publisher of *Campfire Along the Treasure Trail: True Treasure Tales*. Newspapers do much more than bring news to a group of readers, they act as the memory of a town. (Courtesy of Viji Winters.)

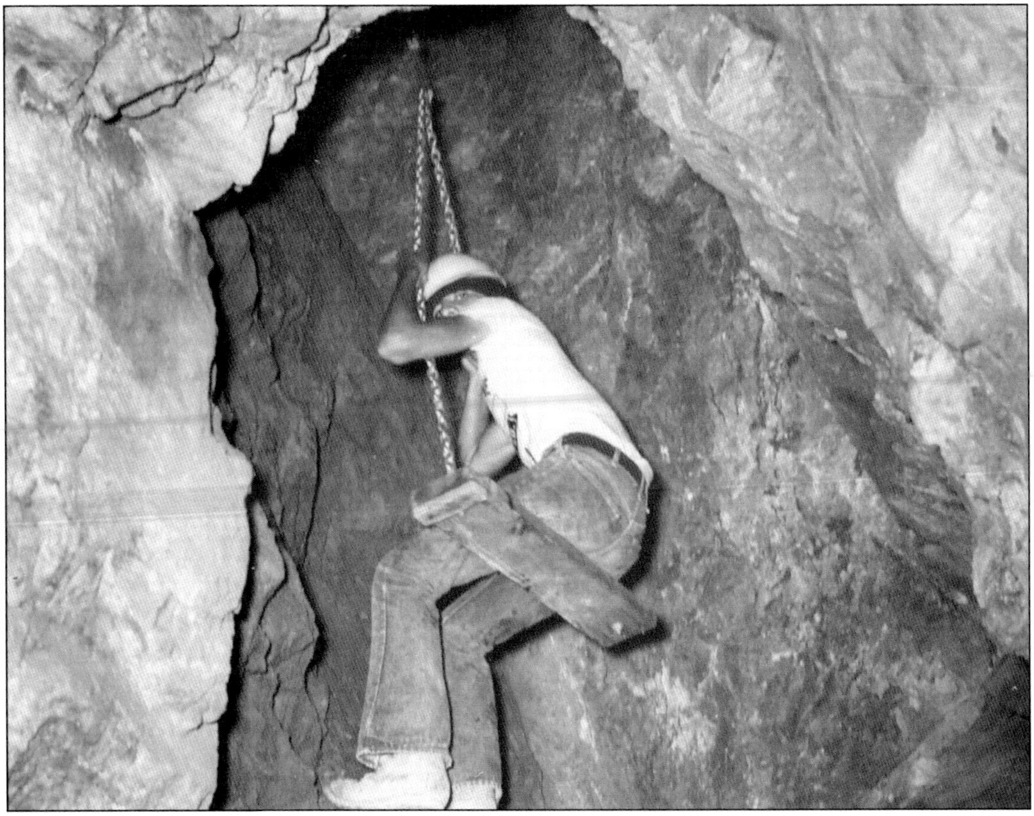

Here Wayne Winters is seen being lowered into an old underground mine. Do not try this at home. (Courtesy of Viji Winters.)

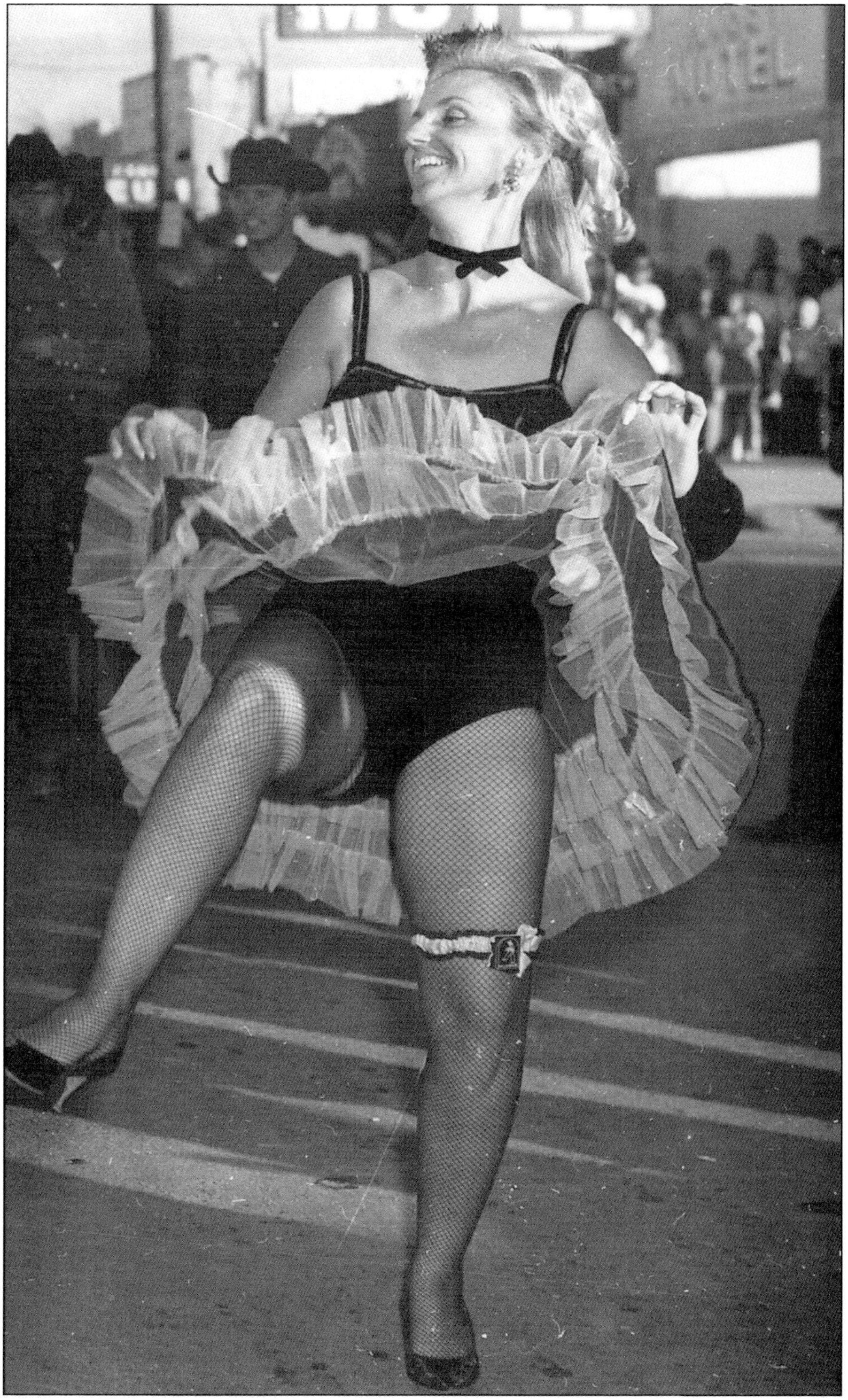

Dancing girls have always been a part of Tombstone's lore, and today they perform on the streets of Tombstone. (Courtesy of Viji Winters.)

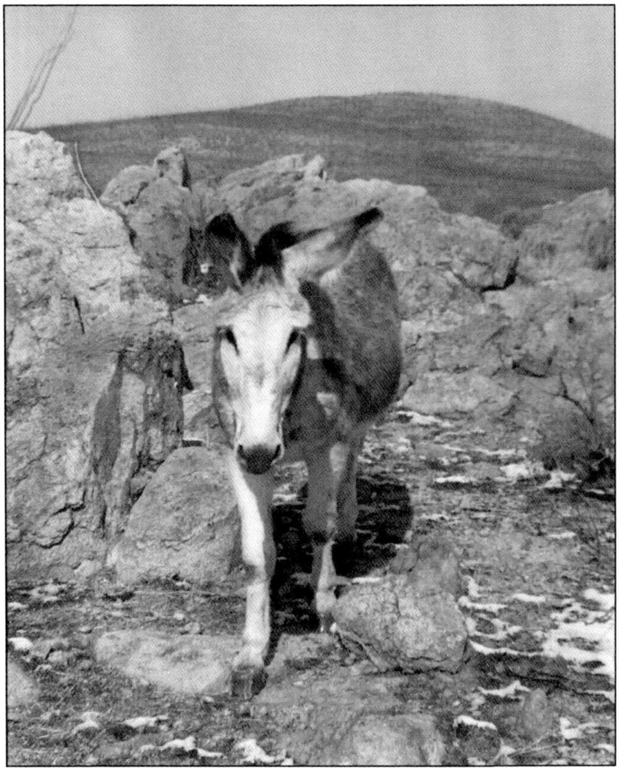

In Tombstone, wild burros range through a desert habitat and do fine as long as they are within 10 miles of water. The wild burro was introduced into the Southwest by Spaniards in the 1500s. They have long ears, a short mane, and reach a height of up to 5 feet at the shoulders. They vary in color from black to brown to gray. Their faces are gentle, but they can have a mean kick. (Courtesy of Viji Winters.)

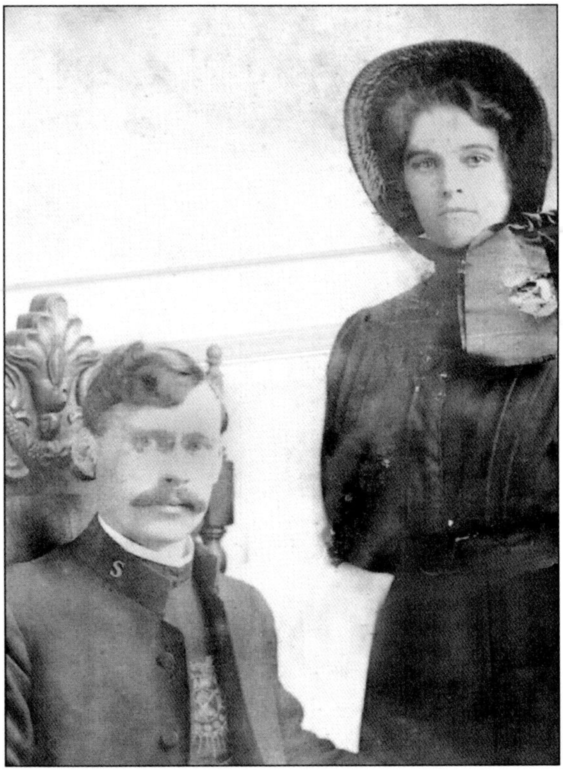

John Escapule Sr., a Basque immigrant, married Emma Trappman. John is listed in the Cochise County Great Register of 1890 as being 34 years old and working as a mill man. He settled near Charleston around 1879. Escapule also ran the Tombstone Assay Office. (Courtesy of Charles and Betty Escapule.)

Early Tombstone pioneers pose for a photograph in their best clothes. Today members of the Vigilante's sister organization, the Tombstone Vigilettes, model late-1880s and early-1900s fashions during Tombstone's special events. They do all they can to make sure it is authentic—no zippers, Velcro, or polyester. (Courtesy of Charles and Betty Escapule.)

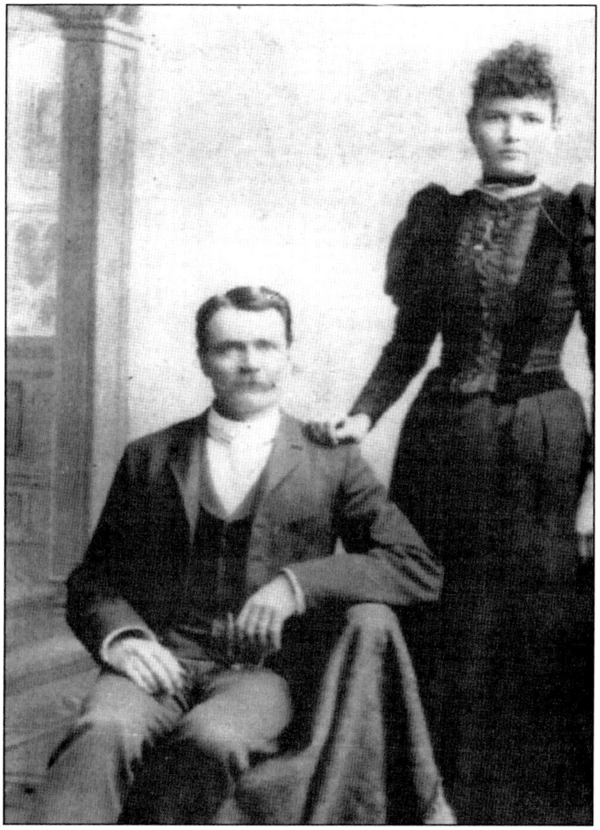

The mining life may have been difficult, but the people always seem to be enjoying themselves. (Courtesy of Charles and Betty Escapule.)

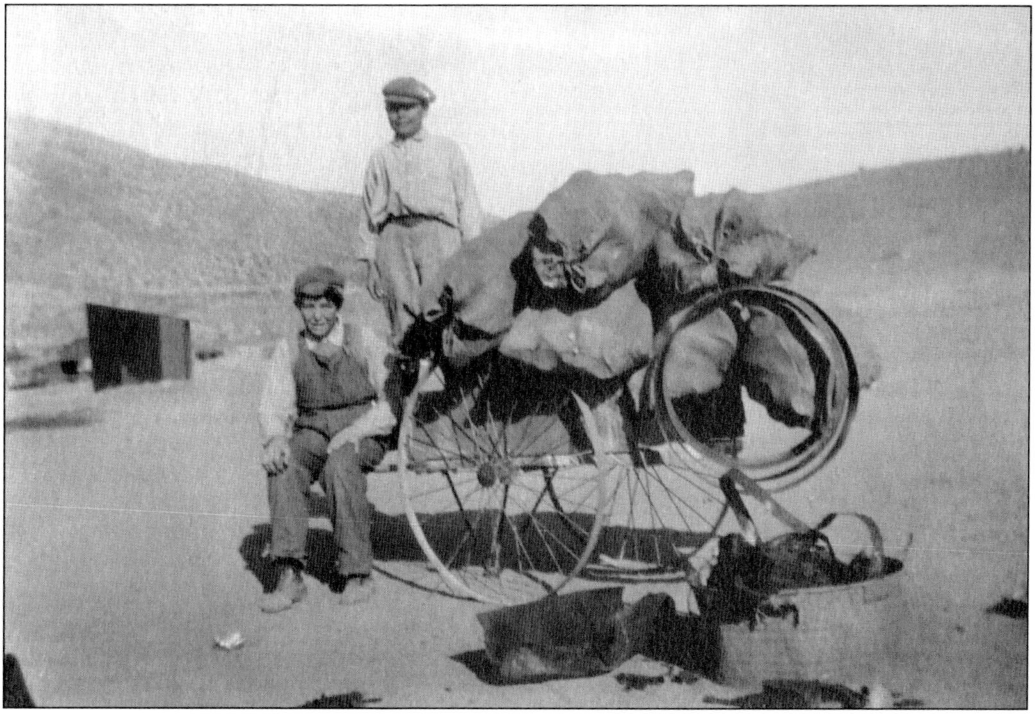

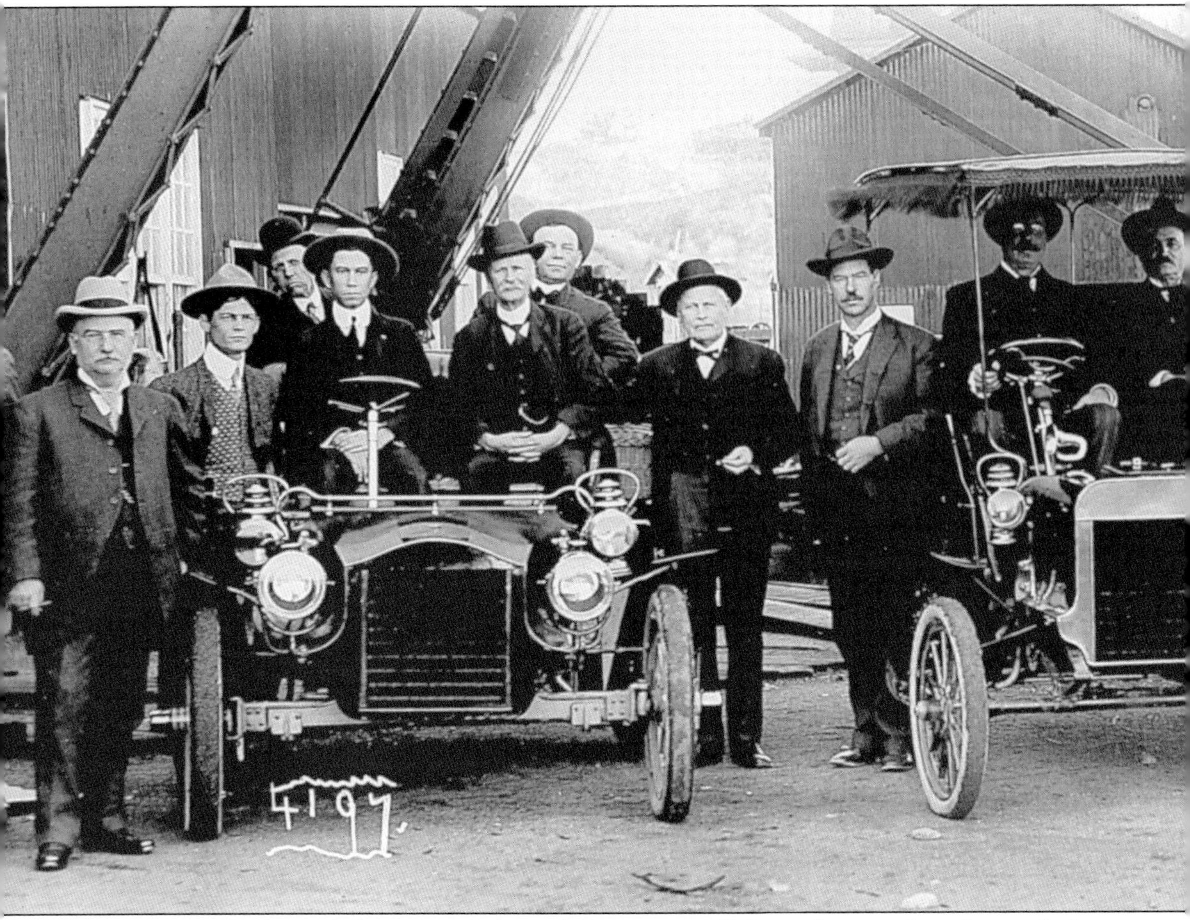

Tombstone embraced the automobile, and these men, all dressed up in their finest clothing, are preparing for a race in the Tombstone hills. (Courtesy of Arizona Historical Society,

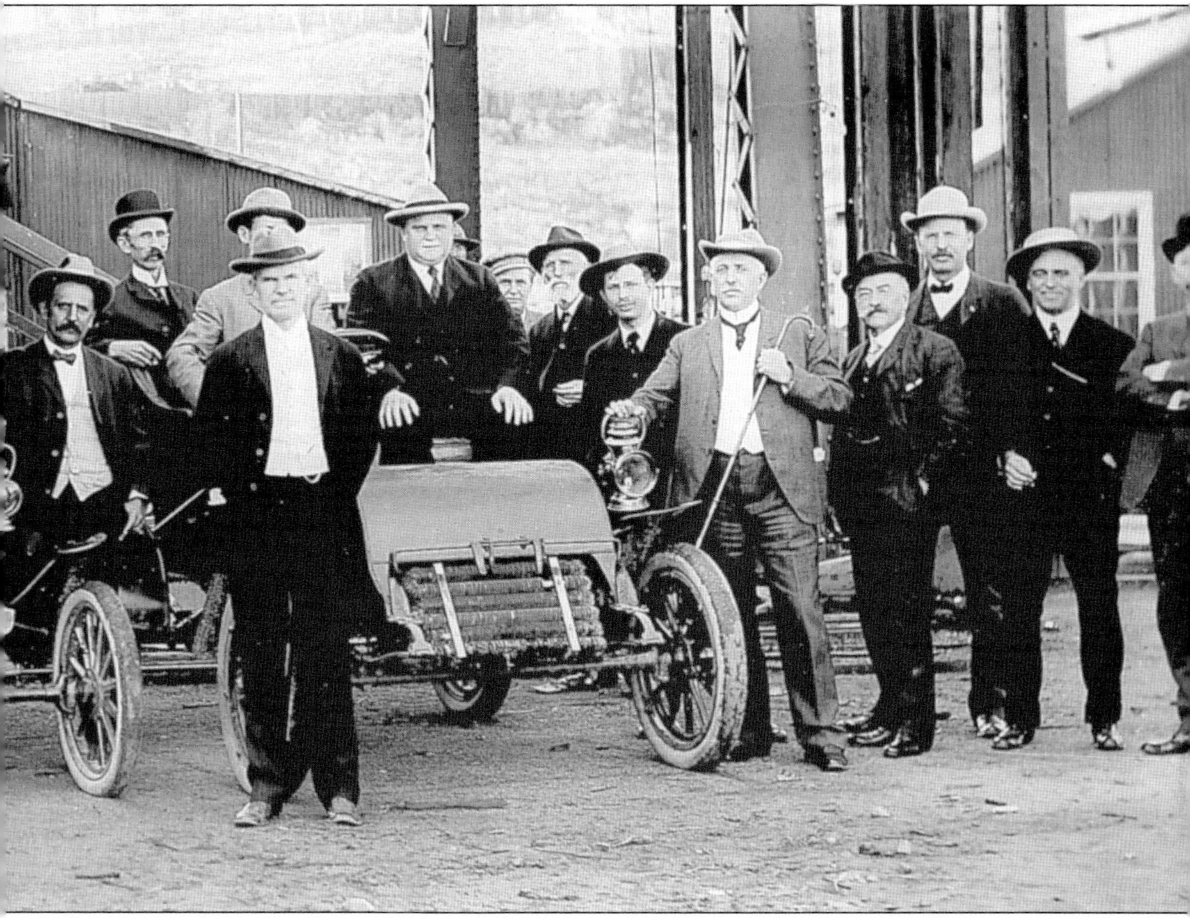

Tucson, Arizona.)

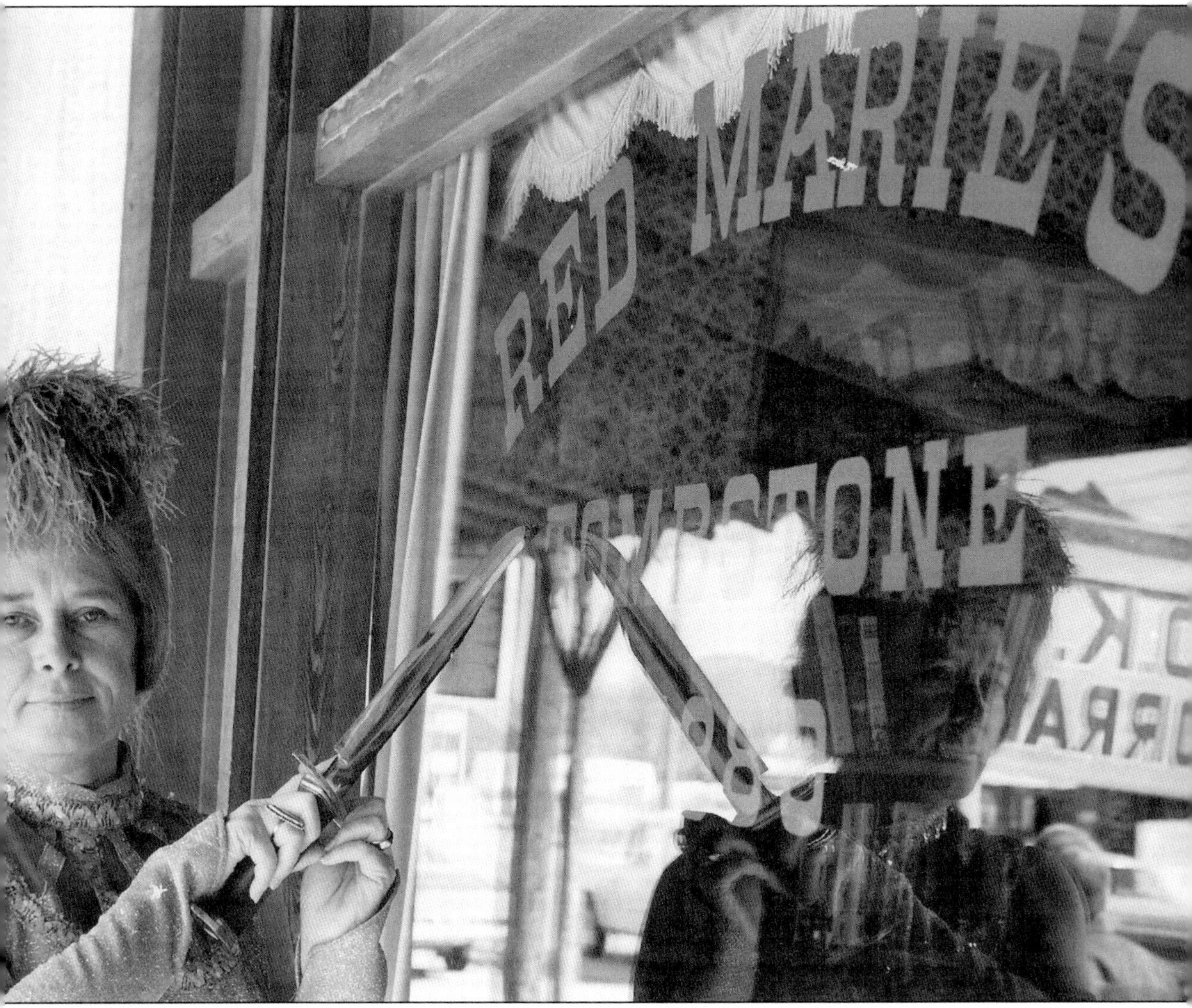

Performances by groups such as the Vigilettes and Hell's Belles help keep Tombstone's sometimes-rowdier history alive. (Courtesy of Viji Winters.)

St. Paul's Episcopal Church is seen here with parishioner George Whitwell Parsons in front. The church, founded by the Revered Endicott Peabody shortly after the famous gunfight, still serves the Tombstone community. Parsons, who was baptized in St. Paul's, chronicled the life of Tombstone in its wild and rowdy days. (Courtesy of Arizona Historical Society, Tucson, Arizona.)

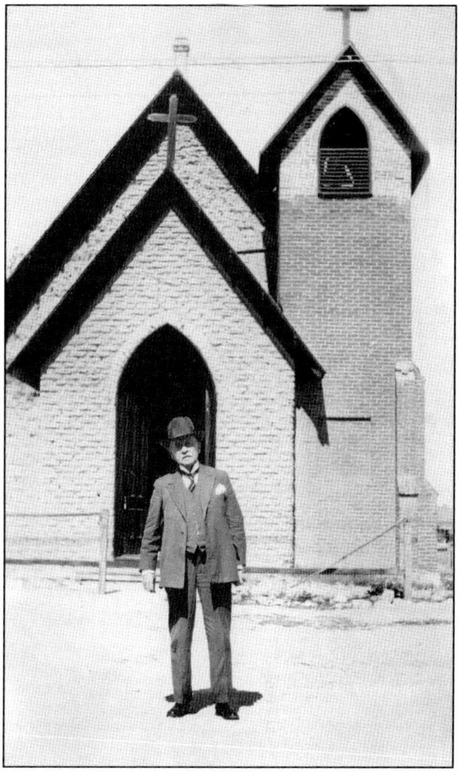

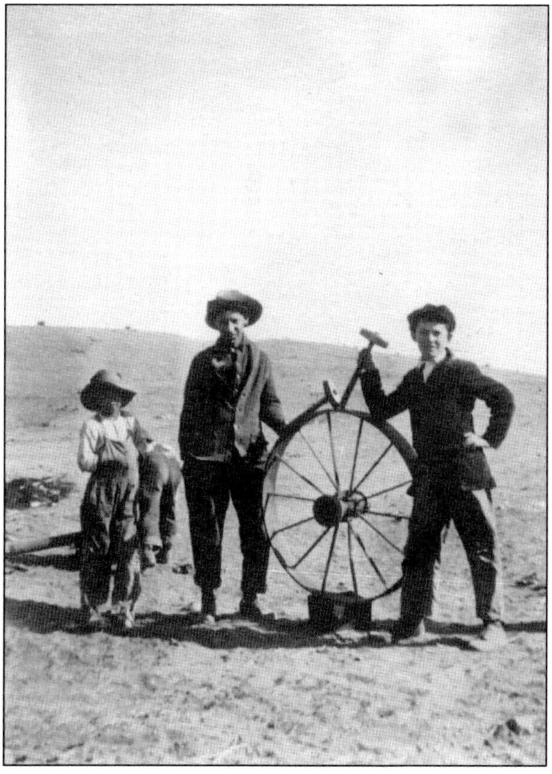

Men are getting ready to install mining equipment in the Tombstone hills. (Courtesy of Arizona Historical Society, Tucson, Arizona.)

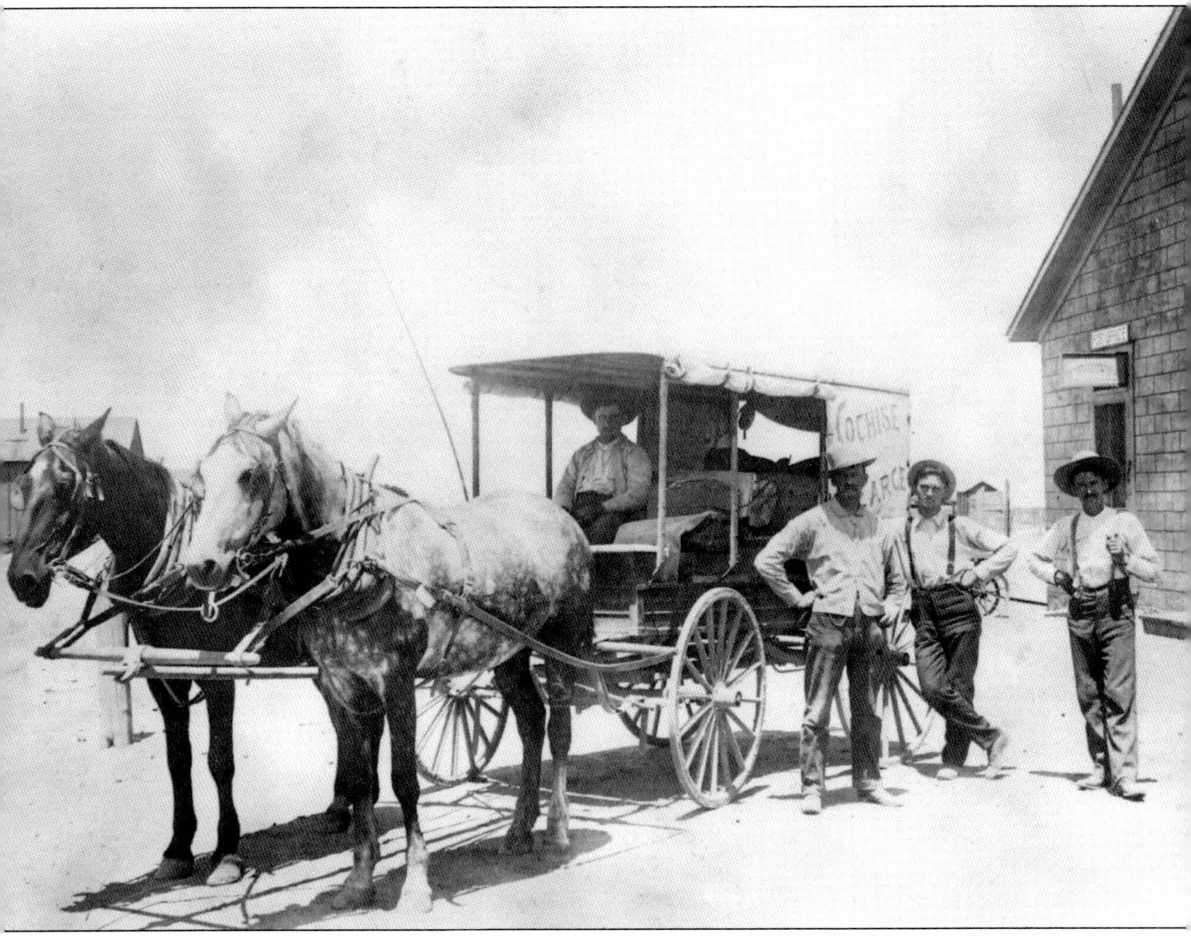

This horse-drawn wagon is parked in front to the Pearce Post Office, which was established on March 6, 1896. It made its run from Cochise, a railroad town, to Pearce. The Cochise Post Office was established on August 28, 1886. (Courtesy of Arizona Historical Society, Tucson, Arizona.)

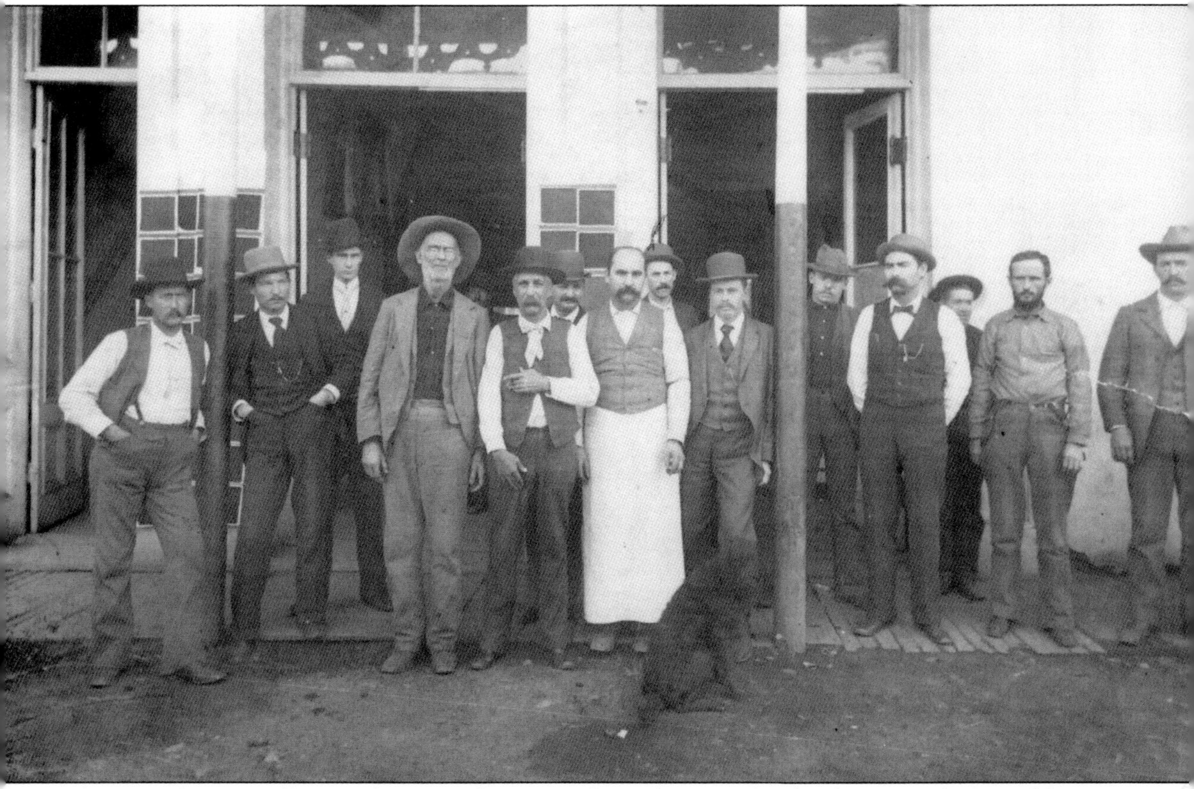

Photography was still a novelty around 1900, and Tombstoners (and at least one dog) would use any excuse to stop what they were doing and get themselves in a picture. Unfortunately, they did not always leave their names with the photographer. There is at least one butcher in the group; he is wearing the long white apron. (Courtesy of Arizona Historical Society, Tucson, Arizona.)

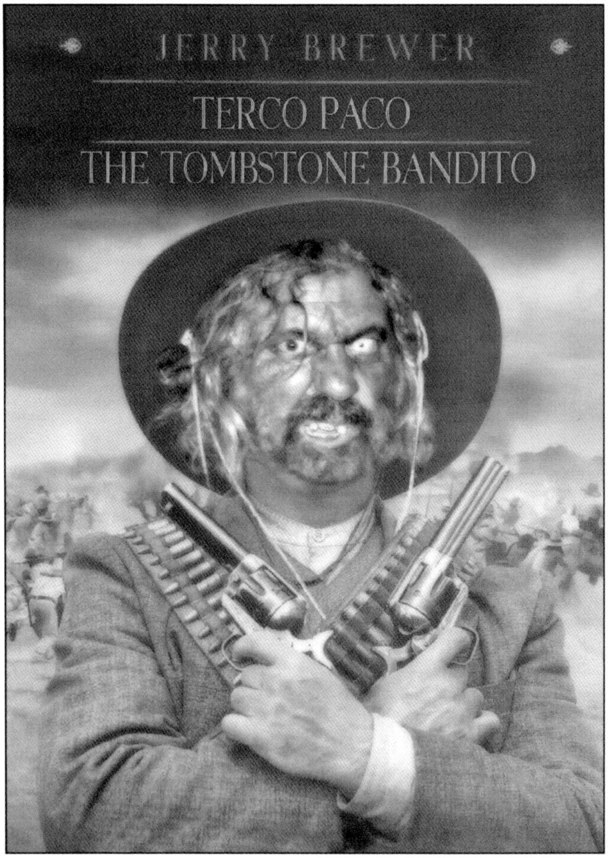

Terco Paco (also known as Jerry Brewer) walks the streets of Tombstone as the town's ugly bad man. When Tombstone's bandito is not scaring the heck out of folks, he lives at Rattlesnake Ranch in the high desert of Dragoon, Arizona, near Tombstone, and raises chickens. (Courtesy of Jerry Brewer.)

George and Nancy Lewis Sosa pose in front of the Old West Bookstore. Nancy, whose roots run deep in Tombstone history and its mining, is emerging as a premier historian, sifting through articles and photographs. She is responsible for collecting material and getting sites on the National Register of Historic Places. (Courtesy of Nancy Lewis Sosa.)

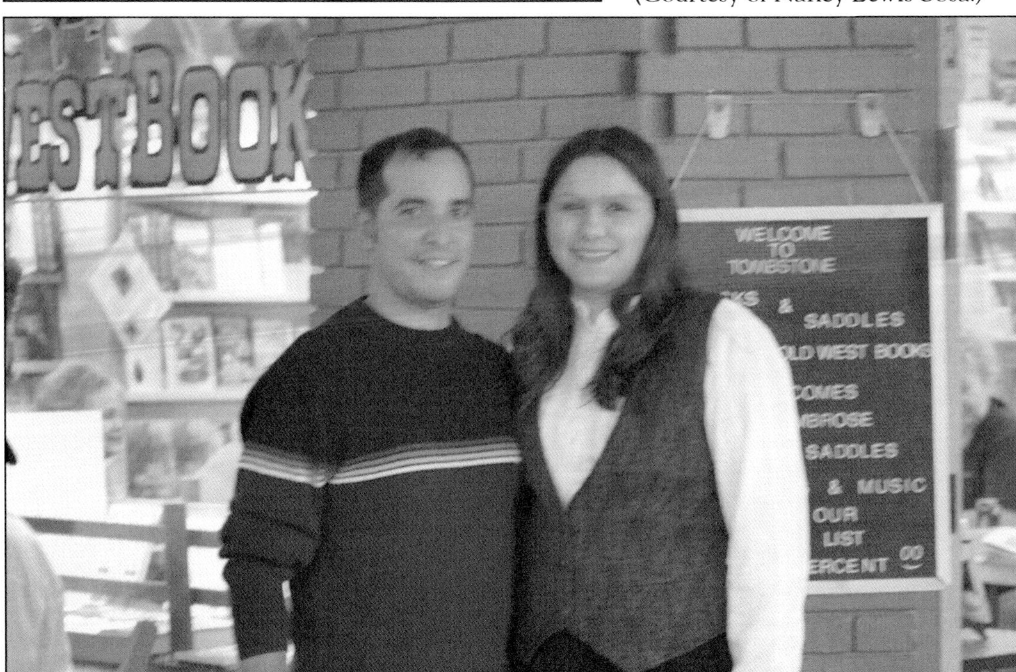

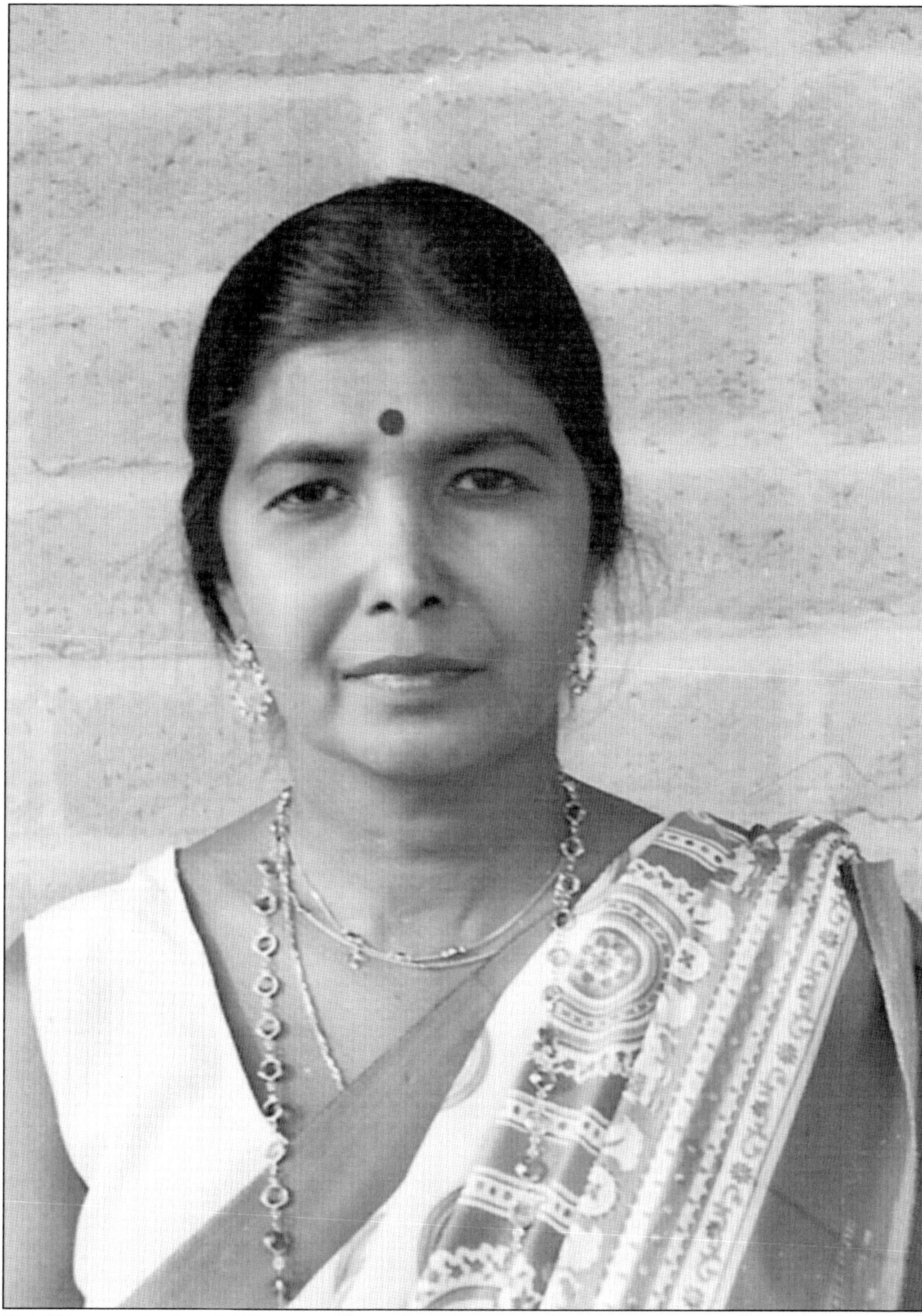

Viji Winters's husband, Wayne, collected much of Tombstone's history in documentation and photographs. She has been the keeper of the lights and generally shared her material with the author. (Courtesy of Viji Winters.)

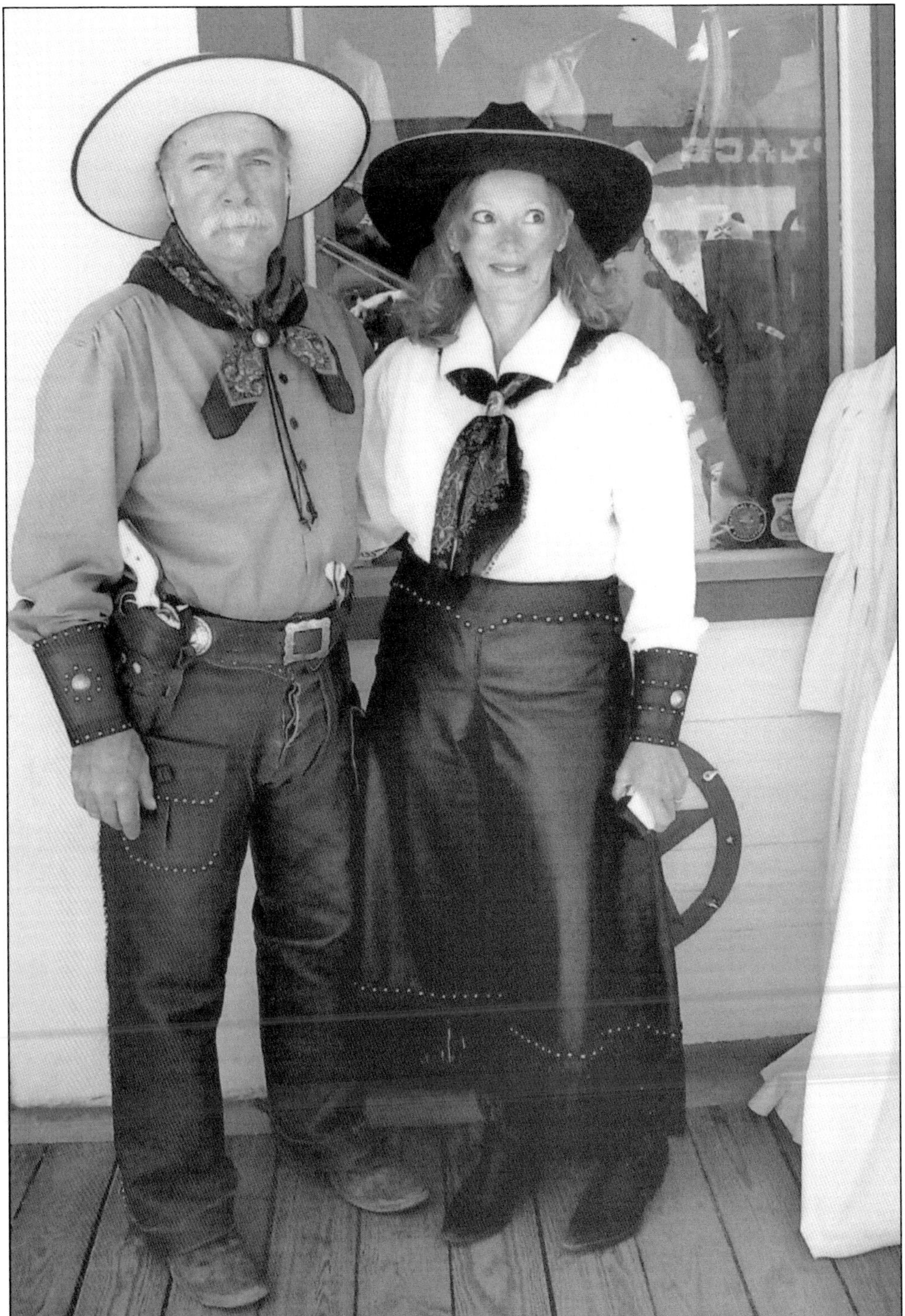

Linda D'Ambrose operates the Old West Bookstore at Allen and Fourth Streets, once the site of the Occidental Hotel in the heart of Tombstone. Here one can find almost everything in print on Tombstone along with other Western literature. Linda's husband, Gino, also showcases his handsome leatherwork in the store. (Courtesy of Linda D'Ambrose.)

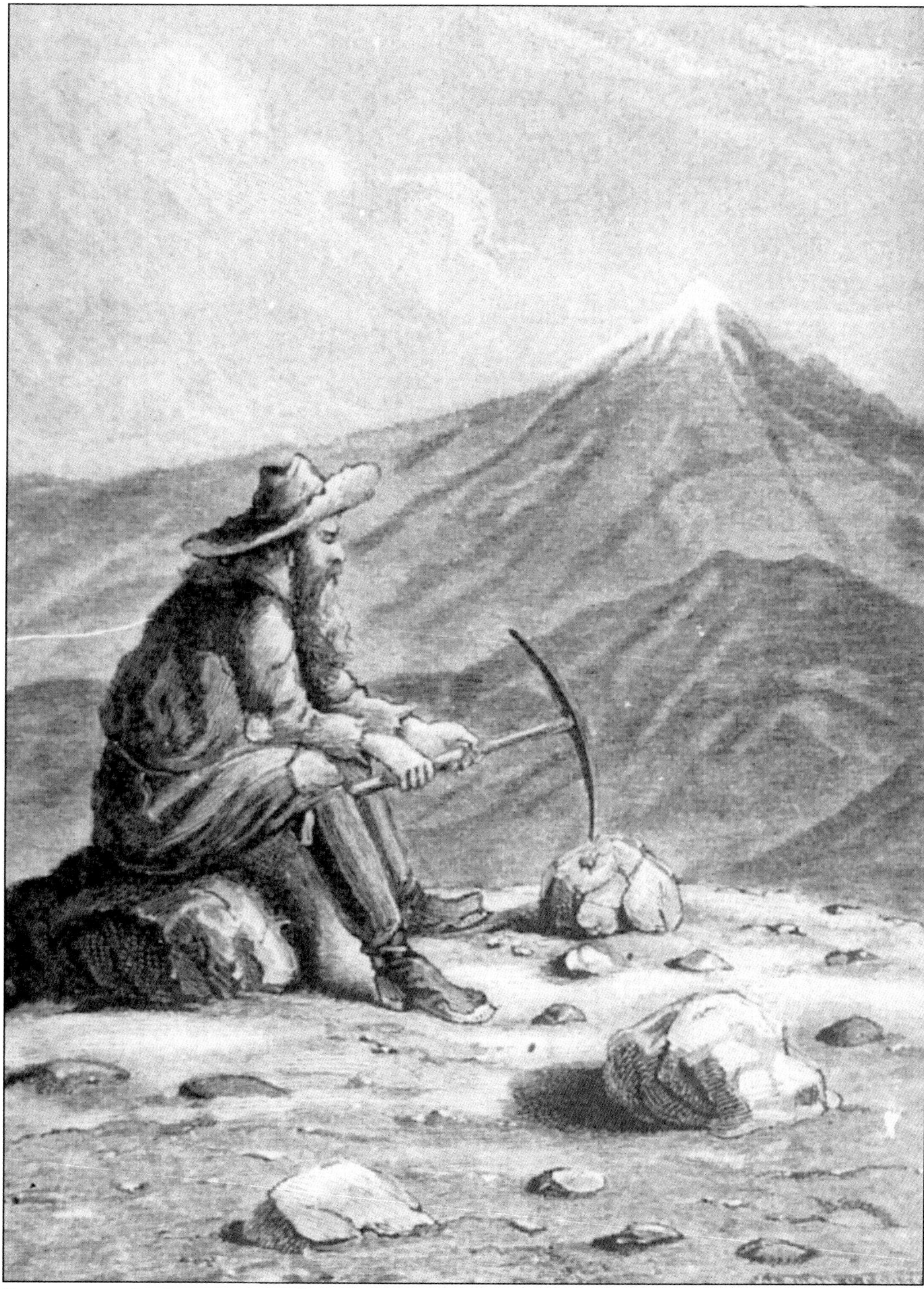

Dreamers and schemers, preachers and prostitutes, and miners and madmen all sought to find their pleasures and profits in the sin and silver in Tombstone. For most, both would be brief. (Author's collection.)

Discover Thousands of Local History Books Featuring Millions of Vintage Images

Arcadia Publishing, the leading local history publisher in the United States, is committed to making history accessible and meaningful through publishing books that celebrate and preserve the heritage of America's people and places.

Find more books like this at

www.arcadiapublishing.com

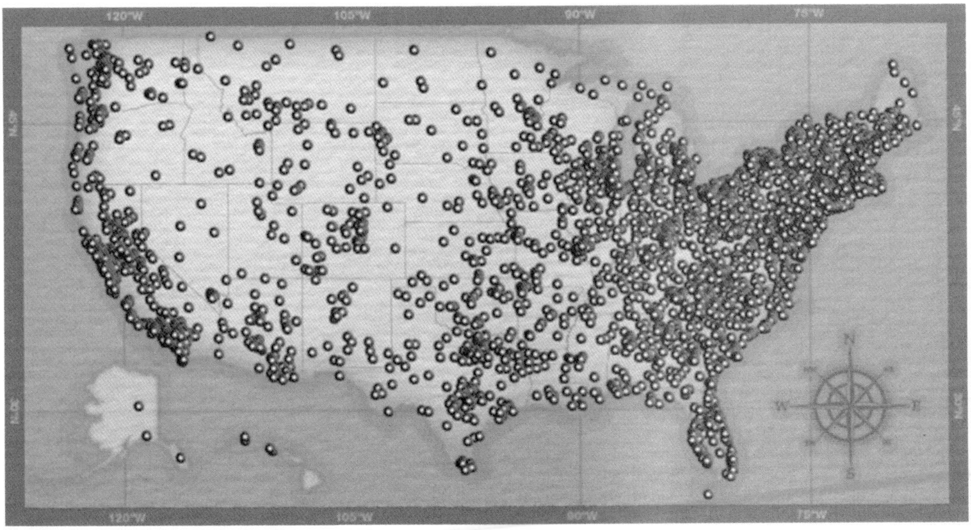

Search for your hometown history, your old stomping grounds, and even your favorite sports team.

Consistent with our mission to preserve history on a local level, this book was printed in South Carolina on American-made paper and manufactured entirely in the United States. Products carrying the accredited Forest Stewardship Council (FSC) label are printed on 100 percent FSC-certified paper.

MADE IN THE USA